1976

ok ma ep

POE'S FICTION
Romantic Irony in the Gothic Tales

POE'S FICTION

Romantic Irony in the Gothic Tales

G. R. Thompson

The University of Wisconsin Press

PUBLISHED 1973
THE UNIVERSITY OF WISCONSIN PRESS
BOX 1379, MADISON, WISCONSIN 53701

THE UNIVERSITY OF WISCONSIN PRESS, LTD.
70 GREAT RUSSELL STREET, LONDON

COPYRIGHT © 1973
THE REGENTS OF THE UNIVERSITY OF WISCONSIN SYSTEM
ALL RIGHTS RESERVED

PRINTED IN THE UNITED STATES OF AMERICA

✳ FOR LC CIP INFORMATION SEE THE COLOPHON

ISBN 0-299-06380-1

For Rose Marie Thompson
and our children
Hallie, Erin,
and Ian

*All that he has to do is to write and publish a very little
book. Its title should be simple—a few plain words—"My
Heart Laid Bare." But—this little book must be* true *to its
title. . . . There are ten thousand men who, if the book were
once written, would laugh at the notion of being disturbed
by its publication. . . . But to write it—there is the rub.
No man dare write it. No man ever will dare write it. No man
could write it, even if he dared. The paper would shrivel
and blaze at every touch of the fiery pen.*

Edgar A. Poe—Marginalia *(1848)*

*. . . there is such a duplicity from first to last. . . . In case the
reader should not be sufficiently observant of the duplicity,
it is the business of the author to make as evident as possible
the fact that it is there. That is to say, the duplicity, the
ambiguity, is a conscious one, something which the author
knows more about than anybody else; it is the essential
dialectical distinction of the whole authorship, and has
therefore a deeper reason.*

Søren Kierkegaard—The Point of View for My
Work as an Author *(1848)*

Contents

Preface

ALTHOUGH IN THIS STUDY I am concerned principally with Poe's Gothic tales, what I have to say about these tales has important implications for his other works. A major point of emphasis is the continuum between the Gothic-occult works and the comic-satiric works. I argue that critics have underestimated his complexity and subtlety in the short story, misconstrued ironic techniques as flaws, and ignored an important aspect of Romanticism that provides a historical context for reading Poe as an ironist instead of a completely serious Gothicist. I attempt to resolve the aesthetic problems of Poe's "flawed" style and to correct the mistaken view that the nearly equal division between the number of his comic and serious tales reflects a "schizophrenic" schism in his world view. At once a Romantic idealist devoted to "transcendental" vision and yet also a satirist, Poe is the preeminent American follower of the European "Romantic Ironists" whose influence was once felt around the world in the larger Romantic movement emanating from Germany.

Although Poe's affinities with the school of Romantic Irony have not been studied before, the possibility that Poe is basically an ironist is not a totally radical suggestion. Indeed, it requires but a few examples to show that in his Gothic tales Poe indulges in ambivalent mockery of man's ability to perceive the world, mockery especially of the rational powers, mockery that includes the ironically and even satirically manipulated responses of the reader.

In placing Poe in a Romantic context, I survey German theories of "transcendental irony," which emphasized the dark possibilities of Kantian idealism. I focus on the Schlegels and Tieck, whom Poe read with care, and on their relationship to "nightside" psychology and philosophy, which Poe used ambiguously in his tales of metempsychosis and mesmerism. After an initial survey of the theories of irony, my basic strategy is to take up in turn the questions of Poe's serious use of the Gothic, of the grotesque and arabesque, and of the occult as the principal problems in the ironic reading of his fiction. In each case, I try to suggest the close link between the Gothic works and the comic works. Regarding Poe's technique, I cite evidence that his Gothic mode was not supernaturalistic but the psychologically realistic, into which he insinuated an element of burlesque. In exploring the meanings of the terms *grotesque* and *arabesque,* which Poe himself applied to his tales, I argue that Poe's Gothic tale developed from a satiric mode into an ironic philosophical concern with the "perverse" as both the structure of man's mind and the structure of the universe. In Poe's universe of misperception and illusion, the fictional hero undergoes extended ironic reverses in fictional structures so ironically twisted and laced with satiric innuendo that the form itself, even the plot, approaches an absurd hoax on the character—just as existence may be God's hoax on man, the ultimate grotesquerie. Thematically, Poe's Gothic works suggest that the deceptive perversity of the universe and of the mind can be transcended only by the Godlike imagination of the ironic artist.

In arguing this, it is not my intention to discredit all those readers who have responded seriously to the sinister, occult element in Poe. Rather, I seek to show other levels of meaning in addition to a surface level of the occult, arguing that a superficially literalist approach to Poe's dark tales in terms of the occult obscures the true complexity of his achievement. It is not so much that previous critics have been wrong, as it is that their readings of Poe's tales have been limited.

Despite occasional appearances to the contrary, I have tried throughout to be suggestive rather than exhaustive. The basic sourcebook for nineteenth-century American "Germanism" is Henry A. Pochmann's massive *German Culture in America: Philosophical and Literary Influences, 1600-1900* (Madison: University of Wisconsin Press, 1957), wherein is to be found the most inclusive and detailed discussion of Poe's knowledge of the German language and his acquaintance with and use of German literature, along with a general discussion of the influence of German literature in America, especially as known in translation. Specific reference to this work is somewhat sparing, however, for Pochmann has little to say about the German theories of irony, which, in fact, seem to have been largely forgotten in our day.

I certainly make no claim to be expert in German literature of the nineteenth century, or even in German literature as known in nineteenth-century America; and much of my presentation derives from previous scholarship rather than from intimate acquaintance with German writers of the period. Moreover, what first-hand knowledge I do have of German literature is principally through translation—which brings me to two important points. First, the evidence presented by Pochmann and others strongly suggests that Poe (who excelled in Greek, Latin, French, and other languages as a schoolboy) could read

German with some facility. Nevertheless, while Poe's ability to read German cannot be proved, the case for German literary influence on Poe does not require reading knowledge of the language on his part. The number of translations, reviews, essays, biographies, and histories of German literature available in English during Poe's lifetime was extraordinary; and I try wherever possible to cite pertinent translations and articles.

Second, I wish to emphasize that the present study is not intended so much as a study of the precise influence of any particular German writer on Poe as it is an attempt to outline what kinds of influential literary and philosophical ideas were "in the air" and thereby provide a plausible historical context for the major subject of the book: a revaluation of Poe's fiction in terms of irony. That is, Poe's irony (this way of reading Poe) is the primary subject, his indebtedness to German writers, a secondary subject.

Since my interest is in Poe as a Romanticist rather than in exact influences and parallels from another literature, much more important than Pochmann's study (or Palmer Cobb's, or any other such study of Poe's knowledge of the German language and indebtedness to German literature) are two other works on which I have relied heavily for the theoretical background of literary criticism. My general debt to René Wellek's *A History of Modern Criticism: 1750–1950*, 4 vols. to date (New Haven, Conn.: Yale University Press, 1956–) is so pervasive that without that study I should simply have never seen the connection between Poe's ironic modes and European theories of irony. I also stand in debt to Wellek's *Confrontations: Studies in the Intellectual and Literary Relations Between Germany, England, and the United States During the Nineteenth Century* (Princeton, N.J.: Princeton University Press, 1965). But the other seminal work for me was Wolfgang Kayser's *Das Groteske: seine Gestaltung in Malerei und Dichtung* (Oldenburg: Gerhard Stalling, 1957), translated by Ulrich Weisstein as *The Grotesque in Art and Literature* (Bloomington: University of Indiana Press, 1965), a book that, whatever its shortcomings, seems to me the most insightful and lucid treatment of the grotesque extant, and which confirmed my sense of the close link between the grotesque and Romantic Irony. To these works I should also add Edward H. Davidson's *Poe: A Critical Study* (Cambridge, Mass.: Harvard University Press, 1957), a work in the tradition of the history of ideas that attempts to see Poe in the aesthetic-philosophical context of Romanticism; and Patrick F. Quinn's *The French Face of Edgar Poe* (Carbondale: Southern Illinois University Press, 1957), which contains what is probably the best general, extended criticism of Poe's works heretofore available.

From this general theoretical background, then, comes what I claim as original here: the basic critical-historical insight into Poe as a man possessed of the temperament of the European Romantic Ironists. The primary impulse for this study came from my initial puzzlement over Poe's entire canon of work and my discovery of a handful of critics who had discussed possible ironic stances in Poe's fiction, notably Darrel Abel and Richard P. Benton, but also Roy P. Basler, Kenneth L. Daughrity, James W. Gargano, Clark Griffith, Terence Martin, Stephen Mooney, William Whipple, and James Southall Wilson. Since then, others have begun to see the compelling logic of ironic masks and modes in Poe. More research into Poe's affinities with and debts to the German Romanticists remains for others better qualified than I to do. But I hope (as my friend and former colleague Davis Dunbar McElroy remarked similarly of his own work on eighteenth-century Scottish clubs) that I have seriously interfered with anyone else hoping to write on the subject.

Regarding critical essays on particular tales, I have made no effort to cite every article. The critical essays on "The Fall of the House of Usher" and "Ligeia" alone run to over a hundred items, many of them highly repetitive of one another. I cite, in the main, what is directly relevant to my argument. Readers seeking a guide to published criticism on a particular tale should consult the annual Poe bibliographies by Richard P. Benton in the *Emerson Society Quarterly* to 1967, and in *Poe Studies* thereafter; the *Checklist of Edgar Allan Poe* compiled by J. Albert Robbins (Columbus, Ohio: Charles E. Merrill Co., 1969); Jay B. Hubbell's chapter on Poe and J. Chesley Matthews's supplementary list of Poe studies, 1955–1962, in *Eight American Authors: A Review of Research and Criticism,* ed. Floyd Stovall (New York: W. W. Norton, 1963; revised, 1971; the revised edition [1971] does not contain the checklist, and the Poe chapter has been rewritten); the first installment of a *Complete Bibliography of Poe Criticism 1827–1967,* J. Lasley Dameron's *Edgar Allan Poe: A Checklist of Criticism 1942–1960* (Charlottesville: Bibliographical Society of the University of Virginia, 1966); and an unpublished Ph.D. dissertation by Esther F. Hyneman, "The Contemporaneous Reputation of Edgar Allan Poe with Annotated Bibliography of Poe Criticism: 1827–1967" (Columbia University, 1968), which catalogs all citations by subject and work. More generally, the annual *PMLA* bibliography and the two volumes by Lewis Leary, *Articles on American Literature* (Durham, N.C.: Duke University Press, 1954, 1970) are useful and dependable. And yet, at the same time, I have tried in the reference matter not only to document my argument thoroughly, but also to provide for those who wish to pursue certain aspects of the subjects of this study a thematic guide through the massive scholarship available.

I have a number of special debts I wish to acknowledge. Edward Avak and Russell Haney gave encouragement at a crucial time. Charles R. Metzger, Eleazer Lecky, and Joseph Boskin, all of the University of Southern California, read the first, more laborious, version of the manuscript as a thesis in 1965–66. Patrick F. Quinn, of Wellesley College, read the same version somewhat later in conjunction with my introduction to *Great Short Works of Edgar Allan Poe* (New York: Harper & Row, 1970) and made so many valuable suggestions that I cannot properly acknowledge all of them. Richard P. Benton of Trinity College read and edited parts of Chapters 3 and 4. The Research Committee of Washington State University awarded me a grant which helped greatly in rewriting and which aided in other related projects. Graduate students here and elsewhere encouraged me to finish the revision sooner than I had intended—to them many thanks. My colleagues in the Department of English at Washington State University, Robert C. McLean, Kathleen McLean, Milton C. Petersen, and especially Conny E. Nelson whose encouragement and good advice kept me at the work, read parts of the later versions of the manuscript and helped me firm it up and trim it down. My colleague in the Department of Foreign Languages and Literatures, David P. Benseler, helped me with some of the difficult German texts.

I wish to thank the following for permission to use portions of my work on Poe that first appeared elsewhere, and in a slightly different form: Harper & Row for the introduction noted above which now forms parts of Chapters 1 and 7; Richard P. Veler and the Chantry Music Press at Wittenberg University for permitting an adaptation of my essay "Poe and 'Romantic Irony,'" which appeared in *Papers on Poe*, a *Festschrift* in honor of John Ward Ostrom, and which is now a long section in Chapter 2; *American Literature* for what is now a part of Chapter 2; Kenneth W. Cameron and Richard P. Benton for material now comprising most of Chapter 3, which originally appeared in the *Emerson Society Quarterly* and was subsequently reprinted in Benton's *New Approaches to Poe* by Transcendental Books; *Poe Studies* and the *Emerson Society Quarterly* for material now a large part of Chapter 4; *English Language Notes* for material now a part of Chapter 5; *Studies in Short Fiction* for material now a part of Chapter 6; and *PMLA* for material now a part of Chapter 7.

G. R. T.

Pullman, Washington
October 1971

CITATIONS IN THE TEXT

The following abbreviations are used in parentheses in the text in an effort to keep the bibliographical apparatus from being too intrusive.

H   Harrison edition. Harrison, James A., ed. *The Complete Works of Edgar Allan Poe.* 17 vols. 1902. Reprint. New York: AMS Press, 1965. The standard edition, though presumably to be superseded by the Mabbott edition now in progress.

B   Borzoi edition. Quinn, Arthur Hobson, and O'Neill, Edward H., eds. *The Complete Poems and Stories of Edgar Allan Poe.* 2 vols. New York: Alfred A. Knopf, 1946. An accurate reprinting from original sources giving earlier verions of some of Poe's first tales. References to this edition occur principally in Chapter 3.

O   Ostrom edition of letters. Ostrom, John Ward, ed. *The Letters of Edgar Allan Poe.* 2 vols. Cambridge, Mass.: Harvard University Press, 1948. Reprinted with a New Foreword and Supplementary Chapter. New York: Gordian Press, 1966.

Also frequently cited for context and translated quotations are:

K   Kayser, Wolfgang. *Das Groteske: seine Gestaltung in Malerei und Dichtung.* Oldenburg: Gerhard Stalling, 1957. Translated by Ulrich Weisstein as *The Grotesque in Art and Literature.* Bloomington: Indiana University Press, 1963. Reprint. New York: McGraw-Hill, 1965. References to this book are primarily limited to the first part of Chapter 5, "Grotesque and Arabesque."

W   Wellek, René. *A History of Modern Criticism 1750–1950.* 4 vols. to date. New Haven, Conn.: Yale University Press, 1956–. References are principally supplementary in the notes.

Parenthetical citations in the text follow this pattern: the code letter is followed by the volume number, then the page number. Thus (H 16:314) is the Harrison edition, vol. 16, p. 314. (B 1:114–17) is the Borzoi Poe, vol. 1, pp. 114–17. (O 2:437) is the Ostrom edition of the letters, vol. 2, p. 437, and so on.

POE'S FICTION
Romantic Irony in the Gothic Tales

1
Perspectives

*Do you know . . . that at Sparta . . . to the west of the
citadel, among a chaos of scarcely visible ruins, is a kind of
socle, upon which are still legible the letters* ΛΑΣΜ. *They
are undoubtedly part of* ΓΕΛΑΣΜΑ. *Now at Sparta were a
thousand temples and shrines to a thousand different
divinities. How exceedingly strange that the altar of Laughter
should have survived the others. . . .*
        "The Assignation" (1835, 1840)

ALTHOUGH FEW WOULD DISPUTE the claim that *Moby-Dick* (1851) is the
masterwork of the Gothic tradition in America, it is clearly Edgar Allan
Poe, rather than Melville or Hawthorne, who is the acknowledged master of American Gothic fiction. But whereas *Moby-Dick* has won its
place in the canon of the classic American works supposedly by transcending its surface genre of the Gothic, no work of Poe has fully won
a place in the lists of classic American writers supposedly because Poe
was unable to transcend the Gothic. Thus it is by a curious irony of
literary history that Poe's intricate manipulation of the genre has resulted in the critical judgment that his was "merely" a Gothic art: the
art of the carney fun house: cheap, obvious, tawdry. And thus Poe's
highly complex use of a Romantic genre has become simplified by reductive critics unable to transcend their own preconceptions of genre.
    Nevertheless, those of us who read Poe past adolescence find our-
selves in a curious position. If we are capable of feeling Poe's massive
impact, we are also likely to feel a little guilty about our response, or
at the very least feel an odd disappointment with Poe's strangely
flawed tales, with their apparently overdone rhetoric, melodramatic
situations, sudden shifts in tone, and seemingly inappropriate intrusions of the comic and absurd. Moreover, the strictures of such critics
as Henry James, D. H. Lawrence, Aldous Huxley, Yvor Winters, and

3

T. S. Eliot are too well known for any student of Poe to feel entirely comfortable about admitting that he does indeed "take Poe seriously."[1]

Even Allen Tate, one of Poe's most able defenders, admits to a persistent ambivalence of response: an attraction and fascination that is somehow constantly undercut.[2] The enigma of Poe's impact, Tate suggests, is his ability to move us on a deep and primitive level despite (sometimes even through) clumsiness. Moreover, because of his view of the Forlorn Demon of the Self, Poe is impressive in the whole corpus of his work, for no other writer in nineteenth-century England, America, or France "went so far in his vision of dehumanized man." This thematic coherence, Tate maintains, is clearer in Baudelaire's translations of Poe into French since the characteristic blemishes of Poe's style do not show so clearly. But when the native English-speaking critic reads Poe, he finds that not one of Poe's works is unblemished, that the "decor" of Poe's Gothic world is often "ludicrous," that the "trappings" of his nightmare world are "tawdry." Tate writes: "I confess that Poe's serious style at its typical worst makes the reading of more than one tale at a sitting an almost insuperable task. The Gothic glooms, the Venetian interiors, the ancient wine-cellars (from which nobody ever enjoys a vintage but always drinks 'deep')—all this, done up in a glutinous prose, so fatigues one's attention that the best will in the world here gives up, unless one gets a clue to the power underlying the flummery" (pp. 467–68). Tate also confesses that he is puzzled by this bad writing because Poe is often capable of direct, simple, unpretentious prose, as in his criticism and in a few of his tales. Tate thus delineates the opposition between Poe's important but narrow themes and horrible but affecting style. The primal fact of death, the perverse fascination of death, the horror of the inhuman and of the dehumanized, and the dramatization and symbolization of subconscious feelings are all done up in glutinous prose and with ludicrous stage-Gothic decor. Thus one of the major problems with Poe's Gothic tales is that, as Gothic tales, they never seem quite wholly to work. "The Fall of the House of Usher," Tate writes, "was a little spoiled for me even at fourteen by the interjection of the 'Mad Tryst of Sir Launcelot Canning'" (p. 455).

A second major problem with Poe's tales (actually another aspect of the first) is that as a single group they seem to lack consistency and wholeness; the body of his fiction splits disturbingly into two large, seemingly inconsistent, groups: flawed Gothic tales on the one hand and flawed comic and satiric tales on the other. Poe's critics have found this duality disturbing not only because the humor of his comic stories seems unpleasantly morbid, really humorless, or finally pointless, but also because Poe has always seemed to them to be, first and last, a

Gothic-Romantic writer. His many attempts at humor and satire, according to the Gothicist view of Poe, show not that he was a humorist, but only that humor was actually "alien" to his personality; when he tried to write humor, he was attempting to put on an incongruous mask, out of keeping with his real self.[3]

Indeed, it has come to be conventional to explain the curious incongruities in Poe's works by means of a pseudo-Freudian biographical approach, as proceeding from his lack of self-identity (Poe as the orphaned child of itinerant actors reared in the home of a tyrannical and unloving foster father). This lack of identity is supposed to have caused him to assume various unsuitable masks or guises and to spend his life in "role-playing."[4] In this mode, one of the most coherent views of the diversity of Poe's career is the suggestion that Poe in his writings borrowed not only the literary symbols of English Romanticism, but also the very personalities of the English Romantic poets. Poe is supposed to have played Byron in his earliest poems, then Shelley, then Coleridge in his later poems. His "unattractive" satire and parody, according to this view, shows, in another dimension, how much he depended on imitation for literary inspiration. This imitative habit of mind is supposed also to be part of Poe's American quality, derived from the empirical habit of mind in the American culture at large. The empirical strain in Poe is supposed to have completely taken over from the Romantic in the early 1840s, when he wrote his first purely "ratiocinative" detective stories. His 1842 review of Hawthorne's *Twice-Told Tales,* in which he discussed the principle of complete unity and totality of effect, thus shows Poe systematizing a formula for the short story; and "The Philosophy of Composition" (1846), in which Poe explained in almost mechanical terms how he came to write "The Raven," step by rational step, shows Poe claiming as his own the analytic mind of M. Dupin, the rational French detective-hero of "Murders in the Rue Morgue" (1841), "The Mystery of Marie Rogêt" (1842), and "The Purloined Letter" (1844).

The scheme falters a little at this point, however, for at the same time that Poe was playing, in the words of Leon Howard, the "coldly calculating emotional engineer" of "The Philosophy of Composition," he was also playing the bereaved Romantic hero of "The Raven" (1845), a Romantic role picked up shortly again in "Ulalume" (1847). And so we return to the easy Freudian view of Poe's inconsistencies: the "personal implications" of "The Raven" as a poem along with the prose account of its composition, according to Howard, are "almost" schizophrenic. Howard does go on to say, however, that Poe's was not truly a "psychological" case, since even before 1846, in the Dupin stories, he was seeking a middle ground of intellectuality that is seen most clearly in the long philosophical essay *Eureka* (1848). Dupin is the man of reason *and* intuition, poet *and* mathematician, whose imagination provides a hypothesis, whose reason controls its application, and whose observation verifies it. This, Poe proposes in *Eureka,* is the true way to knowledge: instead of the creeping and crawling methods of induction and deduction, we must have leaps of intuition "corrected" by reason.[5]

But this view of Poe's imaginative life, attractive and coherent though it may be in general, does not adequately account for the analytic criticism he practiced from the beginning, or for the number of satiric and comic works that appeared throughout his twenty-year career in a pattern of loose alternation with the Gothic works. Poe's first published story, "Metzengerstein," is ostensibly a Gothic tale; but it was one of five that Poe sent to the *Philadelphia Saturday Courier* in 1831, four of which ("The Duc de L'Omelette," "A Tale of Jerusalem," "Loss of Breath," and "Bon-Bon") are comic and satiric. These comic tales, published after "Metzengerstein" early in 1832, were followed in the next three years by four ostensibly Gothic stories ("MS. Found in a Bottle," "The Assignation," "Berenice," and "Morella"). Then came three comic and satiric tales ("Lionizing," "Hans Phaal," and "King Pest") in the middle of 1835, followed by the ostensibly Gothic tale "Shadow." Then two more comic and satiric tales ("Four Beasts in One" in 1836 and "Mystification" in 1837) were followed by two more Gothic tales ("Silence" in 1837 and "Ligeia" in 1838). From the winter of 1838–39 to the winter of 1839–40, we find four satiric tales ("How to Write a Blackwood Article," "A Predicament," "The Devil in the Belfry," and "The Man That Was Used Up") followed by three Gothic tales ("The Fall of the House of Usher," "William Wilson," and "The Conversation of Eiros and Charmion"), followed in turn by the comic "Why the Little Frenchman Wears His Hand in a Sling." This loose pattern of alternation continues to the end of Poe's career, even suggesting conscious self-parody; the Dupin stories (1841 to 1845) are burlesqued in the comic detective story " 'Thou Art the Man' " (1844); the suspended animation of "M. Valdemar" (1845) is made comic in Count Allamistakeo's resurrection in "Some Words with a Mummy" in the same year; the living burials of Madeline Usher and of Berenice are travestied in "The Premature Burial" (1844); the Gothic decor of "The Masque of the Red Death" (1842) and the revenge theme in "The Cask of Amontillado" (1846) became part of an absurd, though savage, fairy tale in "Hop-Frog" (1849).

When, at almost exactly and midpoint of his career, Poe first collected his stories as *Tales of the Grotesque and Arabesque* (1840), the comic and satiric works outnumbered the "serious" works by fourteen to eleven. Of the tales written after 1840, the serious outnumbered the comic and satiric by twenty-four to nineteen (though what is serious and what is comic in about a half-dozen of these later tales may, initially, seem arguable). Thus, of the total of Poe's sixty-eight short tales, thirty-five are ostensibly serious and thirty-three are comic and satiric—a balancing off of the serious and the comic that can hardly be mere accident.

Another, more comprehensive, kind of explanation of these matters and other seeming "inconsistencies" in Poe's work focuses on the basic thesis of *Eureka* (1848), Poe's essay on the origin, meaning, and destiny of the universe. In this book-length work, Poe begins with the proposition that existence implies ultimate annihilation—not only of the individual, but of all things, in a pointlessly pulsating cosmos which endlessly creates and destroys itself. Often self-consciously facing extinction, the forlorn Poe hero gives way to "hysterical" laughter or "draws back," symbolically, toward self-annihilation in a manner paralleling the basic destructive design of the universe as Poe saw it. In Poe, writes Harry Levin, "the premise of knowledge" is that "all men are mortal, and the insights of tragedy culminate in the posture of dying. More than once . . . [Poe] reminds us that Tertullian's credo, 'I believe because it is absurd,' was inspired by the doctrine of resurrection. And though Poe's resurrections prove ineffectual or woefully incomplete, we are reminded by the Existentialists that the basis of man's plight is absurdity."[6] Given Levin's "existentialist" context, Poe's Gothic works, implicitly based on a vision of absurdity, and the mad and half-mad Gothic figures which inhabit these works, seem clearly related to the fierce absurdity of his comic and satiric works.

Although this is a progressive explanation (except for the element of "hysteria") of the whole body of Poe's work and of its fascination for the modern reader, and while it points the way to a more just assessment of Poe, critics have been slow to reexamine thoroughly the corpus of Poe's work. The result has been an incomplete revaluation which has passively reinforced the older, now traditional, view of Poe as merely the schizophrenic genius of the demoniac imagination. The apparent discrepancy between Poe's "unnatural" comic face and his "true" serious face remains a nagging problem for the modern reader. Moreover, even the reader who would allow a simple, natural diversity of interest to Poe finds himself faced with the critical question of just how to read the works of a Gothic humorist—or the works, for that matter, of a humorous Gothicist.

What we need is a new way of reading Poe—a way just as informed as the new readings of Mark Twain and Herman Melville which have in the last few decades saved their works from consignment to the adolescent's bookshelf. We must divorce ourselves from the traditional Gothicist view of Poe, a view which includes not only the image of Poe as the mad genius of the macabre tale but also the contrary image of Poe as the dreamy poet of the "ideal" world of supernal Beauty. The ideal and the demonic are, of course, major elements in Poe's consciously developed image—but so too are the comic and satiric. The real questions are: how to develop a reading inclusive of these divergent tendencies, and how truly divergent are they at last?

In this study, I am concerned primarily with Poe's Gothic fiction. But I attempt to see it within a coherent system provided by the structures of the individual tales, by the entire canon of his work, and by the pattern of his career, as well as in a literary and philosophical context it has not been seen in before. We will take as a given the traditional view of Poe as a man obsessed with the "nightside" of the soul. The depth and insight that characterize this obsession are what make for Poe's power. But an obsession is also a structure of consciousness, however directed by subconscious impulses. A structure of consciousness must find a language, a set of forms to express itself, and this brings us to another given of Poe, his acceptance of the Gothic tradition as the language of forms by means of which his obsession could be articulated. It is at this point that the traditional criticism of Poe stops, with the recognition of the powerful obsession and the less powerful language and form. How many critics have in effect wished that Poe, like Kafka, had found a language adequate to his obsession?

We will go on from this point. We will develop another dimension: the dimension that explains how Poe was able to protect himself from the despair to which such immersion as his in the nightside vision must normally lead, and that also explains the paradoxical intertwining of the comic and the serious in his tales, and indeed in the pattern of his career. The key to this new style of reading Poe is to be found in the twentieth-century emphasis on the concepts of tension and irony. (American "New Criticism," in fact, is the culmination of one line of Romantic literary theory.) The contrast between the ideal and the demonic in Poe's works, between the serious and the comic, the Gothic and the satiric, and, thematically, between hope and despair, is a matter of the balance achieved by the dynamic tension of opposite forces. The view of art and life informing both the tales and the poems, and to an extent the criticism, is that of skeptical dissembler and hoaxer who complexly, ambivalently, and ironically explored the fads of the Romantic Age. Flat statements or commitments in Poe are only seeming. Almost everything that Poe wrote is qualified by, indeed controlled by, a prevailing duplicity or irony in which the artist presents us with slyly insinuated mockery of both ourselves as readers and himself as writer. Irony was the device that allowed him both to contemplate his obsession with death, murder, torture, insanity, guilt, loss, and fear of total annihilation in a meaningless universe, and also to detach and protect himself from the obsession.

In general, the word *irony*, historically and at present, points to some basic discrepancy between what is expected or apparent and what is actually the case.[7] As a literary term, irony implies some deception, which becomes clear with the perception of discrepancy between the immediately apparent intention, or meaning, or circumstance, or stated belief, and a half-hidden meaning or reality. Literary irony is seen in a writer's verbal and structural mode of purporting to take seriously what he does not take seriously, or at least does not take with complete seriousness. In the implied contrasts the ironist sets up, there is often a sense of one term in some way mocking the other. Irony may also be a serious, noncomic, nonsatiric attitude; in such a case irony may mean simply that an expressed attitude is somehow qualified, usually by its opposite possibility. In any event, although there are different ironic tones, irony is more often than not philosophically characterized by a skepticism engendered by seeing opposite possibilities in a situation, as is especially evident in the particularly complex and paradoxical skepticism of the strongly ironic poetry of the seventeenth and twentieth centuries. This style of irony is highly praised in modern literary criticism; and it is in this sense that the term *irony* describes Poe's characteristic mode of writing, his habit of mind, and even his style of Romantic idealism.

But Poe is not only an ironist, he is a satiric ironist. Satire, in general, makes fuller use of comic distortion than irony and is always immediately clearer, since the incongruities show more plainly. Satire distorts the characteristic features of an individual or of a society or of an artistic work in order to ridicule that which the satirist dislikes— usually (or avowedly) the vices and follies of mankind, the lamentable falling away from traditional ideals. When the satirist makes use of irony, he pretends to take his opponents seriously, accepting their premises and values and methods of reasoning in order eventually to expose their absurdity. The relationship of irony to satire, however, is complicated by the problem of emphasis, since either can be the weapon of the other, since either can provide the basic thrust of a work, and since both make use of distortion. But in addition to Poe's ironic and satiric styles, we must consider his closely related style as a hoaxer. Whereas satire makes use of comic surprises and contrasts, irony is usually subtler, and the essential deception involved in literary irony may be so subtle that the work becomes a hoax, and this is often the case in Poe. A hoax is usually thought of as an attempt to deceive others about the truth or reality of an event. But a literary hoax attempts to persuade the reader not merely of the reality of false events but of the reality of false literary intentions or circumstances—that a work is by a certain writer or of a certain age when it is not, or that one is writing a serious Gothic story when one is not. The laugh of the hoaxer is rather private, intended at best for a limited coterie of followers. Just as the satirist limits his circle of understanding readers to those who can perceive the flaws of society, so the ironist limits his circle of understanding readers to those who can discriminate with more subtlety the complexities of art and life.

At the extreme, the hoax can limit the circle of understanding readers to an audience of one. The hoax can in such a case be seen as a kind of supreme irony in which the writer mocks perceptive "eirons" like himself, and even, therefore, himself. Indeed, the German Romantic Ironists of the early nineteenth century, who had great influence on Poe, constructed theories of transcendence of one's mere selfness through almost this very means—what Friedrich Schlegel called "self-parody" and "transcendental buffoonery," which involves achieving a mystical sense of an "ideal" state beyond our limited earthly one by playing, as it were, a cosmic hoax on both the world and oneself.[8] Critical, skeptical detachment was the basis of these formal theories of Romantic Irony which flourished in the late eighteenth and early nineteenth centuries, especially in Germany, and which constitute a major and heretofore unexplored part of the historical context of Poe's literary and philosophical vision. These formal theories of irony will be a major touchstone of this study.

In English, the first instances of the word *irony* reflected its earliest classical meaning. Irony conveyed only a sense of a criticism that blamed through apparent praise, a technique that requires of the writer little more than a sense of the incongruous and an ability to exaggerate or understate. Poe, it is worth mentioning here, in No. 30 of "Fifty Suggestions" shows an interesting awareness of this early meaning. He writes: "A common *trick* is that of decrying, impliedly, the higher, by insisting on the lower, merits of an author." That is, a reviewer may praise "the acumen of Carlyle, the analysis of Schlegel, *and* the style of Macaulay," thereby implying, by praising Macaulay's "style," that he does not have the "acumen" and "analysis" of the others (H 14: 180–81). Gradually, the term was applied to more diverse effects involving some kind of discrepancy and came to be associated with reverses of circumstance and with certain characters and attitudes in tragedy, but especially with the personality of Socrates —with a habit of mind skeptical, dissimulating, and more than a little amused. *Eironeia* and *eiron* were initially terms of abuse for the Greeks, *eiron* suggesting something like deceiver, or sly fox. But Aristotle, and subsequently Cicero and Quintilian, expanded the meanings of irony so that it came to mean a mode of behavior that makes use of pretended modesty or ignorance in order to expose falsehood or to get at some truth possibly concealed under the surface of a situation or statement. In the *Nicomachean Ethics,* Aristotle used the term *eiron* to mean one who understates, as opposed to *alazon,* a pretender who exaggerates, with the ideal lying between the two. J. A. K. Thomson points out, however, that Aristotle, with characteristic Greek hatred of excess, guardedly praised the "eirons." But Cicero conceived of irony, especially "Socratic" irony, as urbane pretense and humane grace; and since then, Socratic irony has meant detached dissimulation in order to get at truth. In the context of Romantic Hellenism, it is easy to see from this background the logic of the impulse toward a "transcendental" irony.

In this connection, it is pertinent to note the meaning of another word. The term *mystic* in the sense of an idealist, of a striver after higher truth (even though through deceptive means), was associated with Socrates' name during his lifetime; and the conjoining of deceptive sly-foxery with idealism, as in Socratic irony, was clearly associated with English and German uses of the word *mystic* up to Poe's time.[9] Poe, in fact, comments on the German literary usage of *mystic* in a review of Thomas Moore's *Alciphron* in 1840. "Mystical" is employed, Poe says, by A. W. Schlegel and "most other German critics" to mean the kind of writing "in which there lies beneath the transparent upper current of meaning an under or *suggestive* one" (H 10:65). Poe goes on to discuss the "soul-exalting *echo*" in some writings of a "more ethereal beauty *beyond*"; but the important point for us in our search for a better understanding of Poe's accomplishment is that Poe links Romantic "ideality" with a suggestive doubleness of meaning and cites Schlegel, a popularizer of the German school of Romantic Irony, as his authority for the concept and the term. By itself, Poe's discussion of "mystical" is not particularly conclusive regarding his familiarity with the theories of Romantic Irony; but such fragments scattered throughout his critical reviews, *Marginalia* notes, essays, and letters, when seen in the literary context of the time, will provide insights that explain how Poe was a skeptical ironist at the same time that he was a Romantic, an idealist, and even a mystic.

It has been insufficiently recognized that it is the Continental movement or school of irony that comprised Poe's basic intellectual, philosophical, and artistic milieu. In the last two decades of the eighteenth century and the first two decades of the nineteenth, writers like Friedrich Schlegel and his brother August Wilhelm Schlegel, E. T. A. Hoffmann, Ludwig Tieck, and others had preceded Poe in the exploration of what they called the "nightside" of the mind and nature. Romanticists generally had come by Poe's time to feel that the secrets of Nature lay deep within the human mind itself. But in their philosophical struggles with objectivity and subjectivity, and in their exploration of mental aberrations, many, especially the "gloomy Germans," became increasingly pessimistic about man's ability to free himself from the web of illusion that existence seemed to present. But the small group of writers and thinkers with which we are here concerned developed a liberating, if still rather gloomy, theory of the darkly comic along with a philosophy of "Transcendental Irony," which could, they felt, free the deep-thinking man from his agonies (at least temporarily).

Romantic Irony has come to mean in our time an awkward and seemingly pointless breaking of dramatic illusion, such as having a stage "audience" interrupt a play with criticisms and even usurp the roles of the "actors," or having a character in a novel observe in Volume 3 that the lake he is now passing by is the very one he had fallen into in Volume 1, page such and such. These techniques, of course, have been used frequently by twentieth-century expressionist playwrights—indeed seem to have been in some sense rediscovered by the practitioners of Theater of the Absurd in their attempt to present an empty, absurd, illusory world. In Poe's time, this kind of irony became (for Poe and the coterie of writers we are talking about) the highest creative, poetic, and philosophical activity, having as its aim the "annihilation" of apparent contradictions and earthly limitations through a liberating perception of the element of absurdity in the mysterious contrarieties of the universe. The Romantic Ironist strove, in his contrariness, deceptiveness, satire, and even self-mockery, to attain a penetrating view of existence from a subliminally idealistic height of aesthetic perception—but always with an eye on the terrors of an ultimately incomprehensible, disconnected, absurd, or at best probably decaying and possibly malevolent universe. The more usual Romanticist wished to penetrate beyond the sensory to the ultimate secrets that lay behind appearance, secrets that, as mentioned, Romantic writers increasingly felt lay within the mind itself. But for the "Dark Romanticist," especially for the Romantic Ironist, the only attainable harmony in all the deceptiveness and chaos which the world presented was a double vision, a double awareness, a double emotion, culminating in an ambivalent joy of stoical self-possession and intellectual control. This kind of Romantic artist-hero held the world together by the force of his own mind—or he watched the world and his own mind crumble under the stress of dark contrary forces. The result, in the works of these writers, is an ambivalent pessimism: a kind of black humor, or black irony, and as well a skepticism engendered by the self-awareness of the subjective human mind insistently reaching out toward an illusive certainty.

The fictional and poetic creations resulting from such philosophical and artistic attitudes were sometimes called "grotesques," sometimes "arabesques," by the German (and French) writers of the day. These two words have complicated and intertwining histories; but clearly Poe was pointing out his philosophical and literary affinities with these writers when he remarked, albeit negatively, on the apparent "Germanism" of his tales in the preface to his first collection, *Tales of the Grotesque and Arabesque* (1840). This distinctively German genre of Romantic fiction (and poetry) is characterized by multiplicity of points of view and yet also by complete dramatization of the imagined world from the viewpoint of a single mind. Thus, in Poe's works, the limited perspective of the ever-present "I" in the tales has, carefully worked up around it, an intricate "arabesque" structure of illusion, misperception, perversity, and grotesque self-torment. Yet, in the complex structure and tone of the tales and poems, all is treated with a seldom recognized half-humorous ironic detachment from the plight of the "I" protagonist.

In Poe's characteristically intricate, even involuted, patterns of dramatic irony, the apparent narrative voice which pervades the surface atmosphere of the work is also seen within a qualifying frame. Several of the tales (for example, "The Black Cat," "The Tell-Tale Heart," "Ligeia," "The Imp of the Perverse," and "The Cask of Amontillado") involve a confessional element, wherein the first-person narrator, like Montresor, seems calmly or gleefully to recount horrible deeds, but which generally implies a listener to whom the agonized soul is revealing his torment. Especially revealing of the ironic structure thus achieved is Montresor in "The Cask of Amontillado." In the surface story, Montresor seems to be chuckling over his flawlessly executed revenge upon unfortunate Fortunato fifty years before. But a moment's reflection suggests that the indistinct "you" whom Montresor

addresses in the first paragraph is probably his death-bed confessor—
for if Montresor has murdered Fortunato fifty years before, he must
now be some seventy to eighty years of age. None of this is explicitly
stated; it is presented dramatically; and we get the double effect of
feeling the coldly calculated murder at the same time that we see the
larger point that Montresor, rather than having successfully taken his
revenge "with impunity," as he says (H 6:167), has instead suffered a
fifty-years' ravage of conscience.[10] Likewise, many of Poe's Gothic
tales seem to involve supernatural happenings; but they too have their
dramatic frames carefully worked up around them. Insinuated into
them, like clues in a detective story, are details which begin to construct frames around the narrative voice of the work. These dramatic
frames suggest the delusiveness of the experience as the first-person
narrator renders it. As in the works of Henry James and Joseph Conrad,
there is often in a Poe tale a tale within a tale within a tale; and the
meaning of the whole lies in the relationship of the various implied
stories and their frames rather than in the explicit meaning given to
the surface story by the dramatically involved narrator.

It has only been within the last ten to fifteen years that critics have
begun to look carefully at Poe's narrators as characters in the total
design of his tales and poems, and to suspect that even his most
famous Gothic works—like "Usher" and "Ligeia"—have ironic double
and triple perspectives playing upon them: supernatural from one
point of view, psychological from another point of view, and often
burlesque from yet a third.[11] But not only is nearly half of Poe's fiction
satiric and comic in an obvious way, also the Gothic tales contain
within them satiric and comic elements thematically related to the
macabre elements.[12] Poe seems very carefully to have aimed at the
ironic effect of touching his readers simultaneously on an archetypal
irrational level of fear and on an almost subliminal level of intellectual
and philosophical perception of the absurd. The result in the Gothic
tales, as in many of the poems, is a kind of ambivalent mockery. We
can respond to Poe's scenes of horror or despair at the same time that
we are aware of their caricatural quality.

Although not really one of Poe's complex tales, and although at the
end ostensibly comic, "The Premature Burial" (1844) is one of the
clearest examples of Poe's double effect, of his Gothic irony. The hero
is an avid reader of Gothic books on burial alive, and he gives us for
three-quarters of the tale horrifying "factual" histories. Terrified of
being buried alive himself, especially since he is subject to cataleptic
fits, the protagonist arranges for a special sepulcher, easily opened from
within, and a special coffin, with a spring-lid and a hole through which

a bell-pull is to be tied to the hand of his "corpse." When he awakes in a cramped, dark, earthy-smelling place, he is convinced that he has fallen into a trance while among strangers and that he has been

> . . . thrust, deep, deep, and forever, into some ordinary and nameless *grave*. . . . this awful conviction forced itself, thus, into the innermost chambers of my soul . . . I once again struggled to cry aloud. And in this second endeavor I succeeded. A long, wild, and continuous shriek, or yell, of agony, resounded through the realms of the subterrene Night.
> "Hillo! Hillo, there!" said a gruff voice in reply. (H 5:271)

The Gothic terror is comically undercut by the reply, and it turns out that the hero has fallen asleep in the narrow berth of a ship, where he has sought refuge for the night, and he is rousted out of his bunk by the sailors he has awakened with his horrible cry. Once we see that this is by no means a straightforward Gothic tale, we can see also the comic exaggeration of the overwrought Gothic style, that is, of what conventionally are "flaws" for twentieth-century readers. The emphasized "deep, deep, and forever," the italicized *"grave,"* the punning meaning of "innermost chambers of my soul," the redundancy of "shriek, or yell," and the capitalized letter of "subterrene Night" are typical of the exaggerations elsewhere in the tale. There can be no doubt that these stylistic exaggerations are part of Poe's burlesque technique once we read the conclusion, for the incident just described strikes the narrator as so ludicrous that he is shocked into sanity: "My soul acquired tone—acquired temper. I went abroad. I took vigorous exercise. . . . I thought upon other subjects than Death. I discarded my medical books. 'Buchan' I burned, I read no 'Night Thoughts'—no fustian about church-yards—no bugaboo tales—*such as this*" (H 5:273). After this jarring, comic, illusion-breaking reference to his own narrative, the hero then tells us that "from that memorable night" his "charnel apprehensions" were "dismissed forever"; and with them "vanished the cataleptic disorder, of which, perhaps, they had been less the consequence than the cause."

The satiric irony of the tale is multiple. The narrator almost terrifies us with his chilling "factual" cases in the first three-quarters of the tale; and then he loses his charnel apprehensions quite suddenly, whereas we are still left entertaining the ghastly possibilities he has suggested. Moreover, the earnestness of his conversion suggests parody of didactic magazine fiction ("out of Evil proceeded Good . . . very excess wrought in my spirit an inevitable revulsion"), especially when we remember Poe's formulation of "the heresy of the Didactic" in "The

Poetic Principle" and elsewhere. Finally, in the last paragraph, just as we are perhaps adjusting to the comic conclusion, the narrator reaffirms ("Alas!") that "sepulchral terrors cannot be regarded as altogether fanciful." The "imagination of man" cannot "explore with impunity its every cavern"; our "Demons" must be allowed to "sleep, or they will devour us" (H 5:273). Thus, the final lines suggest with nice ambiguity both the psychological and the supernatural, and leave us entertaining the serious possibilities of the absurd situation.

Many critics, however, will grant Poe a unified complexity of symbolism supporting the madness of an obviously mad character, like Roderick Usher, but balk at seeing an ironic complexity governing the whole tale in the suggested madness of the narrators of spooky stories like "Usher" and "Ligeia." Edward Wagenknecht, for example, has written that the "absurd notion" that "Ligeia" is "not a story of the supernatural but a study in morbid psychology" requires that we "ignore the text except where it can be perverted" and that we substitute the "fashionable notions of a later period" for those of Poe's own time.[13] "Neither aesthetically nor psychologically," Wagenknecht writes, does this twentieth-century Freudian reading allow us to read the tale "as a nineteenth-century story":

Abnormal as he is, the narrator is a fairly conventional type of Poe hero; if we are to assume that we see the whole story in a distorted mind in this instance, why should not the other stories be interpreted on the same basis? Indeed, once we have decided to ignore the author's intentions and the milieu out of which the story comes, there is no reason why we should confine ourselves to misrepresenting Poe; an unlimited field is opened up. (pp. 248–49)

Wagenknecht's theoretical point is well taken, but his conclusion about Poe is in error, for given the psychological theories of the eighteenth and nineteenth centuries and the techniques of nineteenth-century Romantic fiction, especially in Germany and America, one is forced to conclude that the psychological reading of "Ligeia" is, for the proper audience, indeed a nineteenth-century reading. As Michael Allen has shown in his *Poe and the British Magazine Tradition,* the conception of a coterie audience was an important element in the attitude of the writers of fiction for the influential *Blackwood's Edinburgh Magazine,* whose lead Poe seems to have followed, even though he also subjected the journal to satiric burlesque. There was, in the minds of these writers, on the one hand a large mass audience addicted to the somewhat tawdry melodrama of people caught in impossible predicaments, such as being accidentally baked in an oven (or buried alive), and a smaller coterie of more perceptive readers who could enjoy the sly satire insinuated into such tales.[14] The effect of "Ligeia" is double—for the coterie of the perceptive. The rationale of the tale is psychological. (And who would deny that Poe was interested in abnormal psychology?) But its primary impact is spooky and weird. Yet this double impact is but one part of Poe's irony; "Ligeia" also contains his characteristic satiric innuendo, his ambivalent mockery, for the tale also contains satiric thrusts at transcendentalism and the two kinds of horror materials to be found in the German and English brands of Gothicism.[15]

An obsession and its expressive forms are contingent though different things, just as "code" and "message" are contingent yet different. The device of irony, this way of saying, was itself an obsession; and it could exist in Poe's works separate from the nightside obsession. When it did, it took the form of hoax, parody, satire, and the comic. In attempting to show Poe's constant struggle with his obsessions, I try to delineate his philosophical and literary consciousness in such a way as to show that the element of the horrific was modified by an ability to mock both the vision of the horror that obsessed him and the very forms expressive of it, that Poe's comic face and his Gothic face merged into one ironic face. What was otherwise an inadequate Gothicism became for Poe, in the manner of certain Continental writers, the literary vehicle for his own double and triple vision. With such multiple vision, and with such strategies of duplicity, he could satisfy his public audience, deal with his obsession, and control in intricate structures of opposed forces his simultaneous involvement in, and mocking detachment from, the double horror of the external world and the internal mind. Thus irony, as a device of saying and structuring, became a way of seeing.

The image that opens Poe's difficult poem "Ulalume" catches neatly this tension of involvement and detachment. The self-tortured, bereaved lover, wandering in a "misty mid-region" of numbed forgetfulness, finds that, under the compulsive urgings of his subconscious mind, he has arrived at the tomb of his lost love, whereupon the smoldering agonies of loss burst forth again. Before this, however, he describes the state of his heart as like that of a polar volcano. Although seething with fire within, it was yet encased in ice. This image, I believe, can be seen not only as the objective correlative of the psychological state of the persona of the poem, but also as the emblem of the artistic and philosophical consciousness of Poe himself. Tormenting fire, as well as polar ice, are recurrent images in Poe's works. If the sulphurous currents of fire in "Ulalume" can be taken as suggestive of an inferno of tormented obsessions, the ice which for a time binds them is then equally suggestive of the aesthetic and philosophical control we find forcibly exerted over these obsessive materials which yet continually threatened to break through the cool detachment of his artistry.

Although the ironic vision was natural to Poe, he was by no means alone among Romantic writers in his exploration of irony as a literary device and as a means of ordering the world. Indeed, the artistic consciousness of a writer may be described as the resultant tension between the individual personality and the external givens of the culture. Thus this study is ultimately in the tradition of the history of ideas, and I take up in turn the history and theory of irony, the Gothic, the grotesque and arabesque, and the nightside, in an effort to delineate the intellectual and artistic milieu with which Poe had to deal. And thus ultimately I end where I begin, showing in Poe the pervasiveness and depth of that peculiarly neglected Romantic conception of irony that the early nineteenth-century German aesthetician K. W. F. Solger, for one, called the "consummate fruit" of the Romantic Mind.[16]

2
Romantic Irony

Say something about objectivity and subjectivity.
"How to Write a Blackwood Article" (1838)

THE QUESTION of Poe's Germanism is a curious one. Critics have connected Poe with German Romanticism from the very first. As early as 1833, one of the first editors of the *Southern Literary Messenger* thought it wise to follow Poe's "Berenice" with a mild apology: "Whilst we confess that we think there is too much German horror in his subject, there can be but one opinion as to the force and elegance of his style."[1] Poe, on the other hand, sought to minimize his debt to the Germans in his preface to the *Tales of the Grotesque and Arabesque,* claiming that he could not be so easily categorized: ". . . Germanism is 'the vein' for the time being. Tomorrow I may be anything but German, as yesterday I was everything else" (H 1:150). Poe made this remark in response to the charge by his "critics" that his serious tales are pervaded by "Germanism and gloom." But, Poe says, the grounds of the charge have not been "sufficiently considered," for his particular kind of "terror" is not some kind of horripilation for horripilation's sake, but is instead concerned with the spirit and mind of man, with the inner man, and not with something merely ghostly or grisly:

Let us admit, for the moment, that the "phantasy-pieces" now given *are* Germanic, or what not. . . . But the truth is that, with a single exception, there is no one of the stories in which the scholar should recognize the distinctive features of that species of pseudo-horror which we are taught to call Germanic, for no better reason than that some of the secondary names of German literature have become identified with its folly. If in many of my productions terror has been the thesis, I maintain that terror is not of Ger-

19

many, but of the soul—that I have deduced this terror only from its legitimate sources, and urged it only to its legitimate results. (H 1:150–51)

Scholars have taken this remark both too seriously, and not seriously
enough. For it has been used by some critics as evidence which denies
German influence on Poe. But as Palmer Cobb observes, the preface,
on the contrary, actually suggests Poe's familiarity with German
literature. Moreover, Poe's reviews, *Marginalia* notes, critical essays,
and, of course, his tales, are saturated with references to German
writers, German philosophy, and German critical terms and ideas.
Poe's preface does not, as Cobb points out, contain a denial of the
"motives and technique of the German romanticists" but in fact an admission of a general German influence; and Cobb also suggests that
Poe indirectly acknowledges a kinship between his tales and those of
E. T. A. Hoffmann's *Phantasiestücke* (1814–15) when he refers to his
stories as "phantasy pieces" in quotation marks—to which we might
also add Ludwig Tieck's *Phantasus* (1812–16).[2]

What is rarely observed about German Romanticism, and about such
writers as Hoffmann and Tieck, is that one of its distinctive features
was the development of a comic perspective, eventually reflected in
Coleridge, Carlyle, and Hazlitt, whom Poe read, along with the latest
translations of German works as they became available in America.
This apprehension of the comic, the ironic, and the absurd in an otherwise melancholy and even sinister world has come to be called, rather
loosely, Romantic Irony. And what is striking about German Romanticism in relation to Poe, I submit, is not Gothic gloom and horror, but
the theories of the Romantic Ironists about the subconscious mind,
about "objective subjectivity," about the ultimate "annihilation" of
contradictions through an ironic art, and about the idealistic "transcendence" of earthly limitations through the Godlike immanence and
detachment of the artistic mind. These ideas can be found in two of
Poe's favorite German writers, the dramatist and novelist Ludwig Tieck
(1773–1853) and the critic August Wilhelm Schlegel (1767–1845).
These figures are those most clearly associated (outside of Germany)
with the theories and practices of Romantic Irony, and we shall have
special reference to them in the discussion of the theory of Romantic
Irony that follows.

I

The concept of Romantic Irony is initially confusing. As a leading
authority on the subject, Raymond Immerwahr, points out, the term

Romantic Irony is rather different from the ordinary meanings attached separately to the two words that make up the phrase.[3] As in ordinary usage of the term *irony* by itself, the Romantic Ironist "means something different from what he appears to be saying: His argument, creation, or representation is not to be taken solely at its face value or in dead earnest." But this is only a part of his stance. The Romantic Ironist "does not mean simply the opposite of what he says"; instead, "he is likely to mean at the same time both what he seems to be saying *and* its opposite" (p. 665). Moreover, Immerwahr adds, it is this kind of "interaction" of opposites, especially of "creative enthusiasm and restraining self-criticism" that characterizes Schlegel's conception of Romantic itself . . ." (p. 666).

The simplest meaning of Romantic Irony is found in the technique of mocking or destroying dramatic illusion in the fiction and drama of certain German writers at the end of the eighteenth century and the beginning of the nineteenth. The technique is allied to satire and parody, and Ludwig Tieck's youthful plays, in which the main interest is satire aimed at eighteenth-century rationalism and sentiment, contain some of the clearest examples of this technique. In Tieck's hands, it reveals a development toward an "objective" philosophy of irony through an increasingly "subjective" treatment of reality. This can be illustrated by reference to three of Tieck's early plays discussed by Carlyle in his *German Romance* (1827), a book that probably introduced Poe to Tieck, Hoffmann, Jean Paul Friedrich Richter, De La Motte Fouqué, and Musaeus, as well as to German literature in general.[4] In *Puss in Boots* (1767), for example, Tieck begins the deliberate breaking of the illusion immediately with a prologue in which members of a make-believe "audience" express fears that the play they have come to see may lack "good taste." The "author" then appears on stage to reassure them. When Puss begins to speak, the "audience" objects that a talking cat destroys dramatic illusion; and throughout the play the "audience" thus interrupts the action, so destroying illusion. The same effect is achieved as the characters in the play as well as the audience break into the action to discuss the merits of the piece. The audience expresses views the opposite of Tieck's (which the real audience must infer); the "good taste" they want in the play is for Tieck bad taste: the moralizing sentimentalities of popular dramatists like A. F. von Kotzebue (1761–1819). A similar ironic structure is seen again when the cat talks with a burlesque grandiloquence that causes his master to call him "sublime friend" just before the cat climbs up to the roof to stalk pigeons: "As in a series of mirrors, there is endless romantic-ironic reflection and re-reflection."[5] The work achieves its meaning as a flickering structure of formal as well as situational ironies.

Like *Puss*, Tieck's *Prince Zerbino* (1798) is an allegorical satire of and on popular literature, and in it we find a further development of a philosophy of the ironic and absurd. An old king abdicates in order to play with lead soldiers, observing that the game we play in life is "really a child's game, and what indeed do we do seriously?" Free from the tribulations of actual rule, he finds true happiness with his lead soldiers. But the central action of the play forms a sequel to *Puss*. Zerbino, seriously ill from reading best sellers, sets out on a journey to find good taste, but fails. At one point, however, by sheer force of will, the hero tries to reverse the play: the scenes already presented are staged once more in reverse order, but the author steps in and forces the play to go on. Indeed, it is hard not to wish that Poe might have reviewed each of the translations of Tieck as they appeared in America. *The World Turned Topsy-Turvy* (1799), for example, is an allegorical burlesque, structured around a number of form-breaking ironies, that Poe would have found attractive. The play is indeed topsy-turvy: an epilogue opens it; a prologue closes it; a spectator becomes an actor and yet remains a spectator; and the stage represents a stage. Moreover, in all this, we find a development toward the psychological, or what the Romanticists called the nightside of nature, eerie because of its nonrational aspects—aspects which suggest gloomy subconscious delusion.[6] In *Topsy-Turvy*, which is still principally satire, we find the speculation: ". . . we sit here as spectators and see a play; in that play spectators are also sitting and seeing a play, and in that third play another play is going to be played by those third actors. . . . People often dream that sort of thing and it is terrible . . . many thoughts spin like that into the inwardness."[7] This interest in the human mind, both conscious and subconscious, and the problem of subjectivity and reality soon led to a concept of "objectivity" as ironic detachment.

The mode of such ironic works as Tieck's early plays, however, was actually the logical development of eighteenth-century German admiration for Cervantes, Swift, Fielding, and Sterne, in whom the Germans found "sportiveness" and an overall sense of harmonious synthesis of contrasts and contradictions. *Don Quixote* was the special favorite of Tieck and his followers, who in their fiction continued the German emulation of Cervantes's techniques of addressing the reader, of making mocking references to one's own work, and of generally fashioning a constant interplay of contradictions and ironies.[8] In the mid-eighteenth century, Christoph Martin Wieland (1733-1813) had in his romance *Don Sylvio of Rosalva* (1764) imitated Cervantes in laughing at his own ideals and in organizing his work around contrasts; and in his novel *Agathon* (1767) and in *Peregrinus Proteus*, a work which Poe quotes from twice,[9] Wieland had used the structural principle of contrast in presenting true contentment as lying between two extremes— for Wieland between pious asceticism and worldly sensualism. Goethe in *The Sorrows of Werther* (1773) and more clearly at the end of the century in *Wilhelm Meister's Apprenticeship* (1796) exemplifies the German Quixotic tradition. Like Cervantes, Goethe often referred directly to his reader, even mocking him openly. Goethe frequently gibed at his own novel, mentioning or suggesting the novel in the novel itself; and, like Cervantes, he often mocked the earnestness of his hero, calling attention to his self-conceit, pretended knowledge, selfishness, and confused thinking. Yet Wilhelm Meister to a large extent remains a sympathetic figure. Indeed, in *Poetry and Truth* (1811–1814), Goethe described the objective presentation of the clash of reason and habit as an "irony" within ourselves and with ourselves whereby we treat our faults in a playful spirit.[10]

In German Romantic fiction, multiplicity of points of view, such as in the double effect of creating a sympathetic but absurd hero, merged with philosophical theories of detachment and objectivity wherein, as mentioned, the superior mind transcends its human flaws. We have already seen that Poe sometimes creates a strong illusion, especially of horror, and then breaks it with a shock, absurdly though only half comically, as in "The Premature Burial." It is this more philosophical development of Romantic Irony, emerging from the openly mocking irony we have just examined, that is Poe's "tradition" in his Gothic tales. It found its initial literary form in the subtle duplicity of the distinctively German genre of the "grotesque": a genre which slyly insinuated double and triple perspectives in a vision closely associated with Gothic horror. When we note how the mocking ironic literary tradition represented by Tieck gradually merged with the subjective idealism of Kant and his followers, we understand how Romantic Irony turned from simple mocking and took on those qualities of brilliant suggestion and confusing chaos that Poe saw in German critical theory (H 16:115– 17). It was in this merger that Romantic Irony became intricately involved with metaphysical speculation on the objective and the subjective, on imagination, delusion, and reality, and on a transcendental mastery of the world and oneself through simultaneous detachment and involvement.

Although the work of Leibnitz (1646–1716) laid down the metaphysical groundwork (as Tieck and his colleagues laid down the formal, literary groundwork), it is Immanuel Kant's "Critiques" of *Pure Reason* (1781), *Practical Reason* (1788), and *Judgment* (1790) that are of immediate concern here. These works increased the general interest in the perplexities of human perception and in the workings of the subconscious mind that characterized the German Romantic Ironists who directly influenced Poe. According to Kant, all human knowledge is subjective, and objects are known only by qualities not inherent in the things themselves but given us by our sensory "intuition." The function of human imagination and intellect is to organize sense impressions into meaningful patterns; thus man's mind, to an extent, imposes order on the universe. But Kant postulated another human faculty, the will, which perceives spiritual and moral truths, unrelated to sense experience and unknowable by the intellect. The will, reaching out toward an external reality of universal moral law, operates within an individual as the categorical imperative in a realm of free moral choice which yet determines rightness and directs action without reference to reason—sometimes even directing action in opposition to reason. Aesthetic values in Kant's theory, as in Poe's, are mediational; in the presence of the beautiful we feel a "unification, a harmonious interplay of sense and mind, a perfect freedom from scientific and utilitarian necessity." This harmony is not merely psychological but philosophical and even moral, for the beautiful is the "symbol of the morally good." This beauty may be combined with natural forms or with purposive human creations, though neither is "pure" beauty. As Wimsatt and Brooks note in words that could have meaningful reference to much in Poe: "Kant's idea of beauty was severe; it related (so far as human making was concerned) almost exclusively to the formal, decorative, and abstract: to Greek designs, foliation on wallpaper, arabesques (things which 'mean nothing in themselves'), music without words." [11] Kant also developed ideas of biological and unconscious artistic creation. His analysis of the organic constitution of a tree (with its own moving and formative power and natural purpose) as opposed to the mechanical functioning of a watch seemed to the German "aesthetic organologists," as Meyer Abrams calls them, to prove that there is a "purely internal teleology" as a "constitutive element in living nature." [12]

Now the Romantic Ironists who were to influence Poe proceeded to take Kant's philosophy much further than he had ever intended. Kant's concepts of human subjectivity, necessity, and biological purpose were reworked by the Schlegels, Fichte, Schiller, Schelling, Novalis, Solger, Tieck, and Jean Paul, so as to emphasize the idea of an absolute idealism wherein all reality is arbitrated, if not indeed created, solely by the individual, who is almost a God-in-himself. The importance of this idea in Poe's thought may be seen in a passage in *Eureka*, where Poe says that it is impossible for one to believe, really, that *"anything exists greater than his own soul.* . . . each soul is, in part, its own God—its own Creator. . . . Man . . . ceasing imperceptibly to feel himself Man, will at length . . . recognize his existence as that of Jehovah" (H 16:312–15). This passage has its ironic perspective too, but, in any event, among these German writers it is the more literary Schlegels who, along with Tieck, are the most direct link between Poe and Romantic Irony. That influence is even clearer when we see how the theory of transcendental irony developed from Kant through Fichte, Schiller, and Schelling. For while Poe was most familiar with Tieck and the Schlegels, these lesser figures were also writers whom Poe seems to have read, or read about, for he mentions them frequently, quotes them, criticizes them, and burlesques them.

The first important reinterpretation of Kant was that of J. G. Fichte (1762–1814) in the last decade of the eighteenth century. Fichte developed a dialectical idealism to unify the theoretical and practical aspects of cognition set apart by Kant. He postulated an active individual ego as the source of the structure of experience, though this ego ultimately derives from an absolute ego or universal moral principle (God). Although each man creates his own world and rules it, he is yet restricted by it; but the more "objective," that is, the more detached, he can be toward the world he projects out of himself, the greater freedom of spirit he attains. (Fichte's concept is clearly similar to the modern critical idea of "aesthetic distance.") Moreover, Fichte linked this unfettered freedom resulting from objective detachment in the face of one's own subjectivity with psychological mastery over the irrational: to be able freely to govern the irrational part in man "according to its own laws is the ultimate purpose of humanity." This, said Fichte, is not a completely attainable goal since man is not divine; but man must at least strive to attain such power.[13]

About the same time as Fichte was writing, Schiller and Schelling began to consider the "inevitable" harmony of art, a harmony that eventually reflects either universal morality or spiritual good in Nature.[14] Friedrich Schiller (1759–1805) wrote in his *Letters of Aesthetic Education* (1795) that art arises out of two impulses—a finite material impulse and the "Idea." The reconciliation in art of the material impulse and Idea is the "free play" of the whole person. And in his essay *On Naive and Sentimental Poetry* (1795–96), Schiller elevated satire as a genre that ironically seeks after or affirms the ideal since it looks down on reality from the height of the ideal.[15] Friedrich Schelling (1775–1854), in several works published or circulated from about 1800 to 1803, dwelt on the harmony between man and nature and the probable conscious intelligence manifest and evolving in nature (*Naturphiloso-*

phie). History, he wrote, was a series of stages tending toward harmony with God after man's mythic fall, and he postulated a series of correspondences between nature and art, involving an antithesis between "subject" and "object," alternatively called "intelligence" and "nature," the "conscious" and the "unconscious," "freedom" (of human will) and "necessity" (imposed by Nature). The aesthetic act unites all ideas; it is the highest act of reason. Poetry penetrates the essence of the universe. By the aesthetic act of the imagination, the artist is able to free himself, to "think," and to "reconcile contradictions" in a liberating transcendence of his limiting self-identity.[16] That Poe was perfectly aware of such ideas will become increasingly clear, but we may note here his hanged narrator's comic remark in an early tale: the effect of the gallows rope upon the neck was such that "Schelling himself would have been pleased with my entire loss of self-identity" (H 2:360).

II

But while very real connections between Poe and the writers we have just surveyed may be pointed to, the most direct link between Poe and philosophical Romantic Irony is to be found in the theoretical writings of Friedrich Schlegel and in the practical criticism of A. W. Schlegel. Although the evidence that Poe read Friedrich Schlegel very closely is scanty, the evidence that he read August Wilhelm is conclusive. Poe was clearly aware of Friedrich's independent works, however, as well as with (so he would have us believe) German criticism in general. As noted elsewhere, Poe in "Exordium to Critical Notices" (*Graham's*, January 1842) wrote in praise of German criticism, remarking that the "magnificent *critiques raisonnées*" of "Winckelmann, of Novalis, of Schelling, of Goethe, or Augustus William, and of Frederick Schlegel" are in principle one with the criticism of Kames, Johnson, and Blair; but he added that the Germans differ "in their more careful elaboration, their greater thoroughness, their more profound analysis and application of the principles themselves."[17] From A. W. Schlegel alone, however, Poe could have gotten a sense of Friedrich Schlegel's more extreme concepts of "higher" irony, "self-parody," and "transcendental buffoonery," tempered by August Wilhelm's wistful melancholy and more practical turn of mind.

As we have seen, Fichte, Schelling, and others concerned themselves with the double problem of an "objective" detachment of the writer both from his art products and from the world even while being subjectively involved in art and the world. Maintaining objectivity, while yet subjectively creating a work from the depths of one's own spirit or mind, seemed to them to imply a suprahuman capacity in the artist and suggested ideas of "liberation" and "freedom" from the rather depressing limitations imposed upon the human spirit by the physical world of the senses and of mere appearances. Around 1800, Friedrich Schlegel had conjoined the terms *irony* and *transcendentalism*. Irony was the process of transcending both the illusions of the world and the delusions of one's own limited mind. Such transcendence of the visible world and of the self was, for Schlegel, achieved through a sense of the comic and the absurd in the serious. By comparing successive phases of our own stupidity and shrewdness, Schlegel suggested, we evolve increasingly superior versions of the self, a true sense of irony. Such a true sense of irony is the perception or creation of a succession of contrasts between the ideal and the real, the serious and the comic, the sinister and the absurd, through which the "transcendental ego" can mock its own convictions and productions from the height of the "ideal." As Poe remarked in "The Philosophy of Composition" (1845), one wants in dark and fantastic composition to approach "as nearly to the ludicrous as [is] admissible" (H 14:205). This kind of higher and more objective skepticism can be seen, according to Friedrich Schlegel, in the works of Cervantes and Shakespeare, which are "full of artfully arranged confusion, charming symmetry of contrasts, marvelous alternation of enthusiasm and irony." To this ironic interplay of contradictions in *Don Quixote,* Schlegel gave the name *arabesque.* Schlegel's use of *arabesque* to mean, in this instance, symmetrical interplay of contrasts and confusions, of earnestness alternating with irony, is crucial.[18]

Poe's 1840 title, *Tales of the Grotesque and Arabesque,* takes on new meaning when seen in this context. Poe's idea of the arabesque was the same as that of the Schlegels, if not directly derived from them; and the formal structures and the metaphysical vision implied are fundamental to an understanding of Poe's tales. Therefore we should come to that suspiciously "flawed" effect characteristic of Poe's Gothic tales with a sense of purpose, not of censure. For what we find in Poe, coming out of this distinctively European context, is a habit of mind basically skeptical, despite its immersion in the Gothic and the nightside.

Thus we will be able to see that Schlegel tells us something about Poe when he equates the term *irony* with an aesthetic act of reason that penetrates the essence of the universe, and when he develops further the ideas of Goethe, Herder, and Schiller (though apparently independent of Fichte and Schelling) that the creative powers of the artist are miniature powers paralleling those exercised in divine creation. Just as God's "objective" universe is an "ironical" reminder of the "subjective" Creator pervading all things, so also is the artist's objective literary creation an ironical reminder of his subjective Self pervading and enlivening his whole work. God's creatures appear to live and move independently of any other force than themselves, and yet God is somehow obviously manifest in their existence. Accordingly, even the most objective artist resides subjectively within his work. To combine extreme objectivity and immanence in a state of self-division and self-consciousness is to resemble God. In order to begin informing such a sense of purpose regarding Poe's "flawed" Gothic, we may note echoes of the German ideas we have discussed which are found in some of Poe's reviews, in his tales "The Island of the Fay" (1841), "Monos and Una" (1841), "The Landscape Garden" (1842) and its expanded version "The Domain of Arnheim" (1847), "The Power of Words" (1845), and in *Eureka* (1848).

In his "Drake and Halleck" review (1836), Poe noted that "Imagination is, possibly in man, a lesser degree of the creative power in God," adding that God creates what was not before, whereas man's artistic imitation of God's creative power is the reorganization of what has already been materially created. In his review of N. P. Willis (1845), Poe defined *imagination* as the artistic combining of elements in such a way as to create something truly original; and therein man's creative power resembles God's.[19] In "Monos and Una" disembodied Platonic spirits discourse on the "poetic intellect" and the transcendental truths reached by artistic analogy. In "The Power of Words" Poe dramatized (with some satiric innuendo about drunkenness) the Romantic imagination weeping over a flowered, green, volcano-studded "star" it has "spoken" into actual material existence (H 6:143–44). In *Eureka*, Poe's analysis of conventional, uninspired thought-processes is integral to his concluding remarks that in order to understand the universe (the purpose of *Eureka*), "we should have to be God ourselves," that "each soul is, in part, its own God—its own Creator," that man, through the division, diffusion, and self-consciousness of the God-principle ordering the universe, will eventually evolve into God (H 1:205, 313–15). These apparent affirmations, it may be observed again, have a melancholy irony to them, as we shall see later. In "Island of the Fay" and "Arnheim," which are ostensibly about beauty, especially the pleasures of contemplating God's beautiful natural garden (the world), Poe is actually concerned with the transitoriness of beauty and with the ironic reminders of deep melancholy import to be found in this beautiful "garden": shadows, rocky outcroppings, geological upheavals, and the like, which are "prognostic of *death*" (H 6:184).

Given Schlegel's (and Poe's) insistence that the world is, to the human mind, a dark, even chaotic paradox, it is understandable that Schlegel should have applied the term *irony* to both the form and spirit of a literary work of genius and to the Godlike state of being of the creator of the work. Only an ambivalent attitude can come close to comprehending the world's dark, contradictory totality; ambivalence is the human being's clear-sighted, conscious reaction to his vision of horrible chaos and to his simultaneous detachment from it. As Wimsatt and Brooks have occasion to note in *Literary Criticism: A Short History*, the "transcendental ego" of the Dark Romantics remains "aloof from fixation or satisfaction at any level of insight," and their examples of "dark irony" are perhaps more accurate than they may have realized: ". . . this irony might be very dark, sardonic, misanthropic; the hero stood with cloak pulled round his shoulder thrust out into the cold blast—a Byronic and Poesque figure" (p. 380).

In the *Athenäum* (1800), Schlegel conceived of the ironic attitude not only as one involving "transcendence" of the opaque facts of the world but also as one having the quality of "Socratic irony," the "free play" of the mind upon everything presented to it.

Socratic irony is a unique form of conscious dissimulation. . . . In it is to be included all jest, all earnest, everything transparently open and everything deeply concealed. It embodies and arouses a sense of the insoluble conflict between the finite and the absolute . . . through it one is enabled to rise above himself. . . . It is a very good sign if smug commonplace people do not know how they are to regard this constant self-parody of taking jest for earnest and earnest for jest.[20]

Such then is Friedrich Schlegel's "transcendental irony," which makes fun even of itself—a complex skepticism that yet involves a mystical faith in the ideal, a deceptive personal aloofness from any final commitment, and a "superior" pleasure in the hoaxlike limitation of one's compeers to a select coterie of the perceptive.[21]

III

But for Poe the principal German critic was not Friedrich Schlegel; it was his brother August Wilhelm Schlegel. A. W. Schlegel was in fact the most influential of the German critics outside Germany. The principal influence Schlegel is supposed to have had on Poe, however, was the doctrine of "unity" or "totality" of effect.[22] Indeed, Poe gives Schlegel credit for this influence several times in his reviews.[23] What is less obvious and far more important is Schlegel's conception of irony—derived from the work of his brother Friedrich—but articulated at length in the famous *Lectures on Dramatic Art and Literature*, which was first translated into English in 1815.

The evidence that Poe read A. W. Schlegel's *Lectures* carefully is conclusive. In September 1835 (at the age of twenty-four), Poe reviewed the Classical Family Library translation of Euripides for the *Southern Literary Messenger*, and nearly everything he has to say about Greek drama is a clear echo of A. W. Schlegel, often closely parallel in phrasing to John Black's 1815 translation. Moreover, Poe seems to have tried very hard to conceal his indebtedness, for he carefully avoids mentioning Schlegel directly until the end of the review, so that the reference seems to be brought in casually for the sake of another critic's reinforcing view rather than to acknowledge the derived ideas of the whole essay.[24] But elsewhere Poe admits his indebtedness, usually with extravagant praise, though sometimes with criticisms similar to his fluctuating comments on Coleridge.

Even had Poe read nothing else of German criticism, A. W. Schlegel's *Lectures* would have introduced him to the concept of transcendental irony. As Søren Kierkegaard pointed out in 1841, A. W. Schlegel's *Lectures on Dramatic Art and Literature* would be the place "where one would certainly expect to find an adequate exposition" of the concept of Romantic Irony.[25] But, curiously, the Romanticists kept complaining that one or the other of them did not truly understand the concept of irony. Thus Hegel complained that neither Tieck nor Solger set forth the philosophic significance of "the great unknown—irony" with any clarity. And Kierkegaard complained:

To the extent that one seeks a complete and coherent discussion of this concept [of Romantic Irony], one will soon convince himself that it has a problematic history, or to be more precise, no history at all. In the period after Fichte where it was particularly important, one finds it mentioned again and again, suggested again and again, presupposed again and again. But if one searches for a lucid discussion one searches in vain. Solger complains that A. W. Schlegel in his *Vorlesungen über dramatische Kunst und Literatur*, where one would certainly expect to find an adequate exposition of it, mentions it only briefly in a single passage.[26]

How curiously, or malevolently, the European ironists read one another, however, will be apparent in our examination of Schlegel's *Lectures*, this work that deals with irony only once in a "brief passage." A general survey of the contents of the *Lectures*, for example, reveals discussion in Lecture III of the essence of the comic; in x, of satirical drama; in xI, of mixed comedy and parody, the ideality of the comic, mirthful caprice, and the perception of the absurd in the serious, in xIII, of the varieties of comedy, self-consciousness and arbitrariness in comedy, and the morality of comedy; in xxIII, of far-fetched metaphor, puns, word-play, objective irony, and mixtures of the tragic and the comic, and in xxvIII, a discussion of English comic writers, as well as briefer commentary throughout.[27]

Perhaps the most striking quality of Schlegel's *Lectures* with regard to Poe is Romantic melancholy yoked together with admiration for ironic and comic objectivity. Writing of the intimate (even metaphysical) connection between the tragic and the comic, Schlegel suggested that man's "reason" and "consciousness" are the bases of both the tragic and the comic sense of life. Whereas animals have no self-consciousness, man's reason forces him to try to account for things, especially his own actions. But a "longing for the infinite which is inherent in our being is baffled by the limits of finite existence." In a remark that is highly suggestive of Poe, Schlegel added, "All that we do, all that we effect, is vain and perishable; death stands everywhere in the back ground . . ." (III, 45). When we think of our dependence on a "chain of causes and effects, stretching beyond our ken," of our helplessness against the power of nature, of our conflicting appetites, we see that "we are cast on the shores of an unknown world, as it were, shipwrecked at our very birth . . . we are subject to all kinds of errors and deceptions, any one of which may be our ruin." Although "poetry cannot remove these internal dissonances, she must at least endeavour to effect an ideal reconciliation of them" (III, 46).

The "comic" tone of mind, on the other hand, said Schlegel, is merely a "disposition" to forget "all gloomy considerations in the pleasant feeling of present happiness." The "imperfections and the irregularities of men . . . serve, by their strange inconsistencies, to entertain the understanding. . . ."

But the mind that truly transcends the contradictions of life is one like that of the old ironist, Socrates. To illustrate the quality of mind that understands the "inmost essence of things," Schlegel used an incident from the *Symposium* (one of Poe's favorite works). Having drunk all but Aristophanes and Agathon under the table, Socrates claimed that (in Schlegel's words) "it is the business of one and the same man to be equally master of tragic and comic composition, and that the tragic poet is, in virtue of his art, comic poet also" (xI, 146). Since, according to Schlegel, no Greek tragic poet had ever attempted to "shine in comedy," Socrates' "remark, therefore, can only have meant to apply to the inmost essence of . . . things. Thus at another time, the Platonic Socrates says, on the subject of comic imitation: 'All opposites can be fully understood only by and through each other; consequently we can only know what is serious by knowing also what is laughable and ludicrous'" (xi, 146). Schlegel then suggested that the comic poet forms "an ideal of human nature the direct opposite of that of the tragedians" but that this "converse ideality" is not an aggregation of "moral enormities" but instead is a representation of "the animal part of human nature . . . that want of freedom and independence, that want of coherence, those inconsistencies of the inward man, in which all folly and infatuation originate" (xi, 148).

The comic poet, as well as the tragic, transports his characters into an ideal element . . . where the caprice of inventive wit rules. . . . He is at liberty, therefore, to invent an action as arbitrary and fantastic as possible; it may even be unconnected and unreal, if only it be calculated to place a circle of comic incidents and characters in the most glaring light. In this last respect, the work should, nay, must, have a leading aim, or it will otherwise be in want of *keeping*. . . . But then, to preserve the comic inspiration, this aim must be a matter of diversion, and be *concealed*. . . . (xi, 149–50; my italics)

Schlegel next, in a passage that should give us some insight into Poe's "flawed" Gothic (one need only recall the "Mad Trist of Sir Launcelot Canning" in "Usher"), took up the matter of interruptions and "intermixtures" in comic and tragic writing. In tragedy they destroy the effect; but "to the comic tone these intentional interruptions or intermezzos are welcome, even though they be in themselves serious" (xi, 151). The mixture of the two genres as in classical "New Comedy" results in a merging of "earnestness and mirth" in which "the ridiculous must no longer come forward as the pure creation of his [the poet's] fancy, but must be verisimilar, that is, seem to be real" (xiii, 176–77). New Comedy was a "mixed species, formed out of comic and tragic, poetic and prosaic elements" that aimed at the illusion of reality and therefore sought sources of comic amusement not in arbitrary exaggeration but in the "province of earnestness"; and these sources "it found in a more accurate and thorough delineation of character" (xiii, 183). Comparing the ancient writers and the modern, Schlegel concluded that the modern Romantic mind "delights in indissoluble mixtures; all contrarieties." He added that "nature and art, poetry and prose, seriousness and mirth, recollection and anticipation, spirituality and sensuality, terrestrial and celestial, life and death, are by it [romantic art] blended together in the most intimate combination" (xxii, 342). This combination of contrasts, this continual crossing of opposites, is modern man's attempt to regain the immediacy of perception that ancient man once possessed. Thus metaphor can never be too fantastic; wordplay, puns, contradictions in the works of a poet show a sensitivity to distant relationships that may mirror the whole universe. The "feeling of moderns is, upon the whole, more inward . . . incorporeal, and . . . contemplative." Instead of the Greek ideal of "natural" harmony, "the moderns, on the contrary, have arrived at the consciousness of an internal discord which renders such an ideal impossible; and hence the endeavour of their poetry is to reconcile these two worlds between which we find ourselves divided . . . (i, 27).

In the natural genius of the modern age, then, we find a union of apparently antagonistical elements held together by a cool indifference best characterized as irony. Shakespeare, for example, "unites in his soul the utmost elevation and the utmost depth; and the most opposite and even apparently irreconcilable properties subsist in him peaceably together" (xxiii, 368).

[Shakespeare] makes each of his principal characters the glass in which the others are reflected, and by like means enables us to discover what could not be immediately revealed. . . . Ambiguity of design with much propriety he makes to overflow with the most praiseworthy principles; and sage maxims are not unfrequently put in the mouth of stupidity, to show how easily such common-place truisms may be acquired. Nobody ever painted so truthfully as he has done the facility of self-deception, the half self-conscious hypocrisy towards ourselves, with which even noble minds attempt to disguise the almost inevitable influence of selfish motives in human nature. (xxiii, 369)

This technique of multiple perspectives or points of view Schlegel called a "secret irony of characterization" commanding high admiration; it is "the profound abyss of acuteness and sagacity; but it is the grave of enthusiasm." We arrive at this ironic detachment

only after we have had the misfortune to see human nature through and through; and when no choice remains but to adopt the melancholy truth. . . . Here we therefore may perceive . . . notwithstanding his power to excite the most fervent emotions, a certain cool indifference, but still the indifference of the superior mind, which has run through the whole sphere of human existence and survived feeling. (xxiii, 369)

Most writers take a point of view and "exact from their readers a blind approbation or condemnation of whatever side they choose to support or oppose." The irony of Shakespeare's writing, however, "has not merely a reference to the separate characters, but frequently to the whole of the action." Shakespeare makes

a sort of *secret understanding* with the *select circle* of the *more intelligent of his readers* or spectators; he shows them that he had previously seen and admitted the validity of their tacit objections; that he himself is not tied down to the represented subject, but soars freely above it; and that, if he chose, he could unrelentingly annihilate the beautiful and irresistibly attractive scenes which his magic pen has produced. (xxiii, 370; my italics)

Thus the ironist, in Schlegel's terms, is much like the great artist in Poe's review of Elizabeth Barrett in 1845; he follows extremes, comes back upon himself, and holds within himself a "fortuitous . . . combination of antagonisms" (H 12:34).

In this one book then—by a critic from whom Poe borrowed theoretical principles of beauty, melancholy ideality, "mystical" indirection, and unity or totality of interest or effect, and from whom Poe stole practical criticism—is a rationale of the comic and ironic blended with Romantic idealism that quite clearly fits Poe into that "vortex" of "German" ideas at which he good-humoredly gibed in the *Marginalia* (H 16:3–4). In A. W. Schlegel's *Lectures* alone, Poe found Romantic-Ironic principles of melancholy idealism and a yearning for sublime beauty even in discord and deformity; a fascination with death as the ultimate fact of existence; a belief in the illusiveness of truth, in human alienation from actuality, and in the "one-sidedness" of all "serious" statements. He found a doctrine of unrestrained fancy in the genre of pure comedy and of verisimilitude in the mixed genre of the serio-comic. He found an emphasis on a literary technique of indirection involving a deceptive and even "secret" irony clear only to the reader of superior perceptions; concern for character portrayal within a meaningful plot and with emphasis on "internal discord," "self-deception," and multiple reflections and perspectives. He found a belief in the explorations of novelty through contrasts of incident, through fanciful and even fantastic metaphor, symbol, punning, and general wordplay. And he found, finally, a concept of a superior mind transcending the gloomy chaos of the world through artistic ironic detachment.

IV

We have seen that Poe knew of the works of Kant, Fichte, Schelling, and Friedrich and August Wilhelm Schlegel; yet one would like some evidence that Poe not only knew but approved of the techniques of the German transcendental ironists. In part, such evidence is to be found in Poe's remarks about Ludwig Tieck, whom he read with clear approval. For one thing, Poe seems to have thought Tieck a writer better even than Hawthorne. In his second, cooler, but still commendatory review of Hawthorne in 1847, Poe argued that Hawthorne's "originality" is more apparent than actual since he does what has already been done by "the German Tieck."

Those [wrote Poe] who speak of him [Hawthorne] as original, mean nothing more than that he differs in his manner of tone, and in his choice of subjects, from any author of their acquaintance—their acquaintance not extending to the German Tieck, whose manner, in *some* of his works, is absolutely identical with that *habitual* to Hawthorne. (H 13:144)

Poe's italics here reflect his belief in variety of effect; he considers Tieck not only the more original of the two even in Hawthorne's own special province, but also the more capable of greater variety.

That Poe had not discovered Tieck between 1842 and 1847 is clear from the tale "Von Jung, the Mystic," written ten years earlier (1837). "Von Jung" begins more or less seriously and ends comically; in it Poe had made the hero a cousin of Tieck's, commenting (in the person of the narrator) that Tieck has given us "vivid exemplifications" in the genre of "*grotesquerie*" (H 4:102). In a *Marginalia* reference in which he does not give Tieck's name, thereby presuming a familiarity on his readers' part and implying familiarity on his part, Poe refers to Tieck's *Old Man of the Mountain* for a satiric comparison to John Wilson ("Christopher North"), the notorious editor of *Blackwood's* who had the "power to make or to mar any American reputation." Lashing out against American subservience to British opinion, Poe calls Wilson a "rhapsodist" unworthy the name of "critic," an "ignorant" and "egotistical" "schoolboy" blunderer, who has "ridden us to death like The Old Man of the Mountain. . . ."[28]

But one of the most interesting of Poe's references to Tieck is the *Marginalia* note wherein he reveals an admiration for a comic and ironic stylistic technique of Tieck's, that, taken seriously in his own style, has seemed to critics one of Poe's worst flaws. Harry Levin, for example, particularly dislikes Poe's "excess of capitals, italics, dashes . . . exclamation points . . . superlatives . . . intensitives and ineffables . . . gallicisms . . . sham erudition, scientific pretensions, quotations from occult authorities, and misquotations from foreign languages."[29] "The misapplication of quotations," Poe writes in *Marginalia*, can be "clever, and has a capital effect when well done. . . ."

One of the best hits in this way is made by Tieck, and I have lately seen it appropriated, with interesting complacency, in an English magazine. The author of the "Journey into the Blue Distance," is giving an account of some young ladies, not very beautiful, whom he caught *in mediis rebus,* at their toilet. They were curling their monstrous heads," says he, "as Shakespeare says of the waves in a storm." (H 16:42)

That Poe's own style—whenever quotations, foreign phrases, footnotes, mottoes, typographical devices, and the like are exaggerated or rendered slightly askew—is ironic and satiric is borne out to some extent by his reviews of the novels of John P. Kennedy and William Gilmore Simms, and by his burlesque article-tale "How to Write a Blackwood Article." In his review of Kennedy's *Horse-Shoe Robinson* (*Southern Literary Messenger*, May 1835), Poe noted that:

A too frequent use of the *dash* is the besetting sin of the volumes now before us. It is lugged in upon all occasions, and invariably introduced where it has no business whatever. . . . Now there is no portion of a printer's fount, which can, if properly disposed, give more of strength and energy to a sentence than this same *dash*; and, for this very reason, there is none which *can more effectually, if improperly arranged, disturb and distort the meaning of every thing with which it comes in contact.* (H 8:10; my italics)

Poe went on to say that everything a writer does, even with his punctuation, must have "an object or an end"; and he then reduced seven dashes from one of Kennedy's paragraphs to one subtly climactic dash.[30] In a review of Simms's *The Partisan* (*Southern Literary Messenger*, January 1836), Poe remarked that Simms had been "wiser" than other writers in the matter of the "initial motto":

While others have been at the trouble of extracting, from popular works, quotations adapted to the subject-matter of their chapters, *he has manufactured his own headings.* We find no fault with him for so doing. The manufactured mottoes of Mr. Simms are, perhaps, quite as convenient as the extracted mottoes of his contemporaries. *All, we think, are abominable.* (H 8:157; my italics)

This is a rather remarkable comment in view of the fact that almost all Poe's tales are beset with mottoes, some of which (like that to "Ligeia") have never been identified despite diligent efforts of scholars —remarkable, that is, unless Poe had some satiric, deceptive, ironic object or end.

In "How to Write a Blackwood Article" (1838), Poe has Mr. Blackwood advise Miss Psyche Zenobia on some details of style for a "sensation-paper." She must consider her tone and her manner of narration, Blackwood says:

There is the tone didactic, the tone enthusiastic, the tone natural—all common-place enough. But then there is the tone laconic, or curt, which has lately come much into use. It consists of short sentences. Somehow thus. Can't be too brief. Can't be too snappish. Always a full stop. And never a paragraph.

Then there is the tone elevated, diffusive, and interjectional. . . . The words must all be in a whirl, like a humming-top, and make a noise very similar, which answers remarkably well instead of meaning. . . .

The tone metaphysical is also a good one. If you know any big words this is your chance for them. Talk of the Ionic and Eleatic schools—of Archytas, Gorgias and Alcmaeon. Say something about objectivity and subjectivity . . . and when you let slip anything a little *too* absurd, you need not be at the trouble of scratching it out, but just add a foot-note and say that you are indebted for the above profound observation to the *"Kritik der reinen Vernunft,"* or to the *"Metaphysische Anfangsgründe der Naturwissenschaft."* This will look erudite and—and—and frank. (H 2:275–76)

After these two references to works by Kant, it is only natural that Blackwood should also discuss "the tone transcendental and the tone heterogeneous." He goes on to give Miss Zenobia some advice regarding the very important "air of erudition" or of "extensive general reading" required for a saleable article. Pulling down three or four volumes and opening them at random, Blackwood says:

By casting your eye down almost any page of any book in the world, you will be able to perceive at once a host of little scraps of either learning or *bel-esprit-ism.* . . . You might as well note down a few while I read them to you. I shall make two divisions: first, *Piquant Facts for the Manufacture of Similes;* and second, *Piquant Expressions to be introduced as occasion may require.* (H 2:277)

Blackwood then gives her facts such as these: "there were originally but three Muses" (which if introduced with a "downright improviso air" looks *"recherché"*); "the river Alpheus passed beneath the sea and emerged without injury to the purity of its waters"; "the Persian Iris appears to some persons to possess a sweet and very powerful perfume, while to others it is perfectly scentless" (H 2:277–78). Then Blackwood gives her, in the original languages, several "piquant expressions" from Voltaire *("aussi tendre que Zaïre"),* Cervantes, Ariosto, Schiller,

Lucan, and Demosthenes, for in a *Blackwood's* article "there is no passing muster . . . . without Spanish, Italian, German, Latin, and Greek." The quotation from the Greek must be typographically pretty.

In a Blackwood article nothing makes so fine a show as your Greek. The very letters have an air of profundity about them. Only observe, madam, the astute look of that Epsilon! That Phi ought certainly to be a bishop! Was there ever a smarter fellow than that Omicron? Just twig that Tau! In short, there is nothing like Greek for a genuine sensation-paper. (H 2:281)

Blackwood urges Miss Zenobia to apply these quotations to her sensations while being choked to death by a chicken-bone; the chicken she had been eating, could, for example, have been "not altogether *aussi tendre que Zaïre.*" Psyche, accordingly (in the companion tale "A Predicament"), proceeds to misquote and misapply the "piquant facts" and "piquant expressions" to her sensations while her head is caught in a large steeple clock.

Poe's "Blackwood Article" and Psyche's "Predicament" are obviously comic and satiric. But a slightly less exaggerated version of the *Blackwood's* styles, surrounded by a Gothic atmosphere at least partially effective, could be used for ironic purposes. What makes Poe's reference to Tieck's ironic technique of misapplying quotations in *The Journey into the Blue Distance* particularly important is that in the melancholy library of the House of Usher, the two protagonists of the tale open a copy of this very volume.[31] The half-comic and absurd Schlegelian intermezzo of the "Mad Trist" of Sir Launcelot Canning is, when seen in the literary context suggested here, integral to the seriocomic tone of grotesquerie permeating not only "Usher," but also Poe's other Gothic tales.

3
Flawed Gothic

I read no "Night Thoughts"—no fustian about church-yards—
no bugaboo tales—such as this.
                    "The Premature Burial" (1844)

How DEEP-SEATED and all pervasive the comic, satiric, and absurdist elements are in Poe's Gothic tales is the general question to be explored here, with special reference to Poe's earliest stories. First, we shall note Poe's early plans for a sequential series of burlesque stories, the "Tales of the Arabesque" and the Folio Club tales; then, we shall take a look at the comic technique and satiric thrusts of Poe's first group of comic tales, dating from 1831, in which the hoaxical and comically esoteric are significant factors; and finally, we shall examine the same (but more deceptive) parody and irony in his first Gothic tale "Metzengerstein" (1831–32). Poe's first Gothic tale illustrates in both its exaggerated first version and in its more subtle revised version Poe's development of the burlesque tale into the ironic hoax. Moreover, "Metzengerstein" exhibits in embryonic form Poe's characteristic themes of ultimate annihilation, of hostile and deceptive fortune, of human fear and perversity, and of the absurdity of human existence— but all in burlesque form similar to that of his obvious satires. Poe's themes and techniques in "Metzengerstein" and in the four more clearly comic tales are, I submit, the touchstone for all his subsequent fiction and are exemplary of his style of Romantic Irony.

I

In May 1833, Poe wrote to Joseph and Edwin Buckingham, the publishers of the *New England Magazine,* and offered them a collection of sequential stories called "Eleven Tales of the Arabesque." Critics have generally assumed that when Poe, seven years later, titled his 1840 collection *Tales of the Grotesque and Arabesque,* he meant to separate the comic and satiric stories (grotesques) from the serious Gothic stories (arabesques). The never published collection "Eleven Tales of the Arabesque," however, Poe intended as a burlesque collection. He included with his letter to the Buckinghams, as a representative of the collection, his tale "Epimanes" (later called "Four Beasts in One—The Homocameleopard"), the story of a Syrian tyrant who runs wildly through the streets of Antioch disguised as an animal until the beasts become indignant at the imposture and break out of their cages and lead a protest march through the city—a comic work with many satiric thrusts at American democracy and nineteenth-century concepts of progress. Moreover, the whole series of tales, Poe explained, was a burlesque not only of contemporary styles of tale-writing, but also of current modes of criticism:

They are supposed to be read at table by the eleven members of a literary club, and are followed by the remarks of the company upon each. These remarks are intended as a burlesque upon criticism. In the whole, originality more than anything else has been attempted. . . . If you like the specimen which I have sent I will forward the rest at your suggestion—but if you decide upon publishing all the tales, it would not be proper to print the one I now send until it can be printed in its place with the others. (O 1:53)[1]

The eleven "Tales of the Arabesque" were probably the five tales published in the *Philadelphia Saturday Courier* in 1832, to which Poe added the six tales submitted to the *Baltimore Saturday Visiter* sometime before October 1833, as the "Tales of the Folio Club." These eleven stories included the ostensibly serious Gothic works "Metzengerstein," "MS. Found in a Bottle," "The Assignation," "Silence," and possibly "A Descent into the Maelström."[2] The comic tales, besides "Epimanes," would have been "The Duc de L'Omelette," "A Tale of Jerusalem," "Loss of Breath," and "Bon-Bon" from the *Courier,* and "Lionizing," unpublished. The "Folio Club" scheme thus was clearly in Poe's mind sometime prior to the spring of 1833 and may have been worked out even as early as 1831. Between 1831 and 1835, at any rate, Poe wrote a preface for the Folio Club tales, the manuscript of which survives on two leaves, written on both sides in Poe's small hand. The first two pages give the preface essentially complete, though the style of the document, T. O. Mabbott feels, suggests notes to be more fully developed later.[3] The other two pages contain part of what has often been called a beautiful Gothic tone poem, the tale "Siope" (later titled "Silence"). The latter two pages are numbered 61 and 62; thus, as Mabbott, Harrison, and others have observed, a good deal of material must have lain between the preface and the story, and the surviving fragment may be part of a manuscript that Poe unsuccessfully sent around to various publishers in 1835 and 1836.

The Folio Club is a "Junto of Dunderheadism," which meets once a month at dinner for a reading by each member of "a short tale of his own composition." The author of the best tale becomes president for the month; the author of the worst tale provides dinner and wine for the next meeting. The writer of the preface represents himself as making an exposé of the Club after attending his first meeting. Under the title "The Folio Club" appears a motto from Samuel Butler: "There is a Machiavelian plot/ Though every [n]are olfact it not" (H 2:xxxvi). The implication seems clear: although some of the members' tales may at first seem no more ridiculous than the Gothic and sensational fiction popular at the time, the stories are actually parodies and satires. In fact, the intention of the Club, the narrator says, is "to abolish Literature, subvert the Press, and overturn the Government of Nouns and Pronouns." The membership of the Club is limited to eleven (because on *April first,* in the year three hundred and fifty before the Deluge, there were eleven spots on the sun). The membership includes, besides the newly elected author of the preface, ten "most remarkable men":

There was, first of all, Mr. Snap, the President, who is a very lank man with a hawk nose, and was formerly in the service of the Down-East Review.

Then there was Mr. Convolvulus Gondola, a young gentleman who had travelled a good deal.

Then there was De Rerum Naturâ, Esqr., who wore a very singular pair of green spectacles.

Then there was a very little man in a black coat with very black eyes.

Then there was Mr. Solomon Seadrift who had every appearance of a fish.

Then there was Mr. Horribile Dictu, with white eyelashes, who had graduated at Göttingen.

Then there was Mr. Blackwood Blackwood who had written certain articles for foreign magazines.

Then there was the host, Mr. Rouge-et-Noir, who admired Lady Morgan.

Then there was a stout gentleman who admired Sir Walter Scott.

Then there was Chronologos Chronology who admired Horace Smith, and had a very big nose which had been in Asia Minor. (H 2:xxxviii–xxxix)

Poe expanded the number of tales and members to seventeen in a letter to the Philadelphia publisher, Harrison Hall, on September 2, 1836, stating that all the tales recently printed in the *Southern Literary Messenger* were part of the Folio Club series.

At different times there has appeared in the Messenger a series of tales, by myself—in all seventeen. They are of a bizarre and generally whimsical character. . . . I imagine a company of 17 persons who call themselves the Folio Club. . . . The seventeen tales which appeared in the Mess^r are supposed to be narrated by the seventeen members at one of these monthly meetings. As soon as each . . . tale is read—the other 16 members criticise it in turn—and these criticisms are intended as a burlesque upon criticism generally. The author of the tale adjudged to be the worst demurs from the general judgment, seizes the seventeen M.SS. upon the table, and, rushing from the house, determines to appeal, by printing the whole, from the decision of the Club, to that of the public. The critical remarks . . . *have never been published*. . . . (O 1:103–4)

At this time, Poe had actually published only fourteen tales in the *Southern Literary Messenger:* the five *Courier* stories of 1832, "MS. Found in a Bottle" from the 1833 *Visiter*, "The Visionary" (later "The Assignation") from the 1834 *Godey's Lady's Book*, and seven previously unpublished tales, "Berenice," "Morella," "Lionizing," "Hans Phaal," "King Pest," "Shadow," and "Epimanes." In order of publication, the tales immediately following the fourteen in the *Messenger* were the comic "Mystification," the seemingly serious "Silence" (which was part of the original Folio Club manuscript), the Gothic "Ligeia," the four comic and satric stories "How to Write a Blackwood Article," "A Predicament," "The Devil in the Belfry," "The Man That Was Used Up," and the Gothic "Fall of the House of Usher." Thus, of Poe's first twenty-two tales, from 1832 to 1839, only two ("Ligeia" and "Usher") are not either clearly comic and satiric or deceptively ironic burlesques for the Folio Club—a remarkable corroboration of Poe's ironic intent in even the most Gothic of his tales. The next year, having added to the series two "serious" tales ("William Wilson" and "Eiros and Charmion") and one comic tale ("Why the Little Frenchman Wears His Hand in a Sling") to make a total of twenty-five, Poe finally was able to get a book-length collection of his stories published as *Tales of the Grotesque and Arabesque* (1840).

Poe's overall ironic and satiric intent was only vaguely understood by his contemporaries, however, as is clear from several letters from 1835 and 1836, regarding the "Tales of the Folio Club." Poe began the *Messenger* series of tales with "Berenice" in March 1835, and the editor, as we have seen, added by way of introduction the complaint that the story had too much "German" horror. The next month (April 30, 1835), Poe explained to White his ironic attitude toward German horror, though without reference to the Folio Club. He defends "Berenice" on the grounds that it is typical of the kind of absurd Gothic tale that sells magazines, and he remarks that "Berenice" had "originated in a bet that I could produce nothing effective on a subject so singular," provided it was treated with an ostensible seriousness.

The history of all Magazines shows plainly that those which have attained celebrity were indebted for it to articles *similar in nature—to Berenice.* . . . I say similar in *nature*. You ask me in what does this nature consist? In the ludicrous heightened into the grotesque: the fearful coloured into the horrible: the witty exaggerated into the burlesque: the singular wrought out into the strange and mystical. (O 1:57–58)

This statement is often taken by critics to indicate a series of different effects, but Poe's order and especially his punctuation suggest a continuum; the terms of the last sentence quoted here are linked by colons, not by semicolons, nor by the commas that many critics have carelessly interpolated into the letter. The colon signifies a further development, a second thought, a subsidiary class: and the alternations of "fearful," "witty," and "singular," of "horrible," "burlesque," and "strange" and "mystical" all derive from the larger category of the "grotesque," a genre allied primarily with the ludicrous and the ironic, but curiously fusing these comic qualities with the sinister.

The problem of context and therefore of intent is unquestionably the major difficulty in reading Poe's earliest fiction. This is largely the result of Poe's sometimes esoteric interests and his penchant for transmuting satire proper into hoax. The New York novelist James K. Paulding was one of the first to recognize the satiric point of Poe's earliest tales. In 1836 Paulding wrote to Poe and White about the manuscript (presumably the "Tales of the Folio Club") that had been sent to Harper Bros. for possible publication. Paulding said that the "quiz on Willis" ("The Duke [or Duc] de L'Omelette" or "Lionizing") and the "Burlesque of 'Blackwood' " were "capital" and "understood by all," but that Poe ought to apply his "fine humor" to "more familiar subjects of satire; to the faults and foibles of our own people . . . and above all to the ridiculous affectations and extravagancies of the fashionable English Literature of the day which we copy with such admirable success and servility" (H 17:378). Paulding felt that there was a "degree of obscurity" in the tales that would "prevent ordinary readers from comprehending their drift, and consequently from enjoying the fine satire they convey" (H 17:377). Emphasizing this point, Paulding added, "For Satire to be relished, it is necessary that it should be leveled at something with which readers are familiar" (H 17:378).[4]

Even Poe's good friend John P. Kennedy, the Baltimore novelist, did not fully comprehend the drift of Poe's first tales. In February of the same year that Paulding criticized Poe's "obscurity," Kennedy had written that he doubted Poe really "intended" the satiric thrusts one could find in reading his stories; but Poe replied that Kennedy was "not altogether right" since his tales had indeed been "*intended* for half banter, half satire"—though Poe politely added that perhaps he would not have "acknowledged this to be their aim even to myself" in those tales not "satires properly speaking."[5] But the mixed intention of satire, banter, and seriousness also seemed obscure to Harpers, for they returned Poe's manuscript with the comment that one of the reasons they had decided not to publish the tales was that they "would be understood and relished only by a very few," and that the "numbers of readers in this country capable of appreciating and enjoying such writings . . . is very small indeed."[6]

The five *Courier* tales of 1831–32, then, prove to be especially significant in this regard, for the continuum of the comic, the satiric, the Gothic burlesque, and the Gothic hoax that these tales demonstrate has great importance for the interpretation of Poe's later fiction. In both theme and technique, we find a clear consistency between the light-hearted satiric spoofs "The Duke de L'Omelette," "The Bargain Lost" (later called "Bon-Bon"), and "A Tale of Jerusalem" on the one hand, and on the other hand the Gothic parody "A Decided Loss" (later called "Loss of Breath") and the seemingly serious Gothic tale "Metzengerstein."

II

"The Duke de L'Omelette" must have puzzled most of the *Courier* readers as much as it has the general twentieth-century reader, for the tale appears to be merely a comic exercise, and none too comic at that. A sensitive French nobleman dies in a paroxysm of disgust when served an ortolan without paper ruffles; finding himself in Hell, he plays cards with the Devil to win back his soul, succeeds by cheating, and takes his leave with the remark, in French, that if he were not the Duke de L'Omelette he would have no objection to being the Devil. Reconstruction of the context of the tale reveals the story to be a satiric parody of the literary style and of the elegant manners and cultural pretensions of a contemporary editor, Nathaniel Parker Willis. Poe exaggerates Willis's imitation of the "silver-fork" style of Benjamin Disraeli (thus hitting at Disraeli as well) in Willis's preciously written column, "The Editor's Table," in the *American Monthly Magazine*. In this column, Willis represented himself as a man of culture, fashion, delicate thought, and exquisitely refined taste. He would invite his readers into his editorial apartments where he wrote at a "rosewood" desk, on which were Chinese cupid inkholders, velvet butterfly pen wipers, and a bottle of Hungary water to perfume his quill; when he was not working, he could be found reclining upon one of his treasured ottomans, reflectively eating an olive, while his pet South American bird flew freely about the apartment. The first paragraphs of Poe's story are, as Kenneth L. Daughrity says, "replete with peppery hits"[7] at Willis: "Keats fell by a criticism. Who was it died of 'The Andromache'? . . . Ignoble souls!—De L'Omelette perished of an ortolan. *L'histoire en est brève.* . . . the Duc was to sup alone . . . he reclined languidly on that ottoman for which he sacrificed his loyalty in outbidding his king. . . . The clock strikes! Unable to restrain his feelings, his Grace swallows an olive" (B 1:100–101).[8] Poe's reference to Keats reflects the criticism by other editors that Willis's career would be killed by his affectations; the Peruvian ortolan served naked (and roasted) to the Duke suggests, of course, Willis's pet bird; olives and ottomans were to Willis symbols of refinement; and little French phrases and literary allusions were trademarks of his style.[9] In a moment, Poe has the Devil take the Duke, curiously scented, from a "rosewood" coffin. Ordered to strip, the Duke displays a dainty fastidiousness, mentions the fashionable tailors who have designed his lovely clothes, and objects that it is too much trouble to draw off his gloves. He then gives scrutiny to the bizarre arrangement of the Devil's "apartment," lighted by a ruby hung from a blood-red chain whose upper end is lost (like, variously, Coleridge, Carlyle, or the City of Boston, depending on the version of the tale) in the clouds. Pushed eventually beyond what a gentleman can properly endure, the Duke invites His Majesty to fence—but must settle for cards. Poe's satire seems to be a criticism, like that of the editors suggested in his first sentence.[10] But the events of the tale intimate that such criticism will not even touch Willis, just as the Duke is above ignoble souls like Keats and is able to outwit, politely, even the Devil. But without this context, the tale seems simply pointless.

Certainly, to the general reader of the time, the humor of the other three comic tales in the *Courier* could have seemed only a trifle clearer than that of "The Duke de L'Omelette." The surface story of "A Tale of Jerusalem," for example, in which the Jews (besieged in the Holy City by Pompey's legions) bargain for a sacrificial lamb but are given a hog instead, seems also rather pointless, not especially amusing, and even unpleasantly anti-Semitic. The tale, however, is a satire on the rage for didactic historical novels set in the Holy Land, parodying in particular Horace Smith's *Zillah, A Tale of the Holy City*, a three-decker published five years before in 1828. Poe lifts phrases and whole lines from the novel and fills his story with mock erudition on Hebrew customs, as well as with burlesque names like Abel Shittim, though the later versions of the story are cleaned up somewhat. Like the opening paragraphs of "The Duke de L'Omelette," the first paragraph of "A Tale of Jerusalem" gives the situation entire and immediately achieves a remarkable phony style.

"Let us hurry to the walls," said Abel-Phittim [the revised name of Abel Shittim] to Buzi-Ben-Levi and Simeon the Pharisee, on the tenth day of the month Thammuz, in the year of the world three thousand nine hundred and forty-one—"let us hasten to the ramparts adjoining the gate of Benjamin, which is in the city of David, and overlooking the camp of the uncircumcised; for it is the last hour of the fourth watch, being sunrise; and the idolaters, in fulfilment of the promise of Pompey, should be awaiting us with the lambs for the sacrifices." (B 1:103)[11]

The rest of the tale continues in this manner with, as J. S. Wilson notes, an increasing number of lines from Smith. But although the style is obviously exaggerated, the story line is plausible enough, up to the end, so that one could read the tale as a serious piece of biblical fiction—if he were a bit obtuse to the nuances of English prose style. The conclusion, however, makes clear even to the most unread that Poe is satirizing something, even if only the Jews themselves. The three Sub-Collectors of Offerings draw up a long rope hung over the city wall, expecting the Romans below to have placed a lamb in a basket. After an hour's tugging, Buzi-Ben-Levi exclaims "Booshoh he! . . . Booshoh he! . . . Booshoh he!—for shame!—it is a ram from the thickets of Engedi, and as rugged as the valley of Jehosaphat!"

It was not until the basket had arrived within a few feet of the Gizbarium, that a low grunt betrayed to their perception a *hog* of no common size.
    "Now El Emanu!" slowly, and with upturned eyes ejaculated the trio . . . "El Emanu! —God be with us—*it is the unutterable flesh!*" (B 1:106)

The last line is directly from Smith's *Zillah*, and those readers up on current "indigestible" fiction would have seen much more clearly than the reader a hundred years later, or even the casual reader of Poe's time, that Poe here is satirizing the currently popular brand of the historical novel.[12]

"The Bargain Lost" (later called "Bon-Bon") tells the story of a philosopher chef, who, while completing an absurd metaphysical treatise, gets into a drunken conversation with the Devil (a kind of gourmet of philosophers' souls) and offers his own soul for his Satanic Majesty's delectation only to be turned down. The satiric point of the tale, with its metaphysical conversation, plentiful references to classical authors, and other recondite allusions, seems to be mockery of, on the one hand, German metaphysics, and, on the other hand, of pretended scholarship in contemporary fiction—a topic Poe takes up more directly six years later in "How to Write a Blackwood Article," in which, as we have seen, Blackwood advises Signora Psyche Zenobia to sprinkle her tales with learned quotations in various languages, to quote obscure titles in German, and to get herself into an impossible predicament.[13]

Similar pretense as well as the whole genre of "sensation" tales, or "intensities," featured in *Blackwood's Edinburgh Magazine* are the major satiric targets, along with transcendentalism, of "Loss of Breath" (called "A Decided Loss" in the *Courier*). Despite vividly morbid passages, the absurdities of the tale are quite obvious; and the story in its several versions is worth recounting at some length, since it contains in burlesque form many of Poe's favorite themes, including alienation and the crowd, perversity, the *Doppelgänger*, burial alive, death-in-life, the absurd universe. Moreover, its style at times approaches effective horror at the same time that it employs in exaggerated comic form the supposed flaws of Poe's serious writing. Part of the technique of the sensation tale is the affectation of literary and philosophical learning, most especially of the currently popular German metaphysical speculation. "Loss of Breath" has both a suitable "philosophical" theme and "learned" style. The opening gambit of the tale is similar to that of the other *Courier* stories; the first sentences not only announce the ostensible theme of bearing ill fortune philosophically, but also suggest an overriding satiric theme through stylistic parody, here involving strained mock-erudite analogies that interrupt the narrative progression.

The most notorious ill-fortune must in the end yield to the untiring courage of philosophy—as the most stubborn city to the ceaseless vigilance of an enemy. Shalmanezer, as we have it in holy writings, lay three years before Samaria; yet it fell. Sardanapalus—see Diodorus—maintained itself seven in

Nineveh; but to no purpose. Troy expired at the close of the second lustrum; and Azoth, as Aristaeus declares upon his honour as a gentleman, opened at last her gates to Psammetichus, after having barred them for the fifth part of a century. . . . (B 1:106)[14]

That the absurd exaggerations of incident and predicament which follow, along with the digressive and inappropriately calm and reflective style, are intended to burlesque the sensation fiction of *Blackwood's* is made perfectly clear in the republication of the tale three years later in the *Southern Literary Messenger* by the addition of the subtitle "A Tale a la Blackwood."[15] Moreover, the character of Windenough, the inverse double of the hero of the tale, Mr. Lackobreath, seems to fit Poe's impression of John Wilson ("Christopher North"), an editor of *Blackwood's*. Wilson had published a sentimental poem called "The Convict" in 1816, detailing the predicament of a man wrongly convicted of robbery and murder but rescued at the last moment by the discovery of the real criminal.[16] Poe extends the similar situation of "Loss of Breath," in order to burlesque much more than the predilection of *Blackwood's* and Wilson for predicament tales; Poe makes specific thrusts at the American theater, at contemporary philosophical and literary figures (including Schelling, Kant, Fichte, Godwin, St. Pierre, Crabbe, Coleridge, Bulwer-Lytton, Disraeli, and possibly by implication Wordsworth); but most especially, Poe hits at the transcendentalists.

The thrusts at the sensationists and the transcendentalists begin soon after the opening incident, in which Mr. Lackobreath literally loses his breath in cursing his wife. Finding himself speechless, he retreats to his room and meditates on his misfortune, discovering himself to be "alive, with the qualifications of the dead—dead, with the propensities of the living—an anomaly on the face of the earth—being very calm, yet breathless." He considers at once the idea of suicide, but "it is a trait in the *perversity* of human nature to reject the obvious and the ready, for the far-distant and equivocal" (B 1:107–8; my italics).[17] He then searches for his breath, like Adelbert Chamisso's "Peter Schlemiel" for his shadow, in the corners of his room, in his closet, in his drawers—for it might have a vapory or a tangible form, as "authorities" will confirm.

William Godwin . . . says in his "Mandeville," that "invisible things are the only realities," and this, all will allow, is a case in point. I would have the judicious reader pause before accusing such asseverations of an undue quantum of absurdity. Anaxagoras, it will be remembered, maintained that snow is black, and this I have since found to be the case. (B 1:108)

Hiding his calamity from the sure indignation of his wife, the "multi-tude," and the "virtuous," Lackobreath regains some of his speech by practicing Indian tragedies in "frog-like and sepulchral tones," giving out that he is interested in the theater and observing to himself that any part of the play *Metamora* applies "equally well to any particular subject." Nor is he in his practice ". . . deficient in the looking asquint —the showing my teeth—the working my knees—the shuffling my feet—or in any of those unmentionable graces which are now justly considered the characteristics of a popular performer. To be sure they spoke of confining me in a straightjacket—but, good God! they never suspected me of having lost my breath" (B 1:109). Setting out for another city by mail stage, Lackobreath is crushed between "two gentlemen of colossal dimensions" and sat upon by a third "of a size larger," which dislocates all his limbs. In a scene reminiscent of Field-ing's *Joseph Andrews*, the passengers object to riding with a corpse and throw Lackobreath out of the stage at the Crow tavern, with no further injury to him than the breaking of his arms and the fracturing of his skull. The tavern keeper sells the "corpse" to a surgeon, who, like the surgeons in *Candide*, proceeds to dissect the still-living body.[18] Lackobreath kicks and plunges, but the surgeon attributes this to the effects of a galvanic battery. Lackobreath then becomes interested in the experiments of the surgeon, though he cannot gather enough wind to "make reply to some ingenious but fanciful theories of which, under other circumstances, my minute acquaintance with the Hippocratian pathology would have afforded me a ready confutation" (B 1:110). Then, tied up corpse-fashion and left alone in a garret "to silence and to meditation," he repeats "some passages of the 'Omnipresence of the Deity,' as is my custom before resigning myself to sleep . . ." (B 1:111). Two cats contend for his nose, however, and he leaps out the window into a prison cart containing the mail-robber W——, to whom he bears a singular resemblance, though W—— is gaunt and he corpulent. Then W—— escapes and Lackobreath is hanged in his place.

In the latest version of the tale (*Broadway Journal*, 1846), Lacko-breath forbears to depict his "sensations upon the gallows," merely mentioning that the jerk of the rope gave a "corrective twist" to his dislocated neck and that he did his best to please the crowd: "My convulsions were said to be extraordinary. My spasms it would have been difficult to beat. The populace *encored*. Several gentlemen swooned." He adds, however, that after the performance, "it was thought proper to remove my body from the gallows;—this the more especially as the real culprit had in the meantime been retaken and recognized . . ." (B 1:112). But in the earlier versions, not only his "sensations" while standing on the gallows but also the philosophical speculation to which they give rise is detailed. The deleted passage contains a good deal of Poe's specific satire, unfortunately reduced only to implication in the 1846 version of the tale.[19] As Lackobreath waits reflectively for the trap to be pulled, profound Godwin-like thoughts flood his mind: "I now reasoned, rapidly I believe—profoundly I am sure—upon principles of common law—propriety of that law especially, for which I hung—absurdities in political economy which till then I had never been able to acknowledge. . . ." Then come ideas from Crabbe, St. Pierre, Bulwer-Lytton and, especially, Disraeli:

. . . synonymes in Crabbe—lunar-lunatic theories in St. Pierre—falsities in the Pelham novels—beauties in Vivian Grey—more than beauties in Vivian Grey—profundity in Vivian Grey—genius in Vivian Grey—every thing in Vivian Grey.
Then came, like a flood, Coleridge, Kant, Fichte, and Pantheism. . . .
A rapid change was now taking place in my sensations. The last shadows of connection flitted away from my meditations. A storm—a tempest of ideas, vast, novel, and soul-stirring, bore my spirit like a feather afar off. Confusion crowded upon confusion like a wave upon a wave. In a very short time Schelling himself would have been satisfied with my entire loss of self-identity. (H 2:359–60)

When the rope twists his neck, he has the sensation that the event has occurred in another realm of existence, "some other *Ens*." He is then taken down and "laid out" in a small chamber, which yet

appeared of a size to contain the universe. I have never before or since, in body or in mind, suffered half so much agony as from that single idea. Strange! that the simple conception of abstract magnitude—of infinity—should have been accompanied with pain. Yet so it was. "With how vast a difference," said I, "in life as in death—in time and in eternity—here and hereafter, shall our merest sensations be imbodied!" (H 2:360–61)

As night comes, Lackobreath has the horrible sensation that perhaps his state of limbo is actual death:

. . . this darkness which is palpable, and oppresses with the sense of suffocation—this—this—is—indeed *death*. This is death—this is death the terrible—death the holy. . . . thus, too, shall I always remain—always—always remain. Reason is folly, and Philosophy a lie. No one will know my sensations, my horror—my despair. . . . This—this—this—is the only Eternity!—

and what, O Baalzebub!—*what* an Eternity!—to lie in this vast—this awful void—a hideous, vague, and unmeaning anomaly—motionless, yet wishing for motion—powerless, yet longing for power—forever, forever, and forever!" (H 2:361–62)

By itself, this last passage, as with others in the tale, could be considered fairly effective horror even though overdone—if, that is, the repetitions and the comic lines "no one will know my sensations" and "what, O Baalzebub!—*what* an Eternity!" were removed. It should not be very difficult to see that the style of many of Poe's more famous Gothic tales derives from this kind of burlesque horror in "Loss of Breath" and that in those tales there may be at least two opposing possibilities for interpretation. In "Loss of Breath," however, there is no ambiguity. Immediately after the terrors of philosophical speculation during the night, for example, the hero sees the light of dawn and realizes that he is not dead (but instead merely in danger of being buried alive): "Then—and not till then—was I fully sensible of the fearful fate hanging over me. The phantasms of the night had faded with its shadows, and the actual terrors of the yawning tomb left me no heart for the bugbear speculations of Transcendentalism" (H 2: 362). In both the early and the 1846 versions, Lackobreath is next placed in a tomb where he falls into a deep sleep. He awakes and searches about the sepulchre, complaining eventually of boredom. Finally, he feels his way among the numerous coffins, lifts them down "one by one, and breaking open their lids," busies himself "in speculations about the mortality within" (B 1:112).

Soon Lackobreath discovers two particularly interesting corpses to which he addresses soliloquies, holding one up by the nose. The bodies perhaps bear a vague resemblance to Coleridge and Wordsworth.[20] The familiar-looking, tall, gaunt "corpse," however, turns out not only to be the criminal W—— but also to be Windenough, Lackobreath's *wife's* "friend."[21] Lackobreath receives a "respiration" from him and together they shout until rescued by Scissors, the Whig editor, who, hearing them, has in the meanwhile published a treatise on "the nature and origin of subterranean noises" (followed by a vigorous "rejoinder" from the Democratic *Gazette*). The tale ends with fine symmetry by means of a paragraph on the merits of a proper philosophy to serve as a "sure and ready shield against those shafts of calamity which can neither be seen, felt, nor fully understood" (B 1:115), spun out windily with plentiful learned allusions to Hebrew wisdom, to a plaque at Athens, to Epimenides, and to Laertius. Such is Poe's blatantly comic treatment of the Gothic and the transcendental.

III

The last story of the *Courier* group to be considered is "Metzengerstein," ostensibly a tale of horror and the supernatural, in which two
hereditary family enemies are wedded in mutual destruction. Arthur
Hobson Quinn remarks of the tale that it stands out in contrast to the
other *Courier* stories, "not only in its excellence but also in its general
tone"; unlike the other four tales, it is "no mere burlesque" but instead
a "powerful story of evil passions in a young man's soul," the allegorical
"lesson" of which may be a warning that evil may become so powerful
that one may lose the power to resist.[22] But it is hard to read "Metzengerstein" with such seriousness. It has too many absurd exaggerations
of both content and style, exaggerations too clearly patterned, too
symmetrically developed, for the tale to be a serious work of Gothic
terror.

Poe scholars have occasionally suggested that "Metzengerstein" may
contain elements of burlesque, but little analysis of such elements has
been undertaken. Interest in "Metzengerstein" has centered on noting
"serious" art in Poe's early works, such as the creation of vivid scenes
of terror and the adumbration of themes and techniques characteristic
of his later work. So too the other *Courier* stories, especially the
extravagancies of "A Decided Loss," have been of interest primarily
for their macabre elements. Edward H. Davidson mentions "Metzengerstein" only in connection with Poe's development from "fooling" to
"masterly inquiry into the diseased and sin-ridden soul of man," with
the further comment that "only a slight shift of emphasis" would
remold "Metzengerstein" into "The Fall of the House of Usher."[23]
But this comment, suggestive though it is, seems to be based on a
general similarity of theme and atmosphere rather than on a detailed
consideration of technique; and Davidson does not, in this instance,
note the presence of like elements of "fooling" in "Usher" and other
of Poe's "serious" works. William Bittner suggests the burlesque possibility of "Metzengerstein" but then, in effect, dismisses the idea. He
writes that "the narrative is ridiculous enough"—a horse in a tapestry
becomes real when possessed by the spirit of Metzengerstein's enemy,
Berlifitzing, and during a violent storm carries the fascinated Metzengerstein to his death in his own burning castle, the smoke from which
takes the shape of a gigantic horse. But the story, he concludes,
following the lead of Marie Bonaparte's psychoanalytic study, changed
as Poe wrote; "Metzengerstein" became a working out of Poe's feelings
about John Allan, and the resulting "sincerity" makes the tale an
effective study in horror.[24]

Indeed, the quality of near seriousness is the principal problem in reading "Metzengerstein" as a satire like the other four *Courier* stories, which are quite obvious in their comic touches even if the satiric point needs footnoting. A degree of seriousness, however, is essential for hoaxical parody, the ultimate put on, since the original must be recognized for parody to have any point. If, on a casual reading, the serious elements overshadow the clues to parody by reducing the blatancy of comic touches, of exaggerations, and of verbal and structural ironies, the work either may have failed in its ironic purpose or may have achieved a subtler irony. If the work fails as parody, then both the casual and the perceptive reader can take the work as a serious, though "flawed," effort. If, however, the clues are merely subtle, the work becomes a hoax; the circle of understanding readers is consciously limited, and the casual reader becomes part of the butt of the satire. It is this kind of satire that "Metzengerstein" presents.

When the tale is read carefully, the many seeming lapses in taste and precise control of point of view and style can in fact be seen to form a unified pattern of satiric irony. We discover that the apparent intent of writing a serious Gothic tale is cumulatively undercut by a ridiculous plot, exaggerated stereotypes of melodramatic Gothic scenes and characters, awkward and confused dialog, and a turgid and sometimes shockingly inappropriate manner of narration. Moreover, the literary satire suggested by these flaws is given reinforcement by an exaggerated series of ironies, by multiple innuendoes from the sounds and connotations of words, and by the motifs of meaningless utterance and perverse human behavior. The obvious "lapses" in style, the true subtleties of style, and the semicomic motifs of meaninglessness and perversity interweave with the quality of near seriousness to present a parody a little better in some ways than its original, a burlesque of the Gothic tale that dupes the enthusiastic but unwary devotee of the genre. Or, as Schlegel puts it, the ironist forms a "secret understanding with the select circle of the more intelligent of his readers."[25]

This then widespread enthusiasm for the Gothic tale is the historical literary context that gives the undersurface of "Metzengerstein" its point, especially the enthusiasm in Poe's day for the kind of "German" horror tale imitated abundantly and badly in English and American periodicals.[26] Poe tried to make his attitude to this (the literary context), and thus the satiric point, clearer by affixing to the 1836 republication of "Metzengerstein" in the *Southern Literary Messenger* the subtitle "A Tale in Imitation of the German."[27] It is quite doubtful, however, that "Metzengerstein" reflects any particular German source, as is often claimed; nor is the tale, so far as is known, a parody of any specific non-German work. Rather, the tale burlesques the genre as a whole.[28] German Gothic is reflected primarily in the setting, the atmosphere of which immediately prepares the reader for a tale of the kind in which one accepts—and expects—the conventions of the medieval castle, the aristocratic hero, and a vague, generalized quality of the supernatural and the horrible, as well as such attendant motifs as prophecy, revenge, and dark fatality; but though the German names of the major characters are important for atmosphere, they are comically tongue twisting; Baron Frederick von Metzengerstein and Count Wilhelm von Berlifitzing are hardly the most euphonious and convincing Poe might have chosen had he been serious.

Instead, it is the half-century of English and American Gothic romance that is the target of most of the satiric innuendo. There are in "Metzengerstein" echoes of the Gothic trappings of Horace Walpole's *The Castle of Otranto* (1764), Matthew G. Lewis's *The Monk* (1796), Walter Scott's *The Antiquary* (1816) and *The Betrothed* (1825), and the elder Richard Henry Dana's once popular poem "The Buccaneer" (1827). T. O. Mabbott has written that Dana's poem, in which the ghost of a slaughtered horse carries a pirate to a burning ship and back twice and finally destroys him, is obviously Poe's source.[29] Mabbott takes the tale seriously, but his view of its source is supported by the fact that Dana was an editor of the *North American Review*, a periodical Poe later attacked vigorously in both his criticism and in his satiric fiction as part of a corrupt literary clique that puffed its own and tomahawked all other writers; thus, a popular poem by one of its editors is an obvious candidate for one of the satiric butts of the tale.[30] In any case, yet another echo indicates that the suggestions of well-known Gothic works in the tale do not merely reveal the "sources" of a budding Gothicist. There is a parallel in "Metzengerstein" of both the horse in the tapestry and the horse in the storm from Benjamin Disraeli's *Vivian Grey* (1826–27). This novel Poe burlesques in more than one tale, including, as we have seen, versions of two of the other *Courier* satires, "A Bargain Lost" and "A Decided Loss."[31] Any such "sources," then, are more probably the satiric butts of an accomplished satirist. "Metzengerstein," though for good reasons differing from the others in its near serious tone and in its dark German atmosphere, is of one piece with the other four *Courier* tales. The other *Courier* stories are caricatures (not hoaxes) of specific, visible objects of ridicule. "Metzengerstein" is a parody of a genre in general and a hoax on those pleased by the genre. Displaying similar qualities of technique and the same burlesque intent, it is merely subtler—on a casual reading.

IV

Like the openings of the other *Courier* satires, the first paragraphs of "Metzengerstein" announce the ostensible situation and at the same time suggest a satiric point. The connotations of the opening are quite clear once satiric possibility suggests itself. "Metzengerstein" is prefaced with two paragraphs on "horror," superstition, and the probabilities of metempsychosis, and even the first two sentences immediately suggest satiric overtones: "Horror and fatality have been stalking abroad in all ages. Why then give a date to the story I have to tell?" (B 1:93).[32] The abstractions *horror* and *fatality*, whether taken to mean certain kinds of human experience or cosmological forces, are twisted slightly from these frames of reference and given a quiet comic touch by the use of "stalking," a word through which Poe personifies Horror and Fatality as a couple of demons ranging far and wide in search of prey. What is implied, especially when one is alerted by the later subtitle, is the currently popular German horror tale; the obvious victim implied in the stalking of Horror and Fatality is the reader of such tales. The idea of reader as victim is not a point that Poe makes merely once, nor even a point that he makes indirectly. As we have seen before, one of his clearest statements on his contemporaries' passion for the Gothic tale appears twelve years later at the conclusion of his semi-comic hoax "The Premature Burial." In this tale, Poe hoaxes his credulous readers for several pages before ending his tale with a ludicrous event and a comically blunt explanation: the hero finally loses his fears of being buried alive after the very absurdity of the final incident restores his sense of proportion, which he lost originally through reading Gothic "bugaboo tales—*such as this*" (H 5:273).

The function of the second sentence of "Metzengerstein" ("Why then give a date to the story I have to tell?") is double. It not only emphasizes in an awkward way the artificial "literary" quality of the undated story to follow, it also interposes a narrator between the reader and the story. Since the story is essentially narrated from the third-person after the opening paragraphs, it may seem somewhat out of place to emphasize the common device of a first-person narrator who never figures in the story himself and is perhaps holding forth before the fireplace in the manner of many tellers of supernatural tales. But the dual purpose of announcing the ostensible theme and at the same time suggesting an overriding irony with a satiric theme is focused in the unwitting *persona* of this narrator. The first paragraphs, as well as later ones, have their satiric point to make about the narrator—and he is, after all, not sitting by the fireside but at the Folio Club table reading his manuscript to a group of "dunderheads."

As the story develops, the announced themes of horror and fatality given in the first sentence are carried out through the agencies of a blood feud and metempsychosis, both rooted in an ancient prophecy. The remarks of the narrator about metempsychosis are of special importance; they foreshadow what apparently takes place in the story (even to mentioning in French the shape of a horse as one of several common reincarnations); and these remarks suggest what the qualities of the narrator are. Our "erudite" author, though he says that "some points in the Hungarian superstition . . . were fast verging to *absurdity*" (my italics), claims not to judge "of their falsity, or of their probability." He immediately proceeds, however, to mention, primarily in a "learned" footnote (in the 1840 edition), some eminent authorities to support the "doctrines of the Metempsychosis." Among these, the reference to Ethan Allen, the "Green Mountain Boy," as a "serious metempsychosist" (H 2:185) is not the most appropriate allusion the narrator could have made, since Allen's reputation as a belligerent Deist was still firmly planted in the minds of his countrymen. Indeed, the mere title of Allen's most famous work, *Reason the Only Oracle of Man* (1789), militates against the supernaturalistic atmosphere the narrator is apparently trying to suggest. Moreover, the very sound of the phrase "serious Metempsychosist," with its abundance of *s*'s, is mildly comic and foreshadows the similarly sibilant names of von Berlifitzing and von Metzengerstein. Thus, the "erudition" of the narrator not only mocks such pretense in the tale of horror, it also underscores the obtuse character of the narrator—and by pointing to a thoroughgoing rationalist in Allen, tips Poe's satiric hand.

Who of the Folio Club members is most likely to be the obtuse teller of a German tale of horror? The obvious candidate is Mr. Horribile Dictu, "with white eyelashes, who had graduated at Göttingen." Dictu is a particularly suitable narrator for several reasons. The citing of Allen along with the European "authorities" is an appropriate gesture, and blunder, from a foreign narrator and thus further underscores the genre of the foreign horror tale. Satiric intent is implied not only by the surface humor of Horribile Dictu's name but also by its Latin denotation; it makes a double-edged comment on both the matter and the manner of the story—horrible to tell and horribly told. Thus, with its innuendoes about genre and about the narrator, the opening suggests an overriding irony, the satiric thesis of which is that the Gothic tale is in both concept and style inherently absurd. But though the tale is sly in its opening, and though there is to follow an effective scene of terror, the absurdities and ironies of the story become increasingly obvious.

Beginning with plot, we may note, first, that the sequence of events has the kind of careful design associated with Poe's best works, here, as in many of Poe's tales, rigorously symmetrical and unified by the constant image, stated and implied, of a horse. The story begins with (1) the narrator's suggesting possible forms of metempsychosis, including the form of a horse. Then the story turns to (2) a history of the enmity (originating in a vague prophecy) between old Berlifitzing and young Metzengerstein, wherein we learn that the old Count is obsessed with horses and that the young Baron is a typical Gothic villain, described with ludicrous-grotesque appropriateness as a "petty Caligula" (for, as Mabbott notes, the bloody Caligula wanted to make his horse a consul). Next the story shifts to (3) a closeup scene of the Baron staring at a horse in a tapestry during a fire at the Count's stables, followed by an extended closeup scene focused on the appearance of a gigantic flame-colored horse. The pattern is repeated in the second part of the tale. There follows (1) some dark and equivocal speculation on metempsychosis; then the narrative again shifts to (2) a "history," wherein we learn not only of Metzengerstein's becoming obsessed with the horse (paralleling Berlifitzing's obsession in the first part) and of the vague enmity between horse and man, but also of an absurd curse by the Count's widow (which, like the prophecy earlier, strangely works out). This history is followed by (3) another closeup scene that brings the plot full circle to another fire as the horse carries the Baron to his death.

We may note, second, that the plot involves the careful working out of various ironies. Within the larger hoaxing irony is an irony shaping the plot in terms of the ostensible themes of horrible and fated enmity and revenge; and within this is a series of minor ironic twists that from their sheer number so exaggerate the symmetrical structure of the plot that it becomes comic beyond the absurdity of the bare events. The house of Metzengerstein, for example, is older than the house of Berlifitzing, but in the persons of the two protagonists the reverse is true; Metzengerstein is young and Berlifitzing is nearly senile. This situation is further twisted so that the feeble old Count becomes prodigiously powerful in his horse form while the young Baron weakens, with the added irony that though Berlifitzing is supposedly captive to Metzengerstein, it is actually Metzengerstein who is captive by his "perverse" obsession with Berlifitzing. The comic is added to the ironic in the absurdity of Berlifitzing's metamorphosis, for, as mentioned, in life he is an ardent lover of horses so that he naturally is reincarnated, in young Metzengerstein's view, as a horse—with the letters W. V. B.

branded on his forehead to ensure recognition. And in his immortal horse form he becomes the sole companion and friend of his "mortal" enemy Metzengerstein. Moreover, though we are told at the beginning of the story that it is Berlifitzing who has the "more bitter animosity," what is developed in the tale is the even more bitter enmity of Metzengerstein.

But what gives real unity to the plot—in terms of the apparent themes of fated enmity and supernatural revenge—is the irony involved in the working out of an "ancient prophecy" so ambiguously phrased that it seems merely "silly" to our narrator. And with this judgment, the narrator introduces, though unwittingly, the motif of meaninglessness, expressed throughout the tale, first in the form of vague and confused utterances (the paradoxical prophecy, impotent ranting, bemused exclamations) and second in the intrusions of the narrator himself. The irony of the narrator's repeated interjections is multiple, for his occasional opinion as to the silliness of what the characters say does not merely comment on the absurdity of the characters in the story; the narrator's commentary suggests in a direct way the absurdity of the conventions and style of the German horror tale and in an indirect way the faulty control of Gothic writers, for, since the silly utterances turn out to be not so silly on a plot level, our narrator seems not to understand his own tale very well. In addition, the motif of meaningless words (especially in connection with the plot-structuring prophecy) implies a comment on human behavior beyond what the dull-witted narrator sees, prefiguring Poe's concern in his later tales with order and disintegration and with the rational and the irrational. The ironic implication of the prophecy has to do with the consequences of absurdity and perversity, since the prophecy itself, because of what it merely seems to say, is the primary cause of its own fulfillment. The prophecy reads: "A lofty name shall have a fearful fall when, as the rider over his horse, the mortality of Metzengerstein shall triumph over the immortality of Berlifitzing" (B 1:94). To the house of Berlifitzing, the ominous utterance seems to imply, "if it implied anything," the eventual triumph of the already more powerful Metzengerstein and thus engenders a "more bitter animosity" in Berlifitzing. The paradox involved in mortality triumphing over immortality is similar to that in the emblem of the Montresors in "The Cask of Amontillado" (1846), in which it is not clear who is the crushing heel and who the fanged serpent, a synecdoche of the story itself, in which it is not absolutely clear who is avenged and who is not. And, of course, the ambiguity of the prophecy adds to the ominous quality of its Gothic vagueness. A further twist is provided by the fact that the tale can be seen as the working out of two paradoxes. The first is the prophecy just quoted. The other is the Latin motto to the story, which can be translated as "Living, I was your plague—dying, I shall be your death."[33]

The prediction, of course, works out literally and ironically in every detail. The lofty name fated to have a fearful fall is not Berlifitzing but Metzengerstein. The mere mortal Metzengerstein does triumph for a limited time over the immortal Berlifitzing when he rides the Count in his horse form, an ironic literal occurrence of what in the prophecy is apparently only a figure of speech: "as the rider over his horse." But this triumph soon proves illusory, for the palace cracks and burns and the Count carries the last of the line of Metzengerstein into the flames, presumably to final death, whereas Berlifitzing is metamorphosed once more, this time into a kind of vapor horse rising triumphant above the ruins of the castle.

The reason the prophecy works, however, lies in the perverse and irrational human reaction to its vagueness. The meaninglessness of the prophecy and the absurdity of the enmity between the two families is emphasized quite pointedly at the beginning of the story.

Never before were two houses so illustrious, mutually embittered by hostility so deadly. . . . The origin of this enmity seems to be found in the words of an ancient prophecy . . . [though] the words themselves had little or no meaning. But more trivial causes have given rise—and that no long while ago—to consequences equally eventful.[34]

We learn next that what gives the prophecy its peculiar power to set the two houses at odds is the result of the two estates being "contiguous." The two houses are thus "predisposed" to quarrel, not so much because of political and economic rivalry, but because "near neighbors are seldom friends." This wry axiom, given as a primary cause of the "enmity" between Berlifitzing and Metzengerstein, underscores early in the story the basic absurdity of the events to follow.

But the manner in which this blunt axiom concerning human relationships is presented epitomizes Poe's technique of maintaining an apparent seriousness; the bluntness, and the absurdity, of the comment is modified through paragraph organization, sentence rhythm, and diction so as to present a surface reasonableness that will keep up the hoax. The paragraph begins with the meaninglessness of the prophecy; next gives the fact of contiguity; then introduces the more reasonable ideas of rival political influence and Berlifitzing envy of Metzengerstein wealth, but phrased in lengthy clauses and sentences that tend to bury the twice emphasized axiom that enmity springs from contiguity. The tendency of the paragraph as a whole is to allay the absurdity of this analysis of the origins of human enmity and bring us, with bland surface coherence, aided by diction abstract enough to suggest a little erudition, to the logical conclusion: "What wonder, then, that the words, however silly, of that prediction should succeed in setting and keeping at variance two families already predisposed to quarrel by every instigation of hereditary jealousy?" (B 1:94). It is easy, if reading casually, to fail to note that what "every instigation" consists of is merely this: that near neighbors are seldom friends—a melancholy-comic view of perversity as well as of the absurd.

Such explanation for the feud fits well the personality of the narrator, hinted at by the first two paragraphs. Although he recognizes the absurdity inherent in the vagueness of the prophecy, and although he has an inkling of the absurd element in human behavior, he is, under his surface reasonableness, also rather absurd. This is the first of his obvious intrusions on the story proper, but his personality as a typical teller of terrible tales is stamped on all the scenes and is implicit in the style of the whole.

The account of the plot-shaping prophecy provides one kind of exaggeration; absurd exaggeration of scene, character, and style soon follow. The section of the story concluding the history of Metzengerstein's feud with Berlifitzing maintains the motif of Gothic vagueness and meaninglessness in its characterization of the young Baron as a typical Gothic tyrant. His mother, the Lady Mary, died young, leaving him sole heir to the Metzengerstein estates.

The young Baron Frederick stood without a living relative by the coffin of his dead mother. He placed his hand upon her placid forehead. No shudder came over his delicate frame—no sigh from his flinty bosom. Heartless, self-willed and impetuous from his childhood, he had reached the age of which I speak through a career of unfeeling, wanton, and reckless dissipation. . . . (B 1:94–95)

The exaggerations of this picture of "flinty" Metzengerstein are concentrated in the image of his hand placed on his dead mother's forehead. But the passage might be taken seriously, despite the grotesque image, because of its impressive-sounding diction and sentence patterns, except that we learn next that the Baron's "career" of "dissipation" since "childhood" has not been that of young manhood nor even of a predatory adolescence. "Heartless" and "flinty" Metzengerstein still has most of his adolescence before him, being just "in his fifteenth year." Aware, apparently, that fifteen years may be a rather young age for such flintiness, our narrator adds: "In a city, fifteen years are no long period . . . but in a wilderness—in so magnificent a wilderness as that old principality, fifteen years have a far deeper meaning" (B 1:94). Not only is this comment vague, it is an inversion of conventional ideas regarding the corrupting influence of city life and the virtues of country life. Immediately after the horrendous suggestiveness of this passage, we discover that the fifteen-year-old Baron indulges in "shameful debaucheries—flagrant treacheries—unheard-of atrocities" (B 1:95). The generality of these crimes is underscored by the abstract diction, the triptych order, and the dashes, producing not emphasis and climax but repeated vagueness. Moreover, the narrator chooses to intrude a "comment" at this point, suggesting that Metzengerstein "out-heroded Herod" and adding wryly that he "fairly surpassed the expectations of his most enthusiastic admirers."

Despite the Gothic vagueness of his history of Baron Metzengerstein's hideous career, at least one concrete crime is attached to his name, though there is no certainty that he committed the act; presumably, he is responsible for the fire in Berlifitzing's stables. But, again, the style points up the melodrama of the entire situation; the diction is overly general, inflated, illogically ordered, and redundant. "The incendiary" is added to the "already hideous list" of Metzengerstein's "misdemeanors" and "enormities." But during the "tumult" which is (of all things) "occasioned by this occurrence," the Baron sits in a "vast and desolate" apartment, buried in meditation, or at least "apparently" so, or maybe he wasn't. At any rate, as he sits amid this Gothic splendor, his attention is engaged on a horse in a tapestry, and there suddenly arises on his "lip" a "fiendish expression" (B 1:96). Despite these remarkable powers of "lip," the Baron seems to have been struck with a perverse idea (self-engendered by a guilty conscience?), for the tapestry horse seems to him, possibly, to have changed its position, a phenomenon which strikes "terror" into the heart of the "fiendish," "reckless," "dissipated," "hideous," "heartless," "impetuous," and "flinty" fifteen-year-old. He shudders to perceive that his shadow, thrown by a "flash of red light," fills up the contour of the "relentless and triumphant murderer of the Saracen Berlifitzing." Such a flinty villain, we might suppose, would rejoice in this omen of the fulfillment of the prophecy; instead, he rushes out "to lighten the depression of his spirits." The characterization of the child Baron as a Gothic tyrant is, then, done with absurd exaggeration, jarring contrasts, comic twists.

But in the latter middle part of the tale—the scene in which the fiery horse appears, and the following history of Metzengerstein's obsession and ensuing solitude—exaggerations of manner are more important than those of incident and characterization. Poe exaggerates his narrator's use of four devices in this section. First, the narrator continues the Gothic mode of vagueness; while the young Baron is "apparently" thinking this or doing that, both the aristocrats and the "multitude" are "attributing" and "suggesting" and "hinting" darkly of things of an "equivocal" nature (B 1:97–98). Second, the narrator writes stilted dialog marked by repetitions of exclamations like "Indeed!" and "Shocking!" Third, the narrator makes several interpretive intrusions into the story to underscore the motif of meaningless words, though he has only limited awareness of the larger implications of his judgments on the "silliness" of our utterances. Fourth, the style is exaggerated through plays on the sounds of words, reinforced through implied puns on the word *horse*.

The latter of these, the wordplay, is probably the most revealing. The horse in this section of the tale is repeatedly described as "unnatural," "untractable," "intractable," "intelligent," "impressive," and "impetuous." Other words are used in connection with the horse, but these half dozen are especially noticeable since they are similar in the approximate alliteration and assonance of the first syllables and in being polysyllables of nearly the same length and accent. Among the most emphasized sounds in the middle section of the tale are variants of *un-*, *in-*, and *im-*, repeated enough to keep the figure of the horse constantly in mind as a submerged image. Moreover, the most frequently repeated sounds, not only in the middle of the tale but also in the beginning section, are long and short *e* sounds, at the beginnings of words. Since the *e* recurs frequently as *equ-* in the repetitions of *equerry, equerries, equals, equally, equivocal,* an implied pun on *equus* suggests itself, which along with the other sounds associated with the horse keeps the image literally echoing throughout the passage. I have earlier pointed out symmetrical repetitions of the horse image in the beginning, middle, and end of the tale, as well as in the jesting reference to Caligula; the counterpoint of sound is further evidence of the care with which Poe wrote his tale. But let us note in passing that the single most obvious characteristic of Poe's style in both his prose and his poetry is his manipulation of sound and rhythm.

We next learn that Metzengerstein becomes companionless "utterly . . . unless, indeed, that unnatural, impetuous" horse may be called his friend; he refuses "invitations" of the Count's "imperious" friends, actions they consider "insults not to be endured." "Equivocal" hints become current, as the Baron disappoints "every expectation" of (our narrator inserts) "many a manoeuvering mamma" (B 1:98). The widow is "even heard to express" the hope that the Baron "might be at home

when he did not wish to be at home, since he disdained the company
of his equals; and ride when he did not wish to ride, since he preferred
the society of a horse" (B 1:98). The irony of this passage is multiple.
The widow of the unfortunate Count wishes to be emphatic, but her
speech is so vague that it sounds anticlimactic and her desires for
Metzengerstein's discomfort so unhurtful that she sounds (as our narrator points out) merely "silly." Thus, the perversity of things operates
on the widow—at least, according to our narrator. But perversity as a
kind of cosmic irony also operates for her and beyond her since her
curse, so absurd on the surface, like the prophecy, comes true with
absurd precision. Metzengerstein "realizes" that the horse *must* be
Berlifitzing and forms what the narrator calls a "perverse attachment"
to the animal—perverse to the narrator because unnatural and mali-
cious, but also perverse for Metzengerstein because the attachment is
ultimately against his own best interests. That is, he rides "when he
does not wish to ride" into the flames of his castle and thus is "at home"
when he assuredly does not wish to be. Despite the prophetic quality
of the widow's curse, however, she remains a comic caricature; the
widow's curse is a parody, symmetrically placed, of the first prophecy.
Moreover, the narrator shows no awareness of the ironic working out
of her curse; he notes only the surface bathos of her words and thus
reveals himself further as a dunderhead who does not even understand
the plot of his story very well.

The rest of the tale details Metzengerstein's perverse obsession, speculates ambiguously on the supernatural character of the horse (at least
in Metzengerstein's mind), and concludes with a description of the
climactic plunge into the flames. The manner of narration in one sense
becomes more subtle and in another sense more obvious. The obvious
intrusions of the narrator are reduced; instead, his style intrudes. Rather than commentary on the silliness of what is happening, an enthusiastic recounting of horrible events takes place—rather too enthusiastic,
for in his enthusiasm the narrator from time to time loses control of his
words, sacrificing meaning and connotation to stereotyped phrases. In
attempting to describe the intensity of the perverse attachment between Metzengerstein and the horse, for example, the narrator writes:
"In the glare of noon—at the dead hour of night—in sickness or in
health—in calm or in tempest—the young Metzengerstein seemed rivet-
ted to the saddle of that colossal horse . . ." (B 1:98–99). The use of
the phrase "in sickness or in health," suggestive of the prayer book
marriage service (though it connotes the wedding together of the fates
of the two enemies), is obviously incongruous; but again the incongruous is buried in a triptych, punctuated melodramatically, so that

although the passage is overwrought it also reduces somewhat the blatancy of the contrast between the several frames of reference. When noticed, however, the contrast calls further attention to the cliché-ridden style of the narrator, who here sacrifices meaning and tone to melodrama and trite rhythmic phrases—faults too often attributed to Poe himself rather than to his implied narrators. This kind of incongruity of tone, as well as the different kind involved in inserting such judgments as "many a manoeuvering mamma," turns the narrator's comments against himself. Not only because he does not see the implications of events and utterances in his own tale, but also because his manner is awkward and obtuse to connotation, his intrusion into the tale is a major satiric pattern.

When the reader recognizes this pattern, the egregious violation of tone and of taste at the beginning of the story—the notorious passage in praise of consumption, sometimes used by hostile critics to prove how obtuse Poe himself is as a narrator or to prove how nearly psychotic he was as a man—is critically appropriate, for it roundly burlesques Gothic melodrama. Writing of the circumstances of young Metzengerstein's inheritance, the narrator tells us that both parents have died, and then introduces a paragraph of elegiac lament that ends with an affirmation.

The beautiful Lady Mary! How *could* she die?—and of consumption! But it is a path that I have prayed to follow. I wish all I love to perish of that gentle disease. How glorious—to depart in the heyday of the young blood—the heart of all passion—the imagination all fire—amid the remembrances of happier days—in the fall of the year—and so be buried up forever in the gorgeous autumnal leaves! (B 1:94–95)

Illogical, florid, melodramatically punctuated, subtly unparallel, this parody of Romantic sentimentalism has for a true subject obtuseness itself. It is an example of what, as we have seen, Poe called six years later in "How to Write a Blackwood Article" the "tone elevated, diffusive, and interjectional": the "words must be all in a whirl, like a humming-top, and make a noise very similar, which answers remarkably well instead of meaning. This is the best of all possible styles where the writer is in too great a hurry to think" (H 2:275). The grotesquerie of the consumptive passage is heightened by its surface associative progression. Blood, passion, fire, and autumnal leaves are easily associated with the implied imagery of heat and color, whereas consumption denotes dampness, delirium from fever, and the coughing up of bloody sputum, each horribly implied by the obtuse "affirmations" of the narrator. And it is immediately after this incredible passage that young Metzengerstein stands beside the corpse with his delicate hand placed delicately upon his dead mother's forehead.

Thus, the "flaws" of "Metzengerstein" interweave to form a unified pattern of satire. The narrator of the Gothic tale is not quite successful in his pretensions to erudition, not quite aware of the ironies of his own plot, not quite in control of his own style. The atmosphere and general technique of the Gothic tale are satirized by Poe's display of the obtuseness of his narrator (regarding tone, connotation, the incongruities of event and character), by the Gothic convention of the vague, by the counterpoint of the doubly ironic motif of meaningless words, and by subtler exaggerations of style through rhythm, puns, and repeated sounds. Gothic figures are satirized through the comic exaggerations of the character of Metzengerstein and through the "perversity" of subjective and superstitious human reactions to vague events and utterances. The plot of the Gothic tale is burlesqued through the exaggeration of events, through the very number and symmetry of ironic and mildly comic twists, and again through the faulty understanding of the narrator. In view of these exaggerations of content, structure, and style, it requires an effort to understand the views of careful readers who yet see "Metzengerstein" as radically different in tone and effect from the other *Courier* satires, or of readers who claim that "Metzengerstein" presents a powerful allegorical lesson, or a serious working out of Poe's inner conflicts.

V

Poe's ironic technique is close to the hoax, even in the more obviously satiric first version of the tale. This burlesque imitation of the German horror story is so close that it can, on a casual reading, be mistaken for its original. It seems clear that the circumstances of the reception of "Metzengerstein" caused Poe eventually, in his revision of this tale and in writing subsequent tales, to narrow the circle of the perceptive audience. The devoted readers of Gothic tales are here hoaxed into believing a carefully flawed tale to be a genuine Gothic performance.

The real flaws of the tale are different. The story seems merely clever rather than intrinsically interesting, despite its intricate ironies and sometimes subtle parody; and the satiric usage of the narrator is mildly inconsistent since he is allowed to make wry comic observations on the characters and on human nature while he is yet part of the butt of the satire. The inconsistency here is not merely a matter of casual verbal irony becoming straightforward from time to time; it is a matter of unclearly defined point of view. We do not have Poe imitating the Gothic tale; the character of the narrator is too strongly implied, and his intrusions form a pattern integral to the ironic structure. And because the narrator has two faces, so to speak, *even* in his role as narrator, several implications are left unclear.

Horribile Dictu (if I may be allowed this assumption) says that the prophecy and the widow's curse are both silly, but they both work out literally and ironically in every detail, including, ludicrously the metaphors (a technique we shall see to be operative in such works as "Ligeia" and "Usher"). Dictu then may be duped in some way, in which case the implication would seem to be the serious one that mysterious and supernaturally charged events should not be judged too hastily. Or Dictu may be employing foreshadowing dramatic irony to set his audience up for the twists to follow (including the supernatural occurrences); but he shows no other awareness of the ironies of his plot (indeed, seems obtuse about the matter), and his style and taste prevent one from responding with any serious delight to such "ominous" foreshadowing. On the other hand, one wonders if Dictu may himself be satiric; and yet he seems only to be faintly aware of the operation of perversity in his tale, and the range of his satire is limited on the surface to mild, "witty" sarcasm regarding the behavior of his characters. To expand the ironic framework so that he is satiric beyond the wryness of incidental comment tends to merge him with Poe the ironist too much—especially since in the overall Folio Club scheme the holder of the seventeen manuscripts plans to "expose" the dunderheads and their writings. It is only by noting that Dictu does not seem to understand his tale very well that his comments have real consistency with the overall parody, for then his self-assumed superiority (as announced by the opening paragraphs) is ridiculed in the working of his plot. But even granting this, the problem of finding a consistent point of view in "Metzengerstein" is likely to prove annoying. The Folio Club scheme was left incomplete, and perhaps Poe had not clearly thought out the personalities of his narrators by the time "Metzengerstein" was published.

In any event, the inconsistency is fairly minor; and Poe, as he increasingly used participating rather than merely peripheral first-person narrators, did not have the same kind of problem later. That is, the problem of the separation and the intrusion of the narrator is not an operative matter, for Poe makes fuller and clearer use of even the observing "I" in his subsequent tales. The first-person narrators of "MS. Found in a Bottle," "Berenice," "Morella," "Ligeia," "The Fall of the

House of Usher," "The Man of the Crowd," and "The Oval Portrait," for example, are involved participants in the action; and their bizarre mental states are integral to the deceptively ironic, seriocomic, and satiric perspectives of the tales.

"Metzengerstein" has sometimes been called a false start by critics who wish to consider only half of Poe's fiction and who insist that Poe is solely a Gothicist. But the tale is a false start only in the sense that its ironic point of view is somewhat blurred. In all other respects, this carefully flawed tale is a paradigm for Poe's subsequent Gothic hoaxes. Poe almost uniquely in American literature possessed the power to touch the unseen, unconscious life, to render forcefully certain dark psychological states, to suggest the demoniac in mankind and in nature —and yet at the same time to bring a cool rationality, an ironic skepticism, and even mockery to bear on all that he examines. He both explores the serious possibilities of the Gothic mania of his times and attacks the society that believes in such things. Poe began his career as a satirist, and he remained a satirist to the end of his career. The only real shift was his increased philosophical and artistic irony, which not only informs all his satire but also came to overshadow the satiric impulse. The ironic mode and the ironic vision of the later tales, however, are implicit in the early satires. The history of Poe's career is the history of his simultaneous exploration of the fearful and the ridiculous. Poe exploited the terrors of the absurd as an ironically detached artist, exploring perverse human psychology in a perverse, absurd universe. And though he may not at first have been in complete control, he knew consciously from the first what he was about.

4
Explained Gothic

*. . . I have availed myself of the force of contrast . . . an
air of the fantastic—approaching as nearly to the ludicrous as
was admissible. . . . With the indulgence to the extreme,
of . . . self-torture, the narration, in what I have termed its
first or obvious phase, has a natural termination, and so far
there has been no overstepping of the limits of the real.*
"The Philosophy of Composition" (1845)

ROUGHLY PARALLEL in the late eighteenth and the early nineteenth centuries were seemingly separate developments of the Gothic, the grotesque, and the arabesque—each involving to a degree the psychology of fear. The development of theories of irony, I submit, served in part as a defense against such fear, metaphysical and otherwise. These were related literary extremes of generalized literary experimentation among writers suspicious of neoclassic regularity and stimulated by the subjective philosophies of Berkeley, Hume, and Kant. The terms have an intertwined history of connotation and reference that puts Poe's odd literary techniques into yet another context, related to those we have just examined, and further illuminates what Poe was up to. When seen in his proper Romantic context, Poe turns out to be not "merely" a Gothic showman (which, however, he assuredly is) nor "only" a clever satirist (which, again, he is). By focusing on the Gothic aspect of Romantic literature, I hope to demonstrate that Poe is as well a stunningly complex psychological and philosophical writer in the dark tradition. To accomplish this, it is requisite to trace the development of "terrible," "explained," and "ambiguous" modes of Gothic fiction from Germany to England to America. Then we shall examine Poe's two most famous Gothic tales, "Ligeia" and "The Fall of the House of Usher," as additional touchstones for his Gothic technique. Finally, we shall look at a number of important statements in Poe's letters, essays, and reviews which suggest that his Gothic mode is that of the ambiguously explained supernatural, in which clues to the real psychological action are patterned much like those of a detective story. Moreover, we shall see that the vision of the human mind that emerges from this complex of literary technique and philosophy is one of despair over the ability of the mind to *know* anything, and that the arabesque patterns of the tales parallel for the reader the labyrinth of surmise that the protagonists go through. Only by an objective reconstruction of the total pattern can we come near the overall meaning Poe built into these works. Simultaneously, he gives us a "supernatural" thrill within the weird subjective "reality" of the psychological state of the narrator's mind, all the while slyly insinuating a burlesque, a grotesquerie of both the content of the fictional structure and its mode.

I

In literature, the word *Gothic* normally refers to the kind of work that seeks to create an atmosphere of mystery and terror through pronounced mental horror. Applied to fiction in the eighteenth and nineteenth centuries, the primary and constant element of the term is terror or horror—*terror* suggesting frenzy and *horror* suggesting perception of something incredibly evil or repellent.[1] The secondary element of the Gothic is the supernatural, whether real or fearfully imagined. Actual use of the term *Gothic* in English to describe an artistic effect or structure dates at least from the early seventeenth century; and by the beginning of the eighteenth century, it had already come to have at least two distinct meanings, each associated with a different kind of disapproval.[2] One meaning had to do with any architectural structure not in the classical style. A second meaning had to do with a historical hypothesis regarding Goths or other northern barbarian invaders of the Roman empire. As Arthur Lovejoy points out, John Evelyn in his *Account of Architects and Architecture* (1697) wrote that "Goths, Vandals and other barbarous Nations" destroyed Roman works and introduced in their stead "a certain fantastical . . . Manner of Building . . . full of *fret* and lamentable Imagery . . . [so that] a judicious Spectator is distracted and quite confounded. . . ." But, Evelyn continued, after the Goths "from the North" came the "*Moors* and *Arabs* from the *South* and *East,* over-running the Civilized World" and destroying true art while replacing it with "busy Work and other Incongruities," with unreasonably thick walls, clumsy buttresses, towers, sharp-pointed arches, doors and apertures without proportion, marbles "impertinently placed," and "turrets and Pinnacles thick set with *Monkies* and *Chymaeras.*" All of this, he continued, "rather gluts the Eye than gratifies and pleases it with any reasonable Satisfaction" and so confounds the sight "that one cannot consider it with any Steadiness, where to begin or end."[3] This element of deception or confusion we shall see, later in this chapter, to be of great significance.

The architectural and historical hypothesis was widely accepted, and in 1713 Christopher Wren wrote that what "we now call the Gothick manner of architecture . . . should with more reason be called the Saracen style."[4] At other times the terms *Arabic* or *arabesque* were used as synonyms for Gothic, though by the middle eighteenth century "regular" Gothic and arabesque Gothic were distinguished. The later arabesque style was supposed to have been a reaction to the earlier style of Gothic, both, of course, being periods within the Middle Ages. The earlier Gothic was thought of as ponderous, somber, and depressing. "Gothic gloom," writes Lovejoy, was one of the conventional descriptive phrases for characterizing its effect upon the mind. The later arabesque Gothic was condemned as "light" and "soaring," "frivolous" and "fanciful," "overrefined" and "overladen with ornament," and "confusing the eye with an excessive multiplicity of separate parts and obtrusive details."

The indictments against the modern arabesque Gothic of the thirteenth through fifteenth centuries, made by such men as Berkeley, Montesquieu, and Addison, listed its want of simplicity (in its use of nonstructural ornament), its failure to conform to nature (because not simple), its lack of symmetry (unnaturally militating against "unity of effect"), and its irregularity (lack of exact mathematical proportion). Thus the earliest literary usages of the term *Gothic* seem to have involved disapproval of what was considered unrestrained "fancy" and "confusing" design. One would like immediately to apply the terms *Gothic* and *arabesque* to Poe; but their meanings were to undergo some radical shifts between 1750 and 1830, and the apparent antithesis between the two styles was to blur into a paradoxical fusion. This paradox of meaning is underscored by the usual twentieth-century application of arabesque to Poe's serious Gothic tales, as if it could not with equal justice describe the frivolous, light, soaring, fanciful, wittily ornamented comic and satiric tales.[5]

Between 1750 and 1800, Gothic interiors, with their profuse scrollwork, sometimes called grotesque work, around windows and on ceilings, suggesting branches and groves and animals, began to symbolize to imaginative minds a "natural" landscape. Moreover, the impact of certain pre-Romantic elements in German literature and of the new "Nature Philosophy" began to be felt in England and elsewhere. By the turn of the century, Schelling in his *Philosophy of Art* (1802–1803) had rejected the idea that Arabs or Saracens brought the Gothic style from the Orient and had claimed (or reasserted) a Germanic origin. The "Gothic imagination," he said, was primitive and natural, closer to the spirit of God than was the classical imagination. A Gothic building, Schelling remarked, was essentially a metaphor (or symbol or hieroglyph) for a huge row of trees, or the natural, primitive habitat of man. Poe commented similarly on the qualities of Gothic imagination: "In omitting to envelop our Gothic architecture in *foliage*, we omit, in fact, an essential point in the Gothic architecture itself. Of a Gothic *church*, especially trees are as much a portion as the pointed arch. 'Ubi *tres*, ecclesia,' says Tertullian;—but no doubt he meant that 'Ubi ecclesia, *tres*'" (H 16:169).

But for our purposes, it is more important to note in the concept of Gothic the intrusion of an aesthetic principle of irregularity or deceptiveness into what was considered natural. Edmund Burke, for example, in *The Sublime and Beautiful* (1756–57) had remarked that the idea of exact proportion had not been drawn from a study of nature, but was an artificial intrusion of man into nature. Subsequently, the characteristic "deformities" of Gothic art became virtues in garden design; the effect sought was beauty without perfect regularity and without immediately apparent design, as in Oriental gardens, which were yet intricately designed.[6] This deceptiveness of design in certain Gothic literary productions became, as we shall see, an integral part of Poe's concept of the Gothic, and allied it with Romantic theories of ironic composition.

These feelings regarding what was presumed to be truly natural shifted to a preference for wildness, seen in the taste for landscapes that suggested the "sublime" through their evocation of a sense of the mystery of the supernatural, hinting at grand secrets of another world that stretches away beyond the range of human intelligence. In the middle of the eighteenth century, Horace Walpole, whose novel *The Castle of Otranto, a Gothic Story* (1765) seems to have given real currency to the term *Gothic* in English literature, emphasized the vaults, tombs, stained windows, gloom, and perspective of medieval buildings; in the Gothic cathedral such ornamentation was supposed to generate sensations of Romantic devotion, though of a superstitious kind. Gothic churches and old castles thus became, after Walpole, inextricably associated with the "thrill of mystery and wonder."[7]

The Castle of Otranto is generally regarded as the prototype of the

Gothic romance in English, though the tale of terror has been traced rather directly to Renaissance drama.[8] In the Preface to *Otranto,* Walpole (as the "translator" William Marshall, Gent.) pretended that his "work was found in the library of an ancient Catholic family in the north of England" and that he had translated the manuscript from the Italian of a monk living at the time of the Crusades (1095 to 1253). He apologized for the "miracles, visions, necromancy, dreams, and other preternatural events" no longer believed in by an enlightened age. But when "our author wrote," said Walpole, "belief in every kind of prodigy was so established . . . that an author would not be faithful to the *manners* of the times" if he did not represent supernatural occurrences.[9] Moreover, he seems to have been concerned with the possibility of censure on the grounds of irregularity, lack of simple design, excessive multiplicity of parts, and distraction (caused by fret and lamentable imagery) that had been associated with the Gothic in the first half of the century. He wrote:

If this *air* of the *miraculous* is excused . . . [and we] allow the possibility of the facts . . . [we find] all the actors comport themselves as persons would do in their situation. There is no bombast, no similes, flowers, digressions, or unnecessary descriptions. Every thing tends directly to the catastrophe. Never is the reader's attention relaxed. The rules of the drama are almost observed throughout the conduct of the piece. . . . Terror, the author's principal engine, prevents the story from ever languishing. . . . (p. 4)

Thus, surprisingly, the term *Gothic* was at this time associated with multiple innuendoes, wit, and even with ironic contrasts. In both the first and second prefaces to *Otranto,* Walpole exhibited concern for the overly simple behavior of the domestics in the tale, but justified it on the basis of overall unity, pointing out that such contrast of character set into stronger relief the qualities of the sublime and the pathetic in the protagonists, and citing (pp. 10–11) the example of Shakespeare's "irony." The potential parallels with A. W. Schlegel are obvious.

Thus, while giving literary currency to the term *Gothic,* Walpole shifted its meaning somewhat from unnatural confusion of details to a legitimately medieval and mysterious composition, artfully put together. Then Walpole, in a second preface for the second edition, said that he had tried to "blend the two kinds of Romance, the ancient and the modern. In the former, all was imagination and improbability; in the latter, nature is always intended to be, and sometimes has been, copied with success" (p. 9). He intended to give the "fancy" free play and yet write of real people, though in extraordinary situations (p. 10). Thus, unity of effect, a principle of contrast, and some psychological verisimilitude are among the qualities, theoretically at any rate, of the earliest English Gothic novel.

The connotation in Gothic of the supernatural and the fantastic, however, was heightened into the principal meaning of the term by the extraordinary success of *Otranto* and especially of Walpole's immediate imitators. The medieval atmosphere was a major element, but it served primarily as the backdrop for weird and terrifying events. The usage of *arabesque* meanwhile began to be more clearly associated with the term *grotesque*, metaphorically applied to literature from ancient scroll-work styles that conjoined animal, human, and plant figures in a bizarre manner which was sometimes playful and sometimes ominous. The three terms, then, were likely in the third quarter of the eighteenth century (and lingering well into the nineteenth century) to mean about the same thing. *Arabesque* was a term used to suggest "later Gothic" styles, and *grotesque* was a term associated with the intricate designs ornamenting Gothic buildings or other artworks, early and late.[10]

The Gothic novel became so stereotyped, however, that it fostered a large catalog of often ludicrous conventions, which Poe burlesqued, and also a large subgenre of Gothic satire popular even before Poe's time.[11] Moreover, writers of Gothic tales developed the tale of terror into the psychological tale of sensation, in which the protagonists got themselves into fantastic predicaments (such as being baked in an oven) and then proceeded to analyze their sensations. These sensation tales, as noted earlier, were the mainstay of the fiction of *Blackwood's Edinburgh Magazine* in the early nineteenth century, which Poe lampoons in "The Premature Burial," "How to Write a Blackwood Article," "A Predicament," "Loss of Breath," and "Metzengerstein." The Gothic writers rapidly developed a number of stock-in-trade devices, such as the lonely manor house, the winding staircase, the heavily curtained bedchambers, underground passages, creaking hinges, misty graveyards, forked lightning, howling wind, eerie animal cries, awful darkness, curses and prophetic dreams, animated portraits, mad heroes and sickly heroines, and the presence of giaours, ghosts, and other forms seemingly the product of metempsychosis. These elements, with a little exaggeration, could be made the devices of clever parody; and, if the exaggerations were subtle enough and combined with any effective scenes of horror at all, they could easily become, as in Poe, satiric hoaxes of the genre.

Besides developing such conventions, the Gothic tale itself also developed into subtypes, as Nathan Drake observed at least as early as 1804. Drake distinguished between the "regular Gothic" (the mythology of Scandinavian origin) and the "vulgar Gothic," which, he said, had in turn two types: "the terrible" (which involves the awful ministrations of the specter) and "the sportive" (which involves fancy, humor, and the innocent gambols of the fairy). Terrible or supernatural Gothic developed along two lines especially important for the understanding of Poe's treatment of Gothic materials: the truly supernatural and the apparently supernatural, or preternatural, which is finally explained away in realistic terms.[12]

Discussing the development of the "terrible" mode of Gothic fiction, J. M. S. Tompkins writes that there were two stages which resulted in the two basic types of the English Gothic romance.[13] In the first stage, the characteristic writer was Mrs. Radcliffe, who worked from English models and produced a type of romance in which the heroines never get their feet dusty, in which there is little or no real violence, and in which supernatural phenomena are rationally and scientifically explained. In the second stage, the Gothic novel was greatly affected by the translation of German Gothic stories, and the characteristic English figure was Matthew Gregory Lewis with *The Monk* (1795). Whereas Radcliffe displayed dignity, delicacy, and moral scrupulousness, the Germanic kind of Gothic terror was "frequently hideous," detailing shocking and "protracted butcheries" (p. 245). The English or Radcliffean method was to darken the scene slowly, but the early German method, Tompkins claims, had no twilight and insinuated mystery. (She apparently does not include the later grotesque works of the German Romantic Ironists as part of the German Gothic tradition.) Radcliffe's elements were beautiful and awesome landscapes, Gothic buildings, and "the sensitive mind of a girl, attuned to all the intimations, sublime or dreadful, that she can receive from her surroundings" (p. 253). Her books were "full of the half-revealed"; "deliberate recourse to suggestive obscurity" was her most noticeable technique. "Her theme is not the dreadful happening . . . but the interval during which the menace takes shape and the mind of the victim is reluctantly shaken . . ." (pp. 257–58). The essence of her fiction, then, was human psychology.

The Gothic terror of the Germans, however, worked by sudden shocks and usually with the "real" supernatural, wrenching the mind suddenly from skepticism to "horror-struck belief" (p. 245). Tompkins writes that the taste of the readers was for "the colossal, the impassioned, the dark, the sublime. They wanted to see great forces let loose and the stature of man once more distended to its full height. . . . They wanted to see him ablaze with destructive fire or tempered by his will to an icy ruthlessness; they wanted vehemence and tumult, and measureless audacity and measureless egoism" (p. 287). But the whole sense of the Enlightenment was against such unchecked force and against the propagation of superstition. Thus, not only did the English Gothic novel become moral and doctrinal, but also the supernatural became a matter of misperception on the part of the characters. The eerie events were perfectly explicable in realistic terms. Mrs. Radcliffe secured a weird effect by the lighting of blue flames on the points of the soldiers' lances before the Castle of Udolpho, but she was careful to add in a footnote: "See the Abbé Berthelon on Electricity." Eager "to serve two gods," writes Arthur Ransome, she "gave us our thrill and our electricity together" and her fiction is thus "a little laughable on that account," whereas Poe later, with a clearer understanding of the effect of the weird, avoided such absurdity.[14]

Ransome's assessment of Poe's method is not quite accurate. The technique of explaining the supernatural, according to Tompkins, though unpopular with later generations of readers, was one of the most popular features of the Gothic tale at the end of the eighteenth century, since the explanations preserved "probability." Even Coleridge wrote in a review of *The Mysteries of Udolpho* in 1794 that the "reader experiences in perfection the strange luxury of artificial terror" and yet is not "obliged for a moment to hoodwink his reason, or to yield to the weakness of superstitious credulity."[15] Moreover, the most successful Gothicist in America before Poe, Charles Brockden Brown, was a proponent of the explained rather than the supernatural Gothic, and the interest of his novels resides in both a spooky thrill and a reasonable psychological or scientific accounting.

It is hard to overestimate the importance of this characteristic, for it comprises an essential difference between American Gothic and British Gothic. In a useful essay on "The Gothic Element in American Literature before 1835," Oral Sumner Coad writes that American poets treated their Gothic mysteries as beyond human ken, but he adds that the dramatists and fiction writers usually "explained" everything: "the preponderance of these rationalized phenomena is proof that the dominant influence on the whole body of American Gothic literature was Mrs. Radcliffe."[16] Accurate though this may be as a general description, it is only a half-truth with regard to the major American Gothicists, as William B. Cairns long ago noticed. In a monograph on American literature from 1815 to 1833 (which was, of course, the formative period for the young Poe), Cairns considers the *effect* of Brown's Gothic fiction (despite explanations involving madness, ventriloquism, and spontaneous combustion) to be "purely horrible." While discussing the effects of writers like Brown, Hawthorne, and Richard Henry Dana, Sr., Cairns writes that the horrors in Dana's novel *Paul Felton* (1821) are "real no matter how they are accounted for." The reader is presented with the observable facts of the dramatic situation and then is left to choose between demonic possession and insanity. But the impact is double: if the reader wishes to get the "strongest effect," Cairns suggests, he intellectually apprehends the weird events as the products of the diseased imagination of a madman, but he feels them as supernatural phenomena.[17]

There is, in other words, a genuine American character, other than mere locale, to the best Gothic tales written on this continent during the last century. Except for the obvious explanations of Mrs. Radcliffe and the ambiguities of a handful of German writers, the ghosts, apparitions, demons, witches, succubi, giaours, fiery orbs, bleeding portraits, animated corpses, invisible tormentors, and grotesque monsters of European fiction of the nineteenth century are usually conceived of (in the dramatic structures of the tales) as actually supernatural. That is, except for certain works by the German ironists, the European writer's handling of the supernatural treats it as a reality that can be explained only by recourse to the occult. But the American mode is markedly different. The very ideology of American fiction is different from the European, whatever other debts the American writer may owe to European literary traditions. Despite the "explained" mode of Mrs. Radcliffe's Gothic romances, we find in examples of the Faust legend that Mephistopheles is a devil in the flesh, not an inhabitant of Faust's imagination. The supernatural is also an actuality in M. G. Lewis's *The Monk*, Mary Shelley's *Frankenstein*, Charles Maturin's *Melmoth the Wanderer*, and Bram Stoker's *Dracula*.

But what comparable American work so insists on the supernatural as an actual realm of phenomena? The American writer's characteristic attitude toward the supernatural and toward the genre of the Gothic is instead ambiguous. This is clearly seen in those American writers who made the European Gothic tradition truly American— Charles Brockden Brown, Washington Irving, Poe, Hawthorne, Melville, and James. The persistent question of Brown's *Wieland*, for example, is whether the younger Wieland acts under the influence of a demonic agent when he murdered his family or whether his was merely the act of a madman influenced by environmental forces. In Irving's "Adventure of the German Student," we are never sure whether the young man has made love to a demonic spirit or the incident is totally the product of his crazed imagination—or, for that matter, a more ambiguous twist, whether his "madness" is not the sign of a demonic pact. And did Hawthorne's Young Goodman Brown really see Faith participate in a Witch's Sabbat, or was the event a product of his lack of faith in human goodness? Did Melville's Ahab pursue the demonic agent of a satanic God, or was the significance of the eerie white whale totally the product of his monomania? Did James's young governess wage heroic battle against the demonic spirits of Peter Quint and Miss Jessel, or did she conjure them up out of an abyss of repressed sexuality? Such questions make it clear that the American development of the Gothic tale inclined toward explained Gothic in psychological terms, a mode that preserved some ambiguity as to the real nature of events.

This, then, is also Poe's Gothic genre. The weird events of such stories as "The Fall of the House of Usher" and "Ligeia" are psychological delusions on the part of the narrators, delusions so subtly insinuated that the reader tends to see only from the narrator's point of view even though he announces his madness, or nervousness, or terror, or some oddity or another that should cause the reader to pause for a moment to consider his distorted or eccentric view of the events he narrates. In their intricacy of design, Poe's Gothic tales contain telltale evidences for rational psychological explanation, yet rarely so obtrusive as to destroy the uncanny supernatural effect, though often the events are so bizarre and incongruous that we cannot fully enjoy the "luxury" of the Gothic terror. It is as if Poe sought to blend two kinds of Gothic romance: the shocking, supernatural, Teutonic tale; and the insinuated, explained, English tale. Poe's technique, as I have suggested before, is one of deceptive tripleness: his tales are supernatural on one level, psychological on another, satiric and ironic on another. If the unwary reader is deceived by the apparent verisimilitude of an apparently supernatural tale (a verisimilitude which in Defoe, Poe said, often half-concealed a *"banter"*), so much the better.[18] If the unwary reader is deceived by a satiric and mocking Gothic tale, he is properly served.

II

Direct statement from Poe that his mode is psychologically explained Gothic is scanty. But there are a half-dozen documents that are highly suggestive. One of the most important of these is an ambiguous correspondence with Philip P. Cooke regarding what Poe at one time considered his masterpiece, "Ligeia." In a letter to Cooke on September 21, 1839, Poe wrote that Cooke was "right" about the "flawed" technique of "Ligeia":

The *gradual* perception of the fact that Ligeia lives again in the person of Rowena is a far loftier and more thrilling idea than the one I have embodied. It offers in my opinion, the widest possible scope to the imagination —it might even be rendered sublime. And this idea was mine . . . but then there is "Morella." Do you remember there the *gradual* conviction on the part of the parent that the spirit of the first Morella tenants the person of the second? It was necessary, since "Morella" was written, to modify "Ligeia." I was forced to be content with a sudden half-consciousness, on the part of the narrator, that Ligeia stood before him. . . . Your word that it is "intelligible" suffices—and your commentary sustains your word. As for the mob—let them talk on. I should be grieved if I thought they comprehended me here. (O 1:118)

Critics disposed to see Poe as a supernaturalist have used this letter and Cooke's original to disprove the psychological reading of "Ligeia," first given detailed expression by Roy P. Basler.[19] James Schroeter, for example, notes that Cooke in his letter of September 16, 1839, identified the narrator with Poe; Cooke wrote that the story would have been improved if "you had only become aware gradually that the blue Saxon eye of the 'Lady Rowena of Tremaine' grew daily darker . . . if you had brooded and meditated upon the change. . . ."[20] "Surely," writes Schroeter, "if Poe had intended his narrator to be regarded as a madman, a murderer, and a psychopath . . . he could scarcely have failed to be deeply offended by Cooke's letter . . ." (p. 406). But Schroeter omits the part of Poe's letter in which Poe wrote, with emphatic pauses, that he was forced to be content with "a sudden half-consciousness, on the part of the narrator, that Ligeia stood before him."

The possibility that Poe was offended by such identification of himself with the mad murderer of the tale, however, provides a fine motive for irony even in his reply to Cooke. In this connection, a second major point made by Schroeter for the nonpsychological reading reveals a startling double revision by Poe. Schroeter calls attention to Cooke's criticism that Ligeia as a "wandering essence" too suddenly takes over Rowena and becomes the "visible, bodily Ligeia," and that this violates "the ghostly proprieties." Schroeter then reports that Poe "did make a change after his correspondence with Cooke," which is "detailed clearly in [A. H.] Quinn's book," the standard biography of Poe. This change, Schroeter adds, the psychological critic Basler "did not bother to check." Schroeter, however, misquotes Quinn and writes that Poe inserted a long passage in which Rowena's now gradual struggles with death are characterized by relapses into "sterner" and "more irredeemable death," accompanied by "agony" that "wore the aspect of struggle with some invisible foe," and "succeeded" by "wild change in the personal appearance of the corpse." Actually, only the last phrase about the changes in the appearance of the corpse was added, and that was in 1845 (usually considered the standard reading, from the *Broadway Journal*).

Even this much of an addition, however, would suggest that Poe took seriously Cooke's judgment about the abruptness of the conclusion; and Quinn writes in his biography that "this clause prepares the way for the final assumption by Ligeia of the body of her rival, without appearing to do so" (p. 749). The problem with this "corroboration" of Poe's supernaturalist intentions is that the original version in the *American Museum* in 1838 includes all of the paragraph about the "hideous drama of revivification" taking place in Rowena down to and including the "struggle with some invisible foe"—so that Poe had already laid a foundation for the gradual possession of Rowena by Ligeia before Cooke, a year later, wrote his unperceptive letter.[21]

The next publication of "Ligeia" was in the *Tales of the Grotesque and Arabesque,* dated 1840. On September 29, 1839, eight days after Poe's reply to Cooke, the publishers Lea and Blanchard wrote Poe that they would print his *Tales* (without paying him). Quinn guesses November 1839 to be the month of publication. Thus, Poe had a month or two to make minor revisions. He did: he took out the passage about Rowena's seeming to struggle with an invisible foe, so that Ligeia's final appearance was made more abrupt than in the version Cooke read! Given this context, the undertone of Poe's letter to Cooke is clearly recognizable as ironic and sarcastic:

I have an inveterate habit of speaking the truth—and had I not valued your opinion more highly than that of any man in America I should not have written you as I did.

I say that I read your letter with delight. In fact I am aware of no delight greater than that of feeling one's self appreciated (in such wild matters as "Ligeia") by those in whose judgment one has faith. (O 1:117)

Poe then went on to list a few others, who, like Cooke, had fully "appreciated" him—indeed, had "read my inmost spirit, 'like a book.'" These other readers included Benjamin Disraeli and N. P. Willis, two of Poe's favorite satiric targets in his early tales.[22] Poe also cited Washington Irving's praise of "Usher," but said to Cooke: ". . . I assure you, I regard his best word as but dust in the balance when weighed with those discriminating opinions of your own. . . . Touching 'Ligeia' you are right—all right—throughout."

Poe then wrote that Cooke's way of doing it would have rendered the story "sublime," and he slyly assured Cooke that the ghost of Ligeia *did not live* but was "entombed *as Rowena*." The innuendo regarding the veracity of the opium-bound narrator as a reporter of empirical data is clear. Ligeia exists in the narrator's mind. "But," Poe writes Cooke, "your word that it is 'intelligible' suffices—and your commentary sustains your word. As for the mob—let them talk on. I should be grieved if I thought they comprehended me here." This last statement surely not only clearly illustrates Poe's attitude toward the majority of his readers but also displays his fine and subtle irony, with P. P. Cooke, in this case, its unsuspecting victim.

If "Ligeia" is not a Gothic tale of the supernatural, then what is it? The concept of the arabesque, to which we had reference earlier as a deceptive pattern, provides an initial clue; for the usage of arabesque, which as we have seen was early connected with the true Gothic, in "Ligeia" seems almost an allegorical explanation of Poe's deceptively psychological Gothicism. Poe's narrator describes his second wife's bridal chamber in a way that clearly shows the close association in Poe's mind of the terms *Gothic* and *arabesque*: the "ceiling, of gloomy-looking oak, was excessively lofty, vaulted, and elaborately fretted with the wildest and most grotesque specimens of a semi-Gothic, semi-Druidical device." From the "most central recess" of the ceiling there is a huge gold censer "depended, by a single chain of gold . . . Saracenic in pattern, and with many perforations so contrived that there writhed in and out of them as if endued with a serpent vitality, a continual succession of parti-colored fires" (H 2:259–60). In the first publication of "Ligeia" (1838) and in *Tales of the Grotesque and Arabesque* (1840), the word *Saracenic* was *Arabesque* (cf. H 2:387, 390).

The rest of the bridal chamber exhibits those overdone qualities that critics have either called tawdry or taken as simply part of the Romantic mode of the supernatural. The bridal bed is "of an Indian model . . . sculptured of solid ebony, with a pall-like canopy above." In each of the "angles of the chamber" stands "on end a gigantic sarcophagus of black granite" (H 2:260). But in "the draping of the apartment lay, alas! the chief phantasy of all." The "unproportionably" high walls are covered with "vast folds" of "heavy and massive-looking tapestry" of rich gold cloth. This cloth also is used for the carpet, for the upholstery, for the canopy of the bed, and for the "gorgeous volutes" of the curtains around the window. The material, however, has a peculiar black design. The cloth is:

. . . spotted all over, at irregular intervals, with arabesque figures, about a foot in diameter, and wrought upon the cloth in patterns of the most jetty black. But these figures partook of the true character of the arabesque only when regarded *from a single point of view.* By a contrivance now common, and indeed traceable to a very remote period of antiquity, they were made *changeable in aspect.* To one entering the room, they bore the appearance of simple monstrosities; but upon a farther advance, this appearance gradually departed; and step by step, *as the visiter moved his station* in the chamber, he saw himself surrounded by an endless succession of the ghastly forms which belong to the *superstition* of the Norman, or arise in the *guilty slumbers* of the monk. The phantasmagoric effect was vastly heightened by the artificial introduction of a strong continual current of wind behind the draperies—giving a hideous and uneasy animation to the whole. (H 2:260–61; my italics)

This passage suggests that the arabesque decor as Poe uses it is not merely the monstrousness of supernatural things but is a matter of appearance, of deceptiveness, of perspective and point of view in an overall design. As a kind of allegorical statement about "tales of the grotesque and arabesque," as well as about the single tale itself, the passage suggests that the real subject of such tales is subconscious and obsessive delusion. In "Ligeia," as in Poe's other Gothic tales, what seems simply monstrous or Gothic on the surface becomes "realistically" psychological, a matter of dream and delusion, as one shifts his perspective. For the attentive, Poe develops an ironic distance between the reader and narrator as it becomes clear that the narrator is closely involved in the eerie events of the story. The "bridal" chamber that the narrator prepares for his second wife, Rowena, should surely alert the reader. For the Gothic and arabesque decor of the room suggests not a bridal but a funeral chamber.

Poe plants the first clue to this kind of psychological dramatic irony in the first paragraph of the tale. The mind of the narrator is clouded. His memory is especially tricky; he cannot at the moment remember where or when he met Ligeia. Nor does he know if he ever knew her last name! On one "topic," however, "memory fails me not. It is the *person* of Ligeia" (H 2:249). She was tall, slender, beautiful; her voice was low, sweet, and musical; her footstep light and elastic; her face had "the radiance of an opium-dream" (H 2:249). The opium dream is but a metaphor at this point in the tale, but halfway through, just before and just after the arabesque description of Rowena's bridal chamber, Poe emphasizes his narrator's drug addiction, even noting his "incipient madness."

Poe also provides him with a motive for murder, if the alert reader will look for it. Having moved from Germany, where his first wife, Ligeia, has died, the narrator purchases a ruined abbey—with the money left him by Ligeia (H 2:258). His next move is to take as his wife a titled Englishwoman. Sneering at her parents, who have accepted a large sum of money from him in return for their daughter's hand in marriage, he begins to indulge his taste for the Gothic in the decoration of his new wife's bridal chamber. He explains that he has always been drawn to the Gothic and the bizarre in architecture and interior design, and he attributes his now wilder Gothic fancies to the influence of the opium he is taking in large quantity. But the reader used to Poe's "ratiocinative" method and to Poe's focus on the disintegrating mind knows what to expect from this death-decorated chamber, especially when the narrator mentions his memories of the ideal Ligeia and his growing "hatred" and "loathing" of Rowena (H 2:261): "Now, then, did my spirit fully and freely burn with more than all the fires of her [Ligeia's] own. In the *excitement of my opium dreams* (for I was habitually fettered in the shackles of the drug) I would call upon her name, during the silence of the night . . ."(H 2:261; my italics).

Soon after, Rowena is taken with a "sudden illness," which the narrator describes most vaguely, punctuated by weird dreamlike memories of the lost Ligeia. Near the end of October, he administers a glass of wine to Rowena, and fancies that "three or four large drops of a brilliant and ruby colored fluid," forming invisibly in the air, fall into the goblet, after which Rowena takes "a rapid change for the worse" (H 2:263–64). "*Wild visions, opium-engendered,* flitted, shadow-like, before me. I gazed with unquiet eye upon the sarcophagi in the angles of the room, upon the varying figures of the drapery, and upon the writhing of the parti-colored fires in the [arabesque] censer overhead" (H 2:264; my italics). Next there follows his watch over the changes in the appearance of Rowena's corpse, a deathwatch that the narrator describes as "an agony of superstitious terror" (H 2:264). The clues undercutting the ostensible supernaturalism could hardly be clearer. Poe's real subject is the delusive madness of his narrator, the subconscious welling up of the extremities of emotion—of extreme love, hate, and fearful superstition—in a spirit writhing in fire.

On a second level of irony, "Ligeia" contains some specific satiric mockery. Clark Griffith has suggested that Poe's underlying satiric point in "Ligeia" is similar to that of "Silence" and "How to Write a

Blackwood Article," a double-edged comment about transcendentalism and Gothicism. Griffith suggests that the overdone style and the symbolic contrasts of light and shadow, of gold and black in the furnishings of the settings, and of the fair and dark women are carefully patterned to make an almost allegorical point. Griffith points out that Ligeia's unearthly transcendentalism contrasts with Rowena's dull worldliness; the dark German lady is infinitely more intriguing than the Englishwoman. Moreover, Griffith notes a series of similarities between Poe's Rowena and Scott's Rowena in *Ivanhoe*, as well as some parallels of setting, such as the disproportionately high walls and the odd draperies. Griffith further notes some startling parallels with *Confessions of an Opium-Eater*, which Poe then thought to be a brilliant hoax by Coleridge, and which Poe parodies among other works in "Silence." Griffith's conclusion, given such parallels and echoes, seems quite plausible: Poe's satiric innuendo suggests the triumph of German idealism and Gothicism over its pale imitations in the English-speaking world.[23]

But even if we assume, for the sake of argument, the traditional reading of "Ligeia" as an occultist tale of the power of the will to effect its reincarnation, what are we to make of the then almost inexplicable self-parody presented in "The Man That Was Used Up. A Tale of the Late Bugaboo and Kickapoo Campaign"? This tale, a political satire on Andrew Johnson, appeared less than a year after "Ligeia," and its first few paragraphs burlesque almost phrase by phrase the opening paragraphs of "Ligeia," a perplexing phenomenon noticed recently by Richard Wilbur.[24] "The Man That Was Used Up" presents as its hero a completely artificial man, Brevet Brigadier General John A. B. C. Smith, severely (indeed, almost totally) wounded in the Indian Wars, but fully reconstructed by American technological know-how: he is fitted up with artificial limbs, artificial shoulders, an artificial chest, and artificial hair, eyes, teeth, and palate. When put all together, the General is a handsome figure of a man, six feet tall, and altogether admirable. Of him, the narrator remarks (in the first version of the story) that his appearance gives "force to the pregnant observation of Francis Bacon—that 'there is no exquisite beauty existing in the world without a certain degree of *strangeness* in the expression'" (H 3:336). This is just what the narrator of "Ligeia," also alluding to Francis Bacon, says of her beautifully strange face:

In beauty of face no maiden ever equalled her. It was the radiance of an opium-dream—an airy and spirit-lifting vision more wildly divine than the phantasies which hovered about the slumbering souls of the daughters of

Delos. Yet her features were not of that regular mold which we have been falsely taught to worship in the classical labors of the heathen. "There is no exquisite beauty," says Bacon, Lord Verulam, speaking truly of all forms and *genera* of beauty, "without some *strangeness* in the proportion." (H 2:249–50)

The implications for Poe's detached, ironic attitude toward his materials, toward such details in Ligeia's "strange" and somehow "irregular" beauty of face, are obvious and suggest a further ironic context for Poe's conception of the Gothic quality of such a tale as "Ligeia."

"Ligeia" opens with the narrator's statement: "I cannot, for my soul, remember how, when, or even precisely where, I first became acquainted with the lady Ligeia" (H 2:248). "The Man That Was Used Up" begins: "I cannot just now remember when or where I first made acquaintance of that truly fine-looking fellow, Brevet Brigadier General John A. B. C. Smith" (H 3:259). In "Ligeia," Poe's strategy in the dreamlike opening is to have his narrator "bring before mine eyes in fancy the image of her who is no more" (H 2:249). She was tall and slender, she had a low musical voice, and there was something "strange" about her appearance (H 2:250). The narrator then carefully details her features, noting the "lofty and pale forehead," the whiteness of her complexion, the "gentle prominence of the regions above the temples," the luxuriant, glossy, raven-black hair, the delicate nose, the shape of her lips and chin, and especially the white teeth which send the light "glancing back, with a brilliancy almost startling." Finally, he describes her extraordinary eyes, large, dark, yet luminous, and especially the mysterious "expression" that lies "far within the pupils" (H 2:251). "What *was* it?" the narrator repeatedly asks himself, that was so remarkable about the strange mystery of her expression (H 2:251–52). He connects this strangeness with the mysteries of the cosmos, the invisible force of the stars in the heavens, emphasizing the sense of "intensity in thought, action, or speech" that seemed to result from her "gigantic volition" (H 2:253). The tale then moves along in this Gothic direction, with the slow but steady accumulation of psychological clues to the nervous and agitated condition of the narrator.

In "The Man That Was Used Up," Poe's narrator comments on his lack of "definite impressions" of his first meeting with the General, mentions that he is "constitutionally nervous" and inclined to become most agitated in the face of "the slightest appearance of a mystery" (H 3:259). He then repeatedly observes that there is something "remarkable" about the General, and details his appearance. The General

is tall, with glossy, jetty-black hair and equally black whiskers surrounding his "utterly unequalled" mouth, and has the "most brilliantly
white of all conceivable teeth." His voice is clear and melodious, and
his extraordinary eyes are especially remarkable, large, deep hazel, yet
lustrous—"and there was perceptible about them . . . just that amount
of interesting obliquity which gives pregnancy to expression" (H 3:260).
The tale then moves along in its comic direction, ludicrously repeating
the mysterious *"je ne sais quoi,"* that *"remarkable* something" about
him. Thus, we see here a salient feature of Poe's habitual mode of
composition, the shift to opposites—first a Gothic tale about a mysterious woman, then a comic tale about a "mysterious" man—using the
same opening strategy in both, as though in self-parody the second
time. The narrator of "The Man That Was Used Up" is almost the
comic *Doppelgänger* of the narrator of "Ligeia." This radical about-
face burlesque of one's own compositional technique, characteristic of
the Romantic Ironists, at the very least shows Poe's preoccupation at
this juncture with artificial constructs in both a Gothic and a comic
vein. Not only may Ligeia be the construct of the narrator's agitated
Gothic mind, but she is also quite clearly his "demon," a device of his
own "self-torture"—as Poe says of the student's conception of the
raven—and thus is an absurdist, if serious, parody of the ideal woman
as much as the artificial General is a comic parody of the ideal man.

But the narrator of the Gothic tale digresses with such singular intensity about this strangeness of the face of Ligeia that we need to
give it further attention. He speaks especially of her eyes and of a
"gentle prominence above the region of the temples." Poe's emphasis
on these features of Ligeia's face is so pronounced that Edward Hungerford suggests that Poe was trying to emphasize for his readers a
proper "phrenological" basis for Ligeia's character.[25] One of the first
things we learn about Ligeia, Hungerford says, is the "eloquence of
her low musical language"; language, Hungerford notes, is one of the
"organs" of phrenology, externally indicated by the eyes. "We have
not very long to wait. The description leaves us peering into the large
eyes of Ligeia. And very large eyes they were" (p. 228). Soon after,
we learn of Ligeia's great learning in various tongues. Hungerford,
however, can find in Poe's "phrenological" emphasis on Ligeia's ability
with languages no direct relevance to the themes of the tale; he suggests instead that Poe is trying to show his readers that Ligeia is
"scientifically true according to phrenology," that Poe is setting up
through phrenological details a subtle clue to Ligeia's major trait—
"love of life." But there is an obvious satiric point to this emphasis on
language if we accept Griffith's suggestion that Poe's innuendo in the

tale has to do with the relationship of German and English literatures.

Ligeia's major trait, however, is to be discovered in that "gentle prominence above the regions of the temples," a significant point for the reader of Poe's time, says Hungerford, for "anyone who knew phrenology" would guess that this prominence above the temples suggested one or more of the following traits: "constructiveness," "acquisitiveness," "secretiveness," "destructiveness," "alimentiveness" (a taste for heavy feeding), or one other, "love of life." Only the last, Hungerford says, could possibly apply to Ligeia. Actually, all of them apply in some way.

It is hard not to see "constructiveness" as double-edged, suggesting her ingenuity and her ambiguous existence in the delirious mind of the narrator. But Ligeia is without doubt "destructive," "secretive," and "acquisitive." In the supernatural interpretation of the tale, she kills Rowena, secretly, and acquires her body. At one point, the narrator remarks on her "gigantic intellectual acquisitions," especially of secret, occult knowledge; moreover, she had acquired a fortune large enough to allow her husband to buy an abbey and a titled bride. As to "alimentiveness," Ligeia's relationship with her husband and her "acquisition" of Rowena's body have something of a vampirelike quality; she feeds on other life to preserve her own. Poe, I suggest, is purposefully ambiguous and ironic about that prominent region "above the temples."

But that "love of life" is the dominant idea of the phrenological description of Ligeia's head is quite clear. Poe specifically underscores this characteristic in the narrator's account of her struggle with death: "It is this wild longing—it is this eager vehemence of desire for life—*but* for life—that I have no power to portray . . ." (H 2:256). This idea, too, has its ironies. Ligeia seems to love life itself without any concern for the ultimate principles of philosophy and ethics which her studies of transcendentalism would suggest were prominent traits in her. Poe is again quite clear: "I would have soothed," the narrator says, "I would have reasoned; but, in the intensity of her wild desire for life,—for life—*but* for life—solace and reason were alike the uttermost of folly" (H 2:255). We have seen before Poe's ironic attitude toward American transcendentalism and toward phrenology, the pseudoscientific, and the occult (even Hungerford admits some difficulty in accounting for Poe's satiric remarks about and satiric use of phrenology elsewhere). Poe's mockery here becomes clearer when we note that the concepts of phrenology were closely related to Coleridge's metaphysics, Swedenborg's mysticism, and New England transcendentalism, all of which Poe satirizes in other works. In fact, so closely related were these four mystic-metaphysical-psychological "theories" that F. H. Hedge, late in the nineteenth century, claimed to have been the real founder of the Transcendental Club, for he had published a series of articles on Coleridge, Swedenborg, and phrenology in 1833 and 1834.[26] This relationship further strengthens Clark Griffith's claims for Poe's insinuated mockery of transcendentalism and mysticism in "Ligeia" by linking the tale quite clearly to the satiric subjects of such tales as "How to Write a Blackwood Article" in just the way he suggests.

A further ironic twist can be seen in the description of Ligeia's head. The front-view picture of her face—looming out of the darkness of her hair, with that gentle prominence above the temples, with an ivory complexion in which are set the large, staring, black, almost pupilless eyes, and with a broad chin above which are "the teeth glancing back with a brilliancy almost startling"—is that of a death's-head (H 2:250). Ligeia, the narrator's obsession, is thus first described in a way that, ambiguously, suggests a grinning skull; her head is for the narrator the symbol of death itself. Later, in decorating Rowena's death chamber with pall-like canopies and Egyptian sarcophagi, the narrator reveals his half-conscious love of death, an ironic inversion of Ligeia's apparent love of life. Moreover, the narrator's memory of the strange face of Ligeia, coupled with his blurred memory of her as a real person and his calling upon her name as he wakes from opium dreams in the dead of night, again suggests a demonic and delusive construct in his mind. But real or not, Ligeia is certainly his vampire, his succubus. His blurred memory of her skull-like head is at the very least a symbol of his obsession with death, just as the zigzag fissure and general decay of the arabesque "face" (H 3:279) of Roderick Usher's house are symbolic of *his* crumbling and decaying mind.[27]

IV

The structural configuration of ambiguously explained Gothic informing "Ligeia" and "Usher" may be clarified by reference to another nineteenth-century tale. In *Heart of Darkness* (first published in *Blackwood's*, 1898–99), Joseph Conrad's first narrator comments on the conception of the meaning of a narrative held by Marlow, who is himself the narrator of the basic tale of his pursuit of his psychological double, Kurtz, and to whom Conrad's first narrator listens as one sitting in darkness waiting for light. This first narrator comments that Marlow, unlike other tale-spinning sailors, saw the significance of a narrative not as a core-meaning of some kind but as a system of structures: "The yarns of seamen have a direct simplicity, the whole meaning of which lies within the shell of a cracked nut. [But to Marlow] the meaning of an episode was not inside like a kernel but outside, enveloping the tale which brought it out only as a glow brings out a haze, in the likeness of one of these misty halos that sometimes are made visible by the spectral illumination of moonshine." So it is with "The Fall of the House of Usher," which bears a number of surprising similarities in theme, imagery, and structure to *Heart of Darkness*.[28] Like "Ligeia," "Usher" is a structure of interpenetrating structures that shifts its aspect with a slight shift of perspective by the reader. Given the initial focus of a reader, the primary answer to any question presented by the story varies, though the relationships among the various structures of the story do not.

This can be partially illustrated by reference to the recurrent concerns of critics of the tale; most of the critical commentary returns obsessively to a few central points, compulsively repeating with slightly altered angles of vision the same set of haunting questions. What is the significance of the close resemblance of Roderick Usher and his sister, and are the two the product of, and guilty of incest? Did Roderick intentionally try to murder Madeline, and did Madeline actually return from her tomb, vampirelike, to claim her brother's life? Is the physical house actually "alive" and by some preternatural force of will controlling the destinies of the Ushers? Or is the story not a tale of the supernatural at all, but rather a work of psychological realism? What then is the precise role of the narrator? And can the work be read in Freudian or Jungian terms? If the tale is a psychological or symbolic work, what is the meaning of the interpolated story of the "Mad Trist of Sir Launcelot Canning"? What significance have the titles of the books in Usher's library, and what significance are we to attach to Usher's strange, neurasthenic art works? The very fact that these questions persist year after year suggests that at the dark heart of the story lies an essential ambiguity, carefully insinuated and carefully wrought.

Thus, just as with "Ligeia," it is misleading to conceive of the meaning of the tale as devolving solely upon any single and fixed subject, such as the supernatural character of the house, or of Madeline Usher, *as opposed* to a Gothic homily on the neurasthenia of the ultimate in narcissistic artist heroes, or as opposed to the incestuous guilt and hereditary curse of the family. The tale is a concatenation of all these, and not an either/or question. Nevertheless, there is, as with "Ligeia," a basic structure that integrates all the others, a set or system of relationships that remains constant and primary, enveloping the rest with a further meaning without disturbing each as a coherent system within itself. This primary structure is the product of the objective synthesis generated by our perceiving as readers the double aspects of the tale as simultaneously supernaturalistic (symbolic of deep structures in the human mind or not) and yet also realistic in a conventional sense. This multiple perception of the simultaneous or parallel levels of the tale derives principally from our perception of the subjectivity of the narrator. As in "Ligeia," we experience a series of "supernatural" events (which have Freudian and Jungian resonances) through the mind of a narrator whom we recognize as disturbed—so that we simultaneously are subjectively involved in and detached from these experiences. The whole system of interpenetrating levels or structures of both tales leads ultimately to Poe's ironic mockery of the ability of the human mind ever to know anything with certainty, whether about the external reality of the world or about the internal reality of the mind.

Much of the discussion of "Usher" to follow derives from Darrel Abel's brilliant analysis of the tale as a psychodrama of the mutual hysteria of the narrator and Roderick Usher.[29] What I offer as progressive to our understanding of the tale is principally addenda to such evidence in terms of a reconsideration of the principal symbols of the tale within the primary structural context proposed—that is, the structure wherein the subjectivity of the narrator provides the basic system of structures holding in tension all the others. I shall attempt to demonstrate the pervasiveness of this primary structure principally by reference to the pattern of the double and its redoubled manifestations (Roderick and Madeline, Roderick and the house, Roderick and the narrator, Madeline and the narrator, the narrator and the house). This pattern is again redoubled by the imagery of the face or skull, which ultimately inverts back on the self as a symbol of the "reality" seen from the inward perspective of characters caught in a labyrinth of mental surmise.

On its most obvious level, the tale is concerned with the traditional Gothic subjects of death and madness and fear. The matters of madness (especially Roderick's) and fear have been frequently commented on, but the other pervading subject of death (physical, familial, spiritual, and mental) has not been closely enough linked to the themes of fear and madness. It is curious, for example, that no one has ever seen fit to remark that when the narrator rides up to the house of Usher, he is immediately confronted with a death's-head looming up out of the dead landscape. Poe obviously intended the image of the skull-like face of the house to dominate as the central image of the tale, for he returns to it again and again, placing the most extended descriptions of it at symmetrically located places in the narrative. Eventually, the pervasive image of the psychically split face reflects the internal landscape of the narrator himself (rather than just Usher), so that the primary structure of the tale merges with its central image. Even when the house sinks into the pool at the end, the motifs of the skull and face (Usher's, the house's, that of the mind gone mad in "The Haunted Palace," and the narrator's) represent the internal spiralling of the complete subjectivity of consciousness. That is, the sinking of the house into the reflecting pool dramatizes the sinking of the rational part of the mind, which has unsuccessfully attempted to maintain some contact with a stable structure of reality outside the self, into the nothingness that is without and within.

Usher's weird painting of what might be a tomb for the burial of the body of Madeline, imaging nothing but rays of light rolling throughout a passage without outlet, is also reflective of the death and burial of consciousness and rationality themselves; thus, it is a painting of Usher's internal void, which is objectified by the final collapse of the house into the image of itself in the pool. The spiralling further and further inward leads us to the mocking irony of the ultimate theme of nothingness, which is all the mind can ever truly know, if it can know anything. The nothingness without (in the landscape) and the nothingness within (in the minds of Usher and the narrator) are mirror images or doubles reflecting the theme of nothingness in the tale. And the collapse of the universe of Roderick Usher includes the double collapse of his mind along with the narrator's—productive of an overall structure of collapse mirroring the pattern of the universe itself, as expressed in *Eureka*.

That Usher's mind disintegrates as the tale progresses is obvious. Both Usher and the narrator comment variously on the matter. The inciting event, in fact, is Usher's written appeal to the narrator to preserve him from the final collapse of his mind. Moreover, as mentioned, a major concern in the tale is the mechanism of fear itself, which has perversely operated on Roderick Usher before the narrator arrives, and which operates on the narrator through Usher afterwards, so that we apprehend the basic dramatic action of the tale as psychological—the presentation of the progressive hallucination of the two protagonists. In the supernaturally charged atmosphere of the first level of the story, the narrator seems to serve as a corroborating witness to the actual return of Madeline, and to the strange, simultaneous "deaths" of the Ushers and of their house. But Poe meticulously, from the opening paragraph through to the last, details the development of the narrator's initial uneasiness into a frenzy of terror, engendered by and parallel to Usher's terrors. The tale opens with the narrator's account of his lonely autumn journey through a "singularly dreary tract of country" in response to a "wildly importunate" summons from Usher (H 3:273–74). At nightfall, as the "melancholy" house of Usher comes into view, the narrator feels a sense of "insufferable gloom" pervading his spirit. He pauses to look at the "mere house," trying to account rationally for its total weird effect. But the scene still produces in him "an utter depression of soul which I can compare to no earthly sensation more properly than to the after-dream of the reveller upon opium . . . an iciness, a sinking, a sickening of the heart—an unredeemed dreariness of thought. . . . it was a mystery all insoluble; nor could I grapple with the shadowy fancies that crowded upon me as I pondered" (H 3:273–74). The primary effect of the opening paragraphs, of course, is to suggest something horrible and supernatural about the house of Usher. But, as in Poe's other tales, there is no overstepping of the real; the strange impression of the scene is relegated to the "fancies" of the narrator. Because the narrator tries to account for the effect rationally, however, we are led, for the time being, to attribute the weirdness of the scene not to his subjective impressions but to the scene itself.

Yet Poe uses this apparent rationality to heighten the irrational. The narrator reflects on the possibility that "there *are* combinations of very simple natural objects" that have the power to affect the mind, but "the analysis of this power lies among considerations" beyond our "depth"; and at this moment, he looks down into a "black and lurid tarn," to see the reflected, remodeled, and inverted images of the "gray sedge, and the ghostly tree-stems, and the vacant and eye-like windows" (H 3:274). The effect of this vision in the pool is to produce in him a "shudder even more thrilling than before" and to "deepen the first singular impression": "There can be no doubt that the consciousness of *the rapid increase of my superstition*—for why should I not so term it?—served mainly *to accelerate the increase itself*. Such, I have long known, is the paradoxical law of *all sentiments having terror as a basis*" (H 3:276; my italics). After this objective recognition of an inward self-division that results in yet further subjectivity, he again lifts his eyes "to the house itself, from its image in the pool" and he becomes aware of a "strange fancy" growing in his mind: "I had *so worked upon my imagination as really to believe* that about the whole mansion and domain there hung . . . a pestilent and mystic vapour, dull, sluggish, faintly discernible, and leaden-hued" (H 3:276; my italics). But Poe then reasserts the narrator's rationality: "Shaking off from my spirit what *must* have been a dream, I scanned more narrowly the real aspect of the building" (H 3:276). The paragraph is organized, however, so as to bring the "real" description back again to the "impression" the scene makes upon the narrator's "fancy." Although the narrator begins his "analysis" of the house at the (rational) roof, with its fine tangled web-work of fungi, his eye travels down along a zigzag fissure to become again "lost in the sullen waters of the tarn" (H 3:277), by now clearly emblematic of the subconscious mind.

The apprehensive, fanciful, superstitious, but "rational" narrator then goes into the house to meet Usher, where, during the course of the next several days, he comes increasingly under the influence of Usher's own wild superstitions. "In the manner of my friend," the narrator says, "I was at once struck with an incoherence—an inconsistency. . . ."

To an anomalous species of terror I found him a bounden slave. "I shall perish," said he, ". . . in this deplorable folly. Thus, thus, and not otherwise shall I be lost. . . . I have, indeed, no abhorrence of danger, except in its absolute effect—in terror. In this unnerved—in this pitiable condition—I feel that the period will sooner or later arrive when I must abandon life and reason together, in some struggle with the grim phantasm, FEAR." (H 3:280)

Usher's statement of his own condition applies also to the narrator, who struggles with the same phantasm, heightened by Usher's own phantasms. It is Usher, for example, who remarks to the suggestible narrator that the house is alive and has exerted a malignant influence on his mind. Later the narrator, looking for something to read, finds that the only books in Usher's library are accounts of strange journeys, eerie meetings, and deathwatches (some of which, like Tieck's *Blue Distance* are partially satiric). Then Usher reads his strange poem about the decay of reason (H 3:284–86), the single extended metaphor of which suggests the "face" of the house of Usher itself, and extends the pattern of descent from roof to basement, of rationality to irrationality, and the inverse ascent of irrationality welling up to overwhelm the rational. Soon after the reading, Madeline dies, and Usher and the narrator bury her in a crypt in the cellar. She has the "mockery of a faint blush of life" upon her skin and a terrible "lingering smile" upon her lips, phenomena that the "rational" narrator attributes to the peculiar ravages of her cataleptic disorder but which Usher intimates is something less natural (H 3:289). Then, as Usher's behavior becomes even more distracted (a continual "tremulous quaver, as if of extreme terror, habitually characterized his utterance"), the narrator confesses to himself his own increasing apprehensiveness. Slowly, although he tries to see in Usher's behavior the "mere inexplicable vagaries of madness," the narrator feels growing in himself a vague fear that Usher has some horrible "oppressive secret" to divulge (H 3:289). "Rationally," however, the narrator acknowledges that Usher's "condition terrified . . . it *infected* me. I felt creeping upon me, by slow yet uncertain degrees, the wild influences of his own fantastic yet impressive superstitions" (H 2:289–90; my italics).

Symmetrically, the psychological themes of the first part of the tale are exactly repeated in the second, but with the fears of both Usher and the narrator at a higher pitch. Shortly after Madeline's burial, the narrator is unable to sleep, especially since, as with the reflected image of the house in the tarn, he is aware of his increased terror: "an irrepressible tremour gradually pervaded my frame; and, at length, there sat upon my very heart an incubus" of "utterly causeless alarm (H 3:290). "Overpowered by an intense sentiment of horror," the narrator begins pacing nervously; suddenly he is startled by a light footstep outside his door. But it is only Usher. Usher's intensely agitated condition, however, is the more unnerving, especially when he suggests that a supernatural and luminous vapor has surrounded the house in spite of the rising wind without.

What is perhaps the clearest of clues to the theme of doubled and redoubled fear comes next. The narrator, in an attempt to calm Usher, reads from a volume called the "Mad Trist." The title calls attention to the basic situation in which the narrator finds himself.[30] Usher is about to keep a mad tryst with Madeline, even as the narrator has kept his mad tryst with Usher. The tale, this "Mad Trist," is an absurd parody of a medieval romance about the delusive meeting of the knight Ethelred with a hermit who disappears and changes his form into that of a fearful dragon. The narrator's reading of the "Mad Trist" to Usher is interrupted by strange sounds of creaking wood, of shrieking, and of grating metal. These sounds, beginning at the bottom of the house and moving upward toward them, eerily (and ludicrously) correspond with the sounds evoked in the chivalric romance. The sounds, of course, are supposed to be the results of the cataleptic Madeline's efforts to free herself from her tomb. Usher, at least, tells the narrator that this is so and that she is, in fact, now standing outside the door. And, in the end, the narrator sees her too: bloody, frail, emaciated, trembling, and reeling to and fro, falling upon Usher in her "now final death agonies" and bearing Usher "to the floor a corpse, and a victim to *the terrors he had anticipated*" (H 3:296; my italics). As a last emphatic psychological detail, Poe has the narrator tell us that "from that chamber and from that mansion, I fled aghast." Thus we do not know for sure that the house splits apart and sinks into the tarn in a lurid blaze, for the narrator has by now been revealed to be completely untrustworthy.

Yet, even here, Poe provides one more turn of the screw, for, buried in the details about the house, is the information that the oxygenless dungeon has been a storage place for gunpowder or "some other highly combustible substance" (H 3:288). Thus if the house cracks open and crumbles, rather than a necessarily supernatural occurrence, as it seems to the hysterical narrator, it is explainable as the combustion generated when the lightning of the storm crackles near the previously airless crypt—the inrushing electricity being conducted along the copper floor and igniting the remnants of powder. Yet these mocking clues are not all. The miasma enshrouding the house provides yet another, for marsh gas was then thought to have hallucinatory effects, and Poe elsewhere mentions this very effect.[31]

If the stated terrors of the narrator are not convincing enough for a complete psychological interpretation of the supernaturally charged events, the recurrent dream imagery and the very order of the opening paragraphs regarding the images of the house in the pool should confirm such a reading. The dream images culminate in the return of Madeline and in the "Mad Trist." Madeline, supposedly the victim of a cataleptic fit, is presumably not a ghost or other supernatural manifestation, even though her appearance at Usher's door produces a ghostlike effect in the best tradition of supernatural Gothic. We do get our Gothic thrill, even though she is not a supernatural being. Yet, if she is not, then how, in her frail and emaciated condition, would she be capable of breaking open the coffin, the lid of which, the narrator specifically tells us, had been screwed down tight? Or of pushing open the door, "of massive iron" and of such "immense weight" that its movement "caused an unusually sharp grating sound, as it moved upon its hinges"? (See H 3:288.) These details of Madeline's entombment, given us at the midpoint of the tale, underscore the dream motif and link her dreamlike manifestation directly to the psyche of the narrator; for Poe also makes a point of having the narrator tell us that Madeline's tomb is at great depth, immediately beneath that portion of the building in which was "my own sleeping apartment" (H 3:288). The images of sleep, mist, water, and descent, recurring throughout the tale, forcibly suggest Poe's focus on the subconscious mind. The night of Madeline's return, just before the reading of the "Mad Trist," the narrator cannot sleep, and a detailed description of his troubled drowsiness is given. Neither can Usher sleep, for he is troubled by the dreamy mist enshrouding the house. Finally, the events, the disappearances, the transformations, and the correspondences of sounds in the tale of the "Mad Trist" which follows, all have the order of a dream, and, moreover, move from the depths of the house upward toward Usher and the narrator.

Yet the "Mad Trist" is made purposefully ludicrous; it reads like a parody, and even the narrator comments on its absurdity. The correspondence of sounds, especially, heightens the ludicrous effect. But the intruded tale of the "Mad Trist" also has a clear ironic effect; it destroys the Gothic illusion. As in "Metzengerstein" and "Ligeia," Poe intrudes an ironic distance clearly and suddenly between the narrator and the reader, here calling attention to the real psychological situation of the two protagonists engaged in their own mad tryst.

Connected with the dream images and reinforcing the suggestion of subconscious action is the dreamlike reflection of the house of Usher in the pool and its parallel in Usher's arabesque face. In fact, Usher's famous face (supposedly a pen portrait of Poe's own according to biographically oriented critics), with its parallels in the appearance of "The Haunted Palace" of Usher's wild poem and in the appearance of the house itself, provides a major clue to the irony insinuated into, under, and around the apparent Gothic surface of the story. Usher's face in a sense is the image of the narrator's own, whose mind, if not disintegrating also, is capable of slipping in an instant into the same kind of madness or hysterical fear to which Usher is subject. The narrator, as he becomes absorbed in his "superstitious" reflections, says that he had to shake off from his fancy "what *must* have been a dream." The narrator's first impression of the house is that it is like a human face, especially with its two vacant eyelike windows. Then he looks down into the pool, but sees only the reflection of the "face" of the house. What is equally likely, of course, is that he should see imaged there his own reflected features, since Poe is careful to point out that the narrator wheels his horse up to "the precipitous brink" of the tarn and thus gazes straight down (H 3:274). Then he remembers Usher's hysterical letter and mentions, along with Usher's "mental disorder," that he had been Usher's close and only friend. Next he remembers that the peasants refer to both the building and the family as the House of Usher and immediately returns to the image of the "face" in the pool (H 3:275–76). When he looks up at the house again, he tries to "analyze" its weird effect, and describes once more its prominent details, especially the overspreading fungi "hanging in a fine tangled webwork from the eaves" (H 3:276). The nervous narrator, conscious of his own vague terror and therefore the more apprehensive, goes into the house to meet Usher, and his attention is focused on the odd appearance of Usher's face. Usher's face has a generally decayed aspect, like the house itself, but especially noticeable are his large and luminous eyes and his hair "of more than web-like softness and tenuity." This tangled, "web-like," "silken hair," of a "wild gossamer texture," thus imagistically merges the facelike structure of the house with Usher's face, the "arabesque expression" of which the narrator cannot "connect with any idea of simple humanity" (H 3:278–79). As we have seen, the narrator grows "terrified" and "infected" with Usher's hysteria. He becomes like Usher. In meeting Usher, he is symbolically staring into the face of his psychological double, and when he steps through the "Gothic" archway of Usher's house into the dark, black-floored hall with its carved, niched, fretted architectural features, lit by "feeble gleams" of "encrimsoned" light that barely makes its way through elaborately "trellised panes," it is clear that the narrator has stepped into the confused, subjective world of Gothic terror and horror. Once inside, in another absurdist touch, he is taken by a servant who "ushers" him into Usher's presence (H 3:277). Thus, Usher's "arabesque" face and the face of the house are the same, and when the narrator gazes into the pool, the reflected "arabesque" face is merged with his own—symbolically is his own. The image of the face is then reemphasized in Usher's poem about the attack of "madness" on the "haunted" castle.

The ghosts in the tale of Usher, then, are those of the mind. Such an analysis does not deny the supernaturalistic surface level of the tale, or other significant patterns such as the incest motif, the eerie hint of vampirism, the use of abstract art to suggest sexuality, entombment, or nothingness, or the carefully balanced themes of order and sentience that other critics have noted.[32] Rather, such a reading incorporates them into its overall pattern, while wrapping a layer of dramatic irony about the whole. As in other of Poe's Gothic tales, the delusiveness of the experience is rendered in and through the consciousness of the narrator so that we participate in his Gothic horror while we are at the same time detached observers of it. In the image of the house as skull or death's-head and the merging of the narrator's face with the face of the house which is also Usher's face in the pool, we see once again in Poe the subtly ironic paralleling of the narrative structure of the tale to its visual focal point. And by having the facelike house of Usher sink into its own image, the final collapse into that void which is both the self and the universe simultaneously is complete. This, then, is the larger pattern of meaning generated by the overall narrative system enveloping the other levels of narrative. And yet there is, by implication, a further enlargement. Since, just as in "Ligeia," it is clear that we do not know that anything the narrator has told us is "real," the whole tale and its structures may be the fabrication of the completely deranged mind of the narrator. Nothing at all may have happened in a conventional sense in the outside world—only in the inner world of the narrator's mind. Of this redoubled nothingness, then, also comes nothing. And as with "Ligeia," this further perception of the structures of nothingness becomes our ultimate perception of the tale as simultaneously involved and detached observers.

V

Poe's attitude toward the ghostly and monstrous "constructions" of the human mind and the mind's susceptibility to the force of suggestion finds succinct statement in his review of William Newnham's *Human Magnetism*. That "the belief in ghosts, or in a Deity, or in a future state, or in anything else credible or incredible . . . is universal," Poe observes, "demonstrates nothing more than . . . the identity of construction in the human brain . . ." (H 16:115). A man can "feign [to] himself a sphynx or a griffin, but it would never do to regard as thus demonstrated the actual existence of either griffins or sphynxes" (H 16:114). In an earlier review in the *Southern Literary Messenger* (December 1835), Poe complained that William Godwin in the *Lives of the Necromancers* had dealt with "the great range and wild extravagancy of the imagination of man" rather than with what is more important—"the *manner* in which delusion acts upon mankind" (H 8: 93–94). Later, in 1842, Poe began his "Mystery of Marie Rogêt," a murder story based on a real murder in New York, with a comment on the "supernatural" impact of sheer coincidence: "There are few persons, even among the calmest thinkers, who have not occasionally been startled into a vague yet thrilling half-credence in the supernatural, by *coincidences* of so seemingly marvellous a character that, as *mere* coincidences, the intellect has been unable to receive them" (H 5:2). Although Poe went on to suggest that by reference to a "doctrine of chance," a "Calculus of Probabilities," we can apply mathematics, "the most rigidly exact in science," to "the shadow and spirituality of the most intangible in speculation" (H 5:2), it is important to note Poe's precise phrasing: "*mere* coincidences" take on a "seemingly marvellous character." Poe's ironic attitude here is clarified in his letters (O 1:199–202) to George Roberts and Joseph Evans Snodgrass (both June 4, 1842). He intimates that he is aware of the "manner" in which his readers will receive the correspondence between the case of Marie Rogêt in Paris and that of Mary Rogers in New York: at the same time that he is applying a calculus of probabilities, his readers will be taken with the seeming supernatural coincidences. The effect then is clearly related to the double impact of ambiguously explained Gothicism. This is heightened by the contrast of the rational and the supernatural in the tale. Poe prefaces the story with a motto from Novalis about the divine and earthly correspondences we call coincidence. But the point of the tale is rational analysis of cause and effect, connection and probability.[33]

A few years later, Poe wrote another letter to P. P. Cooke expressing his appreciation of Cooke's recent praise for his latest work, even though "others have praised me more lavishly." Poe suggested that Cooke reread an "improved" version of "Ligeia," and Poe sarcastically commented on the general response to his ratiocinative tales: "You are right about the hair-splitting of my French friend:—that is all done for effect. These tales of ratiocination owe most of their popularity to being something in a new key. I do not mean to say that they are not ingenious—but people think them more ingenious than they are—on account of their method and *air* of method." Poe then patiently explained to Cooke some of the intentional hoaxing involved in the Dupin tales: "In the 'Murders in the Rue Morgue', for instance, where is the ingenuity of unravelling a web which you yourself (the author) have woven for the purpose of unravelling? The reader is made to confound the ingenuity of the supposititious Dupin with that of the writer of the story" (O 2:328).

This half-mocking detachment is found also in Poe's comments on his apparent use of the supernatural in "The Raven" (1845). Four months after his letter about Dupin, Poe wrote in a letter to George W. Eveleth (December 15, 1846) that he had taken great care both with his words and with the studied effect of a sense of the supernatural in "The Raven."

> Your objection to the *tinkling* of the footfalls . . . occurred so forcibly to myself that I hesitated to use the term. I finally used it because I saw that it had, in its first conception, been suggested to my mind by the sense of the *supernatural* with which it was, *at the moment,* filled. No human or physical foot could tinkle on a soft carpet—therefore the tinkling of feet would vividly convey the supernatural impression. (O 2:331)

Poe here defended himself from the same kind of charge of stylistic flaw that T. S. Eliot a hundred years later claimed resulted from Poe's never paying attention to the "actual meanings" of words, though Poe admitted that, although he had carefully considered and planned the effect, he may have failed to make the momentary supernatural effect "felt." In this same letter, Poe also mentioned other general improbabilities in the poem, especially the position of the lamp that throws the shadow of the raven on the floor, which had been objected to by a "blundering" critic in the *Hartford Review*. Poe wrote Eveleth that he had indeed conceived a clear position for the candelabrum, "affixed against the wall, high up above the door and bust—as is often seen in the English palaces, and even in some of the better houses in New York." But to object to the unusualness of this arrangement, Poe wrote, was to miss the point: "For the purposes of poetry it is quite sufficient that a thing is possible—or at least that the improbability be not offensively glaring" (O 2:331). Poe wanted the supernatural effect generated by his Gothic decor to be felt by a reader vicariously experiencing the protagonist's situation. But Poe made it abundantly clear in "The Philosophy of Composition" (1846) that the supernatural effect was not to be taken by the perceptive reader as the true dramatic action of his Gothic works.

In this essay, Poe described the action of "The Raven" as psychological, and repeatedly suggested that there is in the poem a clear separation between the narrator's vision and the reader's. Poe points out that the dramatic center of "The Raven" is the emotional state of the bereaved lover. But this center was arrived at only after his having considered the problem of overall intention, length, specific effect desired (melancholy loss of a spiritualized beauty being most universal), and the unifying devices appropriate. Having decided to give the poem a surface stylistic and emotional unity through the device of a one-word refrain, Poe said, he then considered the difficulties of monotony and decided further upon a nonreasoned response from a nonhuman creature (a parrot or a raven) that should have, above all, *"variation of application."* The one-word nonreasoned refrain would be subject to different interpretations by a distraught human being. The "replies" at first would seem commonplace, but less so with each repetition, as the bereaved lover begins to apply personal and sinister meanings to the raven and his one meaningless word. Poe wrote that:

. . . the lover, startled from his original *nonchalance* [bemused apathy] by the melancholy character of the word itself—by its frequent repetition— and by a consideration of the ominous reputation of the fowl that uttered it—is at length excited to *superstition,* and *wildly* propounds queries of a far different character—queries whose solution he has passionately at heart —propounds them half in superstition and *half in that species of despair which delights in self-torture. . . .* (H 14:201–2; my italics)

One of the major stratagems of the poem would be to deepen the "ultimate impression" by "force of contrast" through the creation of "an air of the fantastic" which should approach "as nearly to the ludicrous as was admissible" (H 14:205), such as when the raven enters the window flirting and fluttering.

At first, the lover banters with the bird. But gradually, as his emotions begin to well up and color his rational state, the lover, wrote Poe, "no longer sees any thing even of the fantastic in the Raven's demeanor. . . . This revolution of thought, or fancy, on the lover's part, is intended to induce a similar one on the part of the reader . . ." (H 14:206). But so far, Poe continued, "every thing is within the limits of the accountable—of the real" (H 14:206).

So concerned was Poe about this point that he next paused to recapitulate the dramatic situation of the poem to show the perfectly real, though perhaps unlikely, quality of all the circumstances and how this reality is insinuated into the poem. The lover even ". . . guesses the state of the case, but is impelled, as I have before explained, by the *human thirst for self-torture,* and in part by superstition, to propound such queries to the bird as will bring him, the lover, the most of the luxury of sorrow, through the *anticipated* answer, 'Nevermore'" (H 14:207; my italics). Despite the irony of this psychological self-division, where the lover objectively sees, or guesses, his true situation yet enmires himself further in his own subjectivity, there is in all this, Poe repeated, "no overstepping of the limits of the real" (H 14:207), although in great literature there are suggestions of something beyond, behind, or under mere appearances. There may be an "under-current, however indefinite, of meaning" that may impart a *"richness"* to the writing. But richness, Poe wrote, "we are too fond of confounding with *the ideal,"* one of the glaring faults of the didactic writings of the American transcendentalists: "It is the *excess* of the suggested meaning—it is the rendering this the upper instead of the under current of the theme—which turns into prose (and that of the very flattest kind) the so called poetry of the so called transcendentalists" (H 14:207–8). Instead, suggested Poe, the writer should try, as he himself had done in the last two stanzas of "The Raven," to convey a symbolic meaning, to "dispose the mind to seek a moral in all that has been previously narrated," to cause "the reader . . . now to regard the Raven as emblematical . . ." (H 14:208), but emblematical not of a message from

Beyond, but of the psychological state of the narrator. The raven, in other words, is the objective correlative of the student's emotional state, just as "The Haunted Palace" and the house of Usher are the objective correlatives of Usher's state of mind. Indeed, just as Usher is emblematical of the narrator's state of mind—and just as Ligeia is of her narrator's state of mind.

Another especially revealing document on this matter is Poe's first review of Hawthorne's *Twice-Told Tales*. Here Poe remarked that the obvious, allegorical "moral" of "The Minister's Black Veil" will be taken by the "rabble" as its "true" meaning, whereas actually the story is a deceptive psychological tale:

. . . to the rabble its exquisite skill will be *caviare*. The *obvious* meaning of this article will be found to smother its insinuated one. The *moral* put into the mouth of the dying minister will be supposed to convey the *true* import of the narrative; and that a crime of dark dye, (having reference to the "young lady") has been committed, is a point which only minds congenial with that of the author will perceive. (H 11:111)

Poe is wrong about Hawthorne's intent, as Hawthorne's later footnote denying any specific cause of Hooper's estrangement from the world bears out.[34] But the very difference between the two writers on this point, their very oppositeness, emphasizes Poe's "realistic" though deceptive technique, as well as his focus on psychological aberration. The reference to the "young lady" occurs early in Hawthorne's tale and is quite brief. Her funeral is the second occasion of Mr. Hooper's wearing the black veil. As Hooper leans over her body, the veil hangs forward so that, had she been awake, she might have gazed into his face; an old lady in Hooper's congregation is almost certain that at this moment the girl's body shuddered. Although the incident increases the uneasiness the villagers feel in the presence of the black veil, it is only a minor introductory event. That Poe took this one reference as the clue to the true meaning of the tale supports what I have said is his characteristic technique: deceptive, ironic, psychological realism, in which the reader must read the clues as a detective in a mystery story. And Poe's comment that such "insinuated" meaning will be "caviare" to the mob corroborates what I have said is central to his characteristic irony: his own hoaxlike mockery.

In this connection, let us conclude with one further item relevant to Poe's ironical use of the psychological mode of ambiguous Gothic. In a review in 1836 Poe commented on an anonymous book called *The Doctor*, which was currently making a great stir as "an imitation of

Sterne—an august and most profound exemplication, under the garb of eccentricity, of some all-important moral law . . ." (H 9:67). But Poe claimed, after a close reading, that the book was a hoax: "That any serious truth is meant to be inculcated by a tissue of bizarre and disjointed rhapsodies, whose *general* meaning no person can fathom, is a notion altogether untenable, unless we suppose the author a madman. But there are none of the proper evidences of madness in the book—while of mere *banter* there are instances innumerable" (H 9:67). Poe thus indicates that madness is a proper literary theme even for moral or philosophical books, and that such madness may be dramatically represented as the bizarre and disjointed rhapsody of a madman if the proper clues are given. Poe may, of course, have reference to some psychological manifestation of madness by the author (unconsciously), since he uses the word *author*; but the context suggests that he is thinking of a literary structure, similar to that of *Tristram Shandy*.

Particularly relevant to Poe's sense of irony, however, is the close association here of banter with madness, though of course he distinguishes between the two—or rather, between two kinds of banter, that of madness and that of pure humor. Disappointed in its lack of reason in madness, what he really likes about the book was that it is "*a hoax*." He particularly relishes the mysteriousness of a monogram on the back cover of the book, the meaning of which he wordily and wittily solved.

This monogram is a triangular pyramid; and as, in geometry, the solidity of every polyhedral body may be computed by dividing the body into pyramids, the pyramid is thus considered as the base or essence of every polyhedron. The author then, after his own fashion, may mean to imply that his book is the basis of all solidity or wisdom—or perhaps, since the polyhedron is not only a solid, but a solid terminated by *plane faces,* that the *Doctor* is the very essence of all that spurious wisdom which will terminate in just nothing at all—in a hoax, and a consequent multiplicity of *blank visages.* The wit and humor of the *Doctor* have seldom been equaled. (H 9:69)

By punning on the meaning of "plane faces" Poe has again connected the "mad" wit and humor of the book with the hoax.

In this connection, we should recall that the term *arabesque* was used in the first three quarters of the eighteenth century primarily to indicate the later Gothic style of ornament in which there was much fret, lamentable imagery, and busy work that so confounded the sight that one could not consider where to begin or end—but which was yet conjoined with congestions of heavy, dark, melancholy, and monkish piles. Moreover, we have seen that one of the earliest literary applications of Gothic indicated inordinate wit and complexity. The historical and psychological association of inordinately complex wit, distraction, and more sinister elements receives one more turn of the screw with the information that the eighteenth century also used the term *arabesque* to mean a madman's rhapsody (W 2:16). The ambivalence of this interlinking congeries is striking; yet a clear basis for the relationship is visible. It is human subjectivity: the extreme reaches of the mind in wit and madness, humor and fear, perception and confusion, the real and the unreal.

Thus, by Poe's own account of his method and intent in "The Raven," and elsewhere, and by his practice in his most famous works, it is clear that his major concern was to make "real" circumstances seem strange or supernatural through unusual decor, through careful consideration of the connotations and dramatic suggestiveness of words, through ludicrous-grotesque contrasts, through careful psychological rendering of an emotionally self-indulgent, distraught, or mad protagonist. The effect of ambiguously real psychological supernaturalism that Poe said he sought in "The Raven" is the same kind of ambivalent effect noted by Cairns in the writings of Poe's immediate predecessors, Charles Brockden Brown and Richard Henry Dana, Sr. The reader is left to choose between the supernatural and the psychological, or for strongest effect, to think one theory and feel the other. Such double effect is, then, also that of "Usher," "Ligeia," and Poe's other "supernatural" tales. As Poe wrote of the "German" terror of the *Tales of the Grotesque and Arabesque:* "If in many of my productions terror has been the thesis, I maintain that terror is not of Germany, but of the soul—that I have deduced this terror only from its legitimate sources, and urged it only to its legitimate results" (H 1:151). What source these "legitimate results" have, clearly, is human psychology. Poe's subject is the precariously logical human mind which is capable of gross misperception, unreal construction, and instant irrationality.

Poe's significance in this cannot be overemphasized. For not only are "Ligeia" and "The Fall of the House of Usher" touchstones for and high points of the technique of such early American Gothic works as *Wieland, Edgar Huntly, Paul Felton,* and tales like Irving's "Adventure of the German Student," "The Spectre Bridegroom," "The Legend of Sleepy Hollow," and even "Rip Van Winkle," but also Poe's two most famous tales are emblematic of the technique and world view of such masterworks of the American Gothic as *The Scarlet Letter, The Marble Faun,* "My Kinsman, Major Molineux," "Roger Malvin's Burial," "Young Goodman Brown," "The Minister's Black Veil," *Moby-Dick,* and "Benito Cereno." As suggested at the outset of this chapter, the vision of the human mind that emerges from these Gothic works is one of despair over the ability of the mind ever to know anything, either about the ultimate reality of the world or about the mind itself.

In "Ligeia," we have a brilliant example of Poe's use of an involved first-person narrator. We are led, first, into the world of supernatural horror, and then out of that world into a world of mental horror, and then, out of that purely mental world into a limbo region of ambiguity where we cannot be sure what did or did not take place. Step by step, we are led to see, objectively, the involved narrator's abnormal condition, all the while subjectively participating in it. Yet, skillful as it is in achieving such ironic ambiguity through simultaneously operative interpenetrating structures, "Ligeia" is surpassed in narrative strategy by "The Fall of the House of Usher" a year later. Indeed, "Usher" represents the next logical step in the manipulation of narrative frames, for Poe gives the narrative one more ironic turn by providing a seemingly objective observer in the person of an initially peripheral narrator who "witnesses" the same preternatural events as does Usher. As we have seen, however, the steadily intensified dramatic irony works in the same way as in "Ligeia": we are again led step by step to draw back, objectively, from both the narrator and Usher, even while participating subjectively in their mutual terror.

In tales like "The Murders in the Rue Morgue," "The Assignation," "The Oval Portrait," "Eleonora," "A Tale of the Ragged Mountains," "Mesmeric Revelation," and others, we shall examine, in the next two chapters, variations of Poe's ironic manipulation of point of view—a technique that began with "Metzengerstein." Moreover, we shall see that coextensive with such narrative strategies is an interrelated image system of dreams, of dreamlike states, and of a limbo region between dreaming and waking. This is an especially significant point, for critics have traditionally seen opium dreams and "sleep-waking" states in Poe's fiction as representative of a Romantic mode of insight, rather than as the forms of delusion they are. This welling up of a subconscious nightside realm of hallucinatory dreamlife that overwhelms the rational daytime mind, however, is critically consistent with Poe's pervasive themes of the deceptive structures of nothingness in the universe and the correlative structures of delusion in the mind. Finally, a total pattern of ironic mockery of absurd self-delusion is all that remains—with reader and narrator left face to face, as it were, staring into each other's luminous eyes, wondering exactly what *has* happened in these subjective encounters with the dark well of the unconscious.

5
Grotesque and Arabesque

*The epithets "Grotesque" and "Arabesque" will be found to
indicate with sufficient precision the prevalent tenor of
the tales here published. . . .*

> *Preface to* Tales of the Grotesque and
> Arabesque *(1840)*

IN 1853 John Ruskin defined the grotesque as the art of a disturbed
imagination and declared it to be an essential part of the Gothic.[1] The
meaning of the word *grotesque* in the twentieth century is likely to be,
loosely, something ugly, distorted, unnatural, with the connotations,
in some contexts, of both the ludicrous and the sinister. Since this very
ambivalence of connotation was in Poe's time the literary denotation
of the term, there should be little difficulty in understanding Poe's
meaning in labeling his tales in 1840 "Grotesque and Arabesque." Yet
it is characteristic of Poe studies that Poe's terms should have been
greatly misinterpreted, grotesque, as we have seen, being defined as
merely satiric and comic, arabesque as emotive and imaginative, and
Gothic.

Such definitions, of course, assert a bifurcation to corroborate the
apparent split between the comic and the Gothic in Poe's whole body
of work. But I remain convinced that Poe did not mean to split apart
the comic and the tragic, or the comic and the serious. Instead, I submit, he conceived of "effect" as a continuum of emotional involvement
with the *grotesque* and the *arabesque* as terms indicating closely proxi-
mate areas of feeling or impact, as that point between laughter and
tears, calmness and frenzy, seriousness and mockery. Arabesque in
fact seems often to be an alternative term for grotesque. If arabesque
has any clear-cut distinction from grotesque in normal Romantic usage, it is only in its stronger suggestion of a deceptive overall pattern,

which is yet intricate and symmetrical, as in an arabesque screen. Arabesque often implies a formal intricacy in the handling of narrative frames; but its psychological meaning is nearly the same as for grotesque. Both terms have as a constant element a tension between opposites that somehow gives one insight, a transcendental vision resulting from the paradoxical fusion of opposing forces.[2]

I

Grotesque as both noun and adjective derives from the Italian words *grottesca* and *grottesco*, which were coined in the latter fifteenth century to designate an ancient Roman ornamental style of sculpture and painting which was discovered through excavations in Rome and other parts of Italy. It was almost immediately realized by Renaissance art critics that this lost style of "grotto-paintings" had been described by Vitruvius, a contemporary of Augustus, who had complained that contemporary Roman artists had rejected "reality" and "verisimilitude" in favor of "bastard forms" wherein human and animal heads and bodies were merged with plants, roots, and tendrils, and in which clear design gives way to a "turbulent entanglement of tools, tendrils, and bastard creatures" to form a sinister background of disorganization to a rationally organized foreground. The Renaissance used the term *grotesque* first to designate the specific scroll type and gradually came to associate the word with both the "carelessly fantastic" and the ominous, with a world almost totally different from the familiar one of reality, "a world in which the realm of inanimate things is no longer separate from those of plants, animals, and human beings, and where the laws of statistics, symmetry, and proportion are no longer valid" (K 21). Wolfgang Kayser speculates that the sinister meaning in part ensued from a phrase so often associated with grotesque in the sixteenth century that it became almost a synonym, as in the phrase "sogni dei pittori," or "dreams of the painters," suggesting a fantastic realm of imagination and fancy welling up from the subconscious (K 21–22). This we shall see to be of major importance in Poe.

Between the fifteenth and the eighteenth centuries, according to Kayser, the terms *grotesque, arabesque* and *Gothic* were "perennially confused" (K 23). Sixteenth-century German usage of the term *grotesque* referred to the monstrous fusion of human and nonhuman elements as the most typical feature of the style and connected this with the "infernal," with devils, tortures, and monstrosities from Ovid, Dante, Giotto, and others. Seventeenth-century French usage, however, emphasized the "pleasantly ridiculous," equally applicable to a person, a manner, a face, or an action; and at the beginning of the eighteenth century (and lingering into the twentieth) the French dictionaries defined grotesque as "silly," "bizarre," "fantastic," "capricious," "ridiculous," "comic," and "burlesque"—usages which are in accord with the usual, reductive, interpretation of Poe's meaning.[3]

But in the eighteenth century, the two usages, the weirdly monstrous and the weirdly comic, developed side by side so that by the last quarter of the century the term *grotesque* was used to mean both simultaneously, and eventually it became a supportive element of the theories of irony developed by the Germans. Wieland, for example, writing on "grotesque caricature" in his *Conversations with the Parson of *** * (1775), seemed to be disturbed by the possibility that the "grotesque" had a hidden meaning of some kind, and frequently returned to the strange impact of the works of the elder Brueghel. The two Brueghels (1520?–1569; 1564?–?1638) and Bosch (c. 1450–1516) painted weird, infernal, flying and creeping creatures, abstracted animate objects, and monsters with both human and animal parts, who seem, as Kayser observes (K 30–32, 38), indifferently to inflict torments on their victims. The elder Brueghel, especially, made the sinister invade an otherwise normal world.

With the German "Storm and Stress" movement and the beginnings of a clear Romantic movement, the concept of the grotesque as a literary form became quite important. Of his play *Confusion, or Storm and Stress* (1776), F. M. von Klinger (1752–1831) wrote, "I have assembled the craziest characters, and the most profoundly tragic feelings frequently alternate with laughing and roaring." Of the reaction of the first audience, he wrote, "There they sat and did not comprehend" (K 44). What they did not comprehend, according to Kayser, was that Klinger's play was neither comedy nor tragedy but a third genre—not a "confusion," as they thought, but a "fusion"—the grotesque, which went beyond mere literary satire and caricature. Another German writer, J. M. R. Lenz (1751–1792), reviewing his own play *The New Menoza* (1775), wrote that German writers of comedy needed to realize that since comedy dealt with serious problems they ought to aim at writing comically and tragically at the same time, as he had (K 44).

The principal literary philosopher of ironic mysticism, Friedrich Schlegel, between 1798 and 1800, linked the terms *comedy, tragedy, irony,* and *grotesque* and *arabesque* together under the banner of irony. We have already seen that in his *Lectures on Poetry* (1800) Schlegel praised the works of Shakespeare and Cervantes for their "artfully regulated confusion, that charming symmetry of contradictions, that strange and constant alternation between irony and enthusiasm present even in the smallest parts of the whole," a structure he called "arabesque." In *Fragment 418* of the first *Athenäum* volume (1798) Schlegel characterized Tieck's works as "poetic arabesques," composed with a sense of irony and endowed with fantasy and gaiety. In *Fragments 75, 305,* and *389* Schlegel associated the "grotesque" with a contrast between form and content, with the explosiveness of the paradoxical antithesis and fusion of the ridiculous and the terrifying, and with sophisticated caricature (K 50–53). Thus, although both terms are associated with irony (contrasts, discrepancies, mockery) in Schlegel's view, again there is a curious inversion of the meanings of grotesque and arabesque as they are usually interpreted with reference to Poe: the arabesque suggesting deceptive point of view and general duplicity; the grotesque suggesting a powerfully emotive fusion of the ridiculous and the terrifying. Yet Friedrich's brother, August Wilhelm, had at the same time associated the grotesque with charm, humor, tenderness, wantonness, and sublimity, a connection apparently derived from Goethe's essay *On Arabesques* (1789) in which Goethe defended the grotesque-arabesque style (making no distinction) from the strictures of the classicists.

As Raymond Immerwahr points out, in Friedrich Schlegel's thought the term *grotesque* is "frequently synonymous" with *arabesque,* just as Schlegel's concept of the arabesque tends to merge with his concept of irony. Immerwahr makes several important historical distinctions among the three terms *grotesque, arabesque,* and *irony* which yet underscore their similarity. He suggests that the origin of the Romantic concept of arabesque is to be found in the "romances" of the Middle Ages and the Renaissance, in which the author has, with full awareness, carefully insinuated into his narrative incongruity in detail and antithesis in character and structure. He cites the works of Wolfram, Boiardo, Ariosto, and Berni as prime examples of this "playful" tradition and traces it through Cervantes, Swift, and Sterne, to the German writers Wieland, Jean Paul Friedrich Richter, and Klinger (see pp. 673–82). Schlegel's concept of the arabesque, Immerwahr claims, is "centered in the generally playful treatment of artistic form," especially as manifested in two closely related ways.

The first is "discussion within the work of the form or medium along with the actual object of portrayal," or the "portraying of this form or medium instead of the object" (p. 673). (We have looked at this effect earlier as characteristic of Tieck's Romantic Irony and have observed it in such Poe tales as "The Premature Burial.") The second, and more important here, is the writer's development of "incongruities in the relationship between a framing narrative and one or more inner strands which break or severely strain the narrative illusion" (p. 678). Immerwahr, from a wide historical perspective, thus defines *arabesque*, as the Romanticists came to know it, as a technique of "deliberate intricacies and inconsistencies in the handling of narrative frames and direct treatment within the narrative of the conditions of the narrative . . ." (p. 683). The close similarity of this concept of arabesque to Romantic Irony in general is most important, for it corroborates Poe's ironic intent in his *Tales of the Grotesque and Arabesque*. Indeed, it is precisely this latter arabesque technique that I have been arguing is the operative strategy, though with very subtle frames, in "Ligeia," "The Fall of the House of Usher," and other of Poe's Gothic tales from "Metzengerstein" to "The Cask of Amontillado." As Immerwahr observes, *arabesque* is a term applicable to the "form of a narrative" which is an "outward manifestation of irony" (p. 683), or a term signifying the "ironic potentialities inherent in the use of a narrative frame" (p. 681).

Thus, the constant element in the Romanticists' usage of *grotesque* and *arabesque*, I suggest, is a carefully patterned union of ironic opposites giving rise to a transcendent vision of the true state of things. The grotesque suggests more strongly a yoking of the chaotic, the fearful, and the comic; the arabesque suggests more strongly a sense of ironic perspectives in the midst of confusion and ominousness. Both suggest the struggle to understand the incomprehensible, neither term meaning anything absolutely exclusive of the other, both focused on the tension between conscious control and subconscious fear and delusion. Friedrich Schlegel called Jean Paul's "grotesques" the "only romantic products of our unromantic age"; and Jean Paul in his *Introduction to Aesthetics* (1804) characterized the genre of the terrifying and the ridiculous, of the tragic and the comic, of the serious and the satiric as true "humor." Humor, Jean Paul wrote, is that "skepticism" which is "born when the mind's eye surveys the terrible mass of martial opinions which surround it," and which leads downward to "the abyss" and upward toward the "idea of infinity" (K 55). This formulation of Romantic "skepticism" we shall later see to be most useful in describing Poe's stance toward art and the world.

Only four years before Poe sent his first tales to a publisher, Victor Hugo, a writer to whom Poe has frequent reference, in the preface to *Cromwell* (1827) used the word *grotesque* to indicate an ambiguous comic genre, creating what is on the one hand "deformed and horrible," and on the other what is "comic and farcical" (K 57). Moreover, Hugo's grotesque exhibits precisely that concern for a union of opposites, a harmony of contrarieties, and a resultant transcendental vision that is characteristic of philosophical Romantic Irony. In art, said Hugo, "an ugly, horrible, hideous thing," transformed by "truth and poetry," becomes "beautiful, admirable, sublime, without losing anything of its monstrosity." For Hugo, the grotesque involved a structural principle of ironic contrasts leading to "a vision of the great infernal laughter." Burton R. Pollin has pointed out that not only was Hugo's preface to *Cromwell* a "widely discussed and extensively publicized document" but also that the June 1828 number of the *Foreign Quarterly Review*, a journal that Poe read regularly, carried a review of *Cromwell* with a summary of Hugo's conception of the historical development of literature (from the ode, to the epos, to the drama and the modern sensibility). The reviewer characterized this modern sensibility with the assertion, derived from Hugo, that "the burlesque is the just and distinguishing feature of the . . . present age" and is born of "the jumbling of tragedy and comedy, terror and buffoonery" as human society progresses toward its present state of clearer vision.[4] The parallels with, and perhaps indebtedness to, the German critics are obvious. There seems little doubt that in calling his tales "Grotesque and Arabesque," Poe did not mean to split them into the comic and the serious but instead to indicate the fusion of the comic and serious into that vision the German Romanticists were calling irony. This conviction is deepened by yet another article in the *Foreign Quarterly Review* the year preceding (July 1827), an essay-review of the works of E. T. A. Hoffmann by Sir Walter Scott.

II

Scott's review, titled "On the Supernatural in Fictitious Composition: and Particularly on the Works of Ernest Theodore William Hoffmann,"[5] has long been associated with Poe's conception of the Gothic and the grotesque and arabesque. But little detailed analysis of what Scott actually said has been offered. Pollin, naturally enough, given his subject of the pervasive influence of Hugo on Poe, seeks to minimize the importance of the discussion of the grotesque that Scott gives. While I do not deny the importance of Hugo's discussion of the grotesque—indeed, I am convinced that Poe must have been aware of it—the Scott article is undoubtedly the more significant.[6] Whereas the influence of Hugo's preface must have been general, the influence of Scott's review was specific: it is clear that Poe not only read Scott's article with care but also that he appropriated Gothic materials from it in a manner similar to the way he appropriated critical materials from A. W. Schlegel's *Dramatic Lectures.*

As with Schlegel's *Lectures*, the evidence that Poe read Scott on Hoffmann is conclusive. The summary of Hoffmann's story "The Entail" that Scott gives in this essay is clearly the source for some of the Gothic elements of Poe's "Metzengerstein" and "Usher," and the parallels provide some striking evidence for Poe's careful perusal of Scott's article. The background of the "Entail" involves an eccentric prince named Roderick, who had in the past (as in "Metzengerstein") given wild parties in a frenzied attempt to achieve good spirits, but who remained essentially alone in a castle surrounded by ghastly vegetation growing blackly up to the very walls. At the time of the story, part of the castle is in ruins, split by a deep fissure "which extended from the highest turret to the dungeon of the castle," rather obviously the source for Roderick Usher's house and its zigzag fissure extending from the roof down into the tarn. A magistrate visits the castle with his nephew (the narrator), who, Scott said, is a vain, "romantic," "enthusiastic" "coxcomb," "trained . . . in the school of Werther" (p. 85), a suggestive judgment if applied to the "nervous" narrator of "Usher." This young man spends the night in a lonely hall of the castle, and at one point (as in "Usher") the storm outside suddenly stops, and the moonlight streams through the windows to illuminate strangely lifelike portraits of ancestral knights and fantastic carvings upon the walls and the ceiling, which project weirdly and in the "uncertain light of the moon and the fire, gave a grisly degree of reality" (p. 87). The narrator (as in "Usher") comments on the influence of environment over the human imagination, and reveals that he has drunk too much. He then decides to indulge his half-pleasant apprehensiveness (like the lover in "The Raven") with a ghost story, the "Ghost-Seer" of Schiller. (Schiller's "Ghost-Seer," we may note in passing, is a rationally explained tale.) He reads Schiller's tale up to the wedding feast of Count von B—— ("Count von Berlifitzing," of course, figures in "Metzengerstein"), that is, to that point where the ghost appears. At this moment, the door to the hall bursts open, and the narrator drops his book; but he explains to himself that it is the wind or something else equally natural, and continues reading, only to be interrupted by the sound of footsteps outside the door. This timing of incidents in the tale to events in the book is like the episode of the "Mad Trist" in "Usher," though Poe makes it more extended, dreamlike, and psychologically delusive.

Other evidence of Poe's reading of Scott's review (though Hoffmann was available in translation) is primarily additive after these parallels. In *Pinakidia*, writing on the derivation of the term *assassin*, Poe mentions Von Hammer (H 14:45), whose work the *History of the Assassins* (1818) is extensively reviewed in the same volume of the *Foreign Quarterly Review* (1:449–72). There is also in this volume a review of Manzoni's *Betrothed* (498–515) from which an extract, concerning death carts used in the plague in Milan in the seventeenth century, may have been used by Poe (there is some doubt about his authorship) in his 1835 review of Featherstonhaugh's translation of the *Betrothed* (H 8:12–19). Scott also makes particular reference in his essay to the burlesque tales of County Anthony Hamilton and to Pulci's comi-heroic poetry (pp. 65–66), both of whom Poe mentions briefly (H 10:189; 14:185; 16:123; 14:43), referring to Pulci as "the sire of the half-serious rhyme." Scott also refers to the horror tales of the "secondary names" of German literature, the very phrase that Poe uses in the preface to the *Tales of the Grotesque and Arabesque*.

More important, Scott in this essay extensively discussed Hoffmann's techniques and compared them to the normal use of the supernatural in Gothic tales, concluding by commenting on Hoffmann's propensity to indulge in the sickly fantasies of the grotesque or arabesque. This Scott disapproved of, preferring the more regular Gothic. According to Scott, Hoffmann's "Entail" has a legitimate human interest, whereas his "The Sandman" belongs to that unsatisfactory genre of "half horror and half whim," and is merely "ingenuity thrown away" (pp. 93–94).

Wolfgang Kayser has observed that the development of Hoffmann's career involved a shift from a kind of allegorical explanation of odd happenings in which inexplicable and vaguely demonic figures turn out to be the traditional devil (which thus tends to undercut the sinister impact of the true grotesque) to an art that permits doubt about unnatural and improbable behavior, encouraging the reader to seek an explanation, within the limits of verisimilitude, but which normally will not be forthcoming. The result of this double effect is the "estranged" world of the true grotesque. Although a little different, this parallels the supernaturalist, explained, and ambiguous modes of the Gothic we examined in the last chapter. Kayser offers a clear example of what he means by ineffective allegorized fairy tale in the figure of the polite stranger in Hoffmann's "Life of a Well-Known Man." The Stranger, when offered help in crossing a street, jumps six feet high and twelve feet across it. At night, dressed in white, he knocks at various doors, his purpose never quite clear, his explanations never quite satisfactory. The weird, estranged world conjured up by these bizarre incidents tends to evaporate, however, when we learn that the stranger is simply the devil (K 75–76, 69–70). Grotesque effect, on the other hand, resists a tendency toward a firm frame of reference, and we are left with a sense of the mysterious.[7]

A major part of this effect lies with the narrative point of view, and it is here that the arabesque merges into the grotesque. Thus a narrator begins with some rationality and separation from the events and characters and gradually moves closer to the events, adopting the perspective of other characters or becoming a deeply affected eyewitness. As we have seen, this technique is typical of many of Poe's stories, especially "Usher" and "Ligeia." Kayser uses as his principal example of this kind of weird psychological verisimilitude Hoffmann's "Sandman" which so puzzled Scott. Kayser characterizes Hoffmann's "Sandman" as a tale with the double effect of the weird and the real—weird when seen from the point of view of the protagonist, but realistically understandable as a psychological study of trauma and obsession. The shifting and contrasting points of view, of terror, apprehension, commonsense, clear perception, willful delusion, and madness, produce in their total ambiguous interaction a large arabesque pattern of irony. Indeed, in the preface to his *Phantasy-Pieces* (1814–15), Hoffmann praised Jacques Callot's etchings of the *commedia dell'arte*, the quality of which he proposed to imitate in his writings, not only for their dreamlike vision but also for their "irony."

Scott also in this essay tries to account for the psychology of the supernatural in literature in terms of effect. In the process he comments on the grotesque and arabesque styles and effects with reference to the comic possibilities of the Gothic, thus further linking Poe's "Gothicism" with the German concepts of ironic horror and whimsy. After some initial remarks on the propensity of even the most incredulous and rational of men to be affected by suggestions of the supernatural, Scott proceeded to this "comic side of the supernatural," which, he said, may either entirely travesty and hold up to laughter the Gothic or generate a sort of "imperfect excitement" (p. 66). This latter species of the supernatural romance, he says, is well executed by French and German writers, like the German Wieland; and there is also a large area of "comi-heroic" poetry that belongs to this class, Scott noted, including the works of Luigi Pulci, Francesco Berni, and Ariosto. Scott found Ariosto only occasionally humorous; but "in some passages at least," said Scott, Ariosto "lifts his knightly vizor so far as to give a momentary glimpse of the smile which mantles upon his countenance" (p. 66). These remarks, I submit, were seminal for the young Poe, interested in the Gothic and yet possessed of a sardonic turn of mind.

When Scott considered the collections of fairy tales, like those of the brothers Grimm, he found them to glut the appetite with too much of the supernatural, remarking, in addition, that there is yet another species of supernatural romance, allied to the satiric, to the comic, to the comi-heroic, to the eccentric, and to the fairy tale, but specifically resulting from the "attachment of the Germans to the mysterious" (p. 72). "This," writes Scott, "may be called the FANTASTIC mode of writing,—in which the most wild and unbounded license is given to an irregular fancy, and all species of combination, however ludicrous, or however shocking, are attempted and executed without scruple" (p. 72). Commenting on recent translations of Chamisso and Hoffmann, Scott described Hoffmann's works in general as "grotesque" pieces of "diablerie" (p. 77), which do not have quite the quality of the true supernatural, and linked the terms *grotesque* and *arabesque* tightly together:

. . . the grotesque in his compositions partly resembles the arabesque in painting, in which is introduced the most strange and complicated monsters, resembling centaurs, griffins, sphinxes, chimeras, rocs, and all other creatures of romantic imagination, dazzling the beholder as it were by the unbounded fertility of the author's imagination, and sating it by the rich contrast of all the varieties of shape and colouring, while there is in reality, nothing to satisfy the understanding or inform the judgment. . . . [His] sickly and disturbed train of thought . . . led him to confound the supernatural with the absurd. . . . (pp. 81–82)

Scott's notion of grotesque, then, is much like the eighteenth-century usage of "arabesque Gothic," as he himself suggested; and, applying rather classicistic standards, Scott found Hoffmann's grotesquerie unsatisfactory. Scott especially found Hoffmann's admission of a sense of kinship with Callot puzzling, and contrasted the engravings of Hogarth with Callot's etchings; in examining the "diablerie" of Callot, he suggests, we find instances of "ingenuity thrown away," whereas Hogarth has a sense of the human and of the social world in which human beings move (pp. 93–94). This comment rather strikingly bears out what Kayser feels is the essential characteristic of the grotesque, an "estranged" world. Scott's attempt to define grotesque writing by reference to arabesque painting again tends to confirm the probability that Poe, too, conceived of the two terms as near synonyms.

In part, Scott's disapproval of the grotesque was the result of his having misconstrued the aims of the genre; especially did he fail to see its concern for ambivalent irony, an effect Hoffmann tried to make clear in the preface to his *Phantasy-Pieces.* And in part he was the victim of a prejudgment which associated such works with a "sick mind." The parallel with the critical reception of Poe is striking. Yet

Scott admitted that it could sometimes be "pleasing to look at the wildness of an Arabesque painting executed by a man of rich fancy" (p. 93). But he complained that the grotesque writers ask us not only to be tolerant of "startling and extravagant caprice," but also of the "horrible" and even the "disgusting." The underlying element of this mixture of whimsy and horror, according to Scott, is "overstrained feelings," which always tend ultimately toward pain and even madness. We, "possess in a much greater degree [he writes] the power of exciting in our minds what is fearful, melancholy, or horrible, than of commanding thoughts of a lively and pleasing character. The grotesque . . . has a natural alliance with the horrible; for that which is out of nature can be with difficulty reconciled to the beautiful" (p. 93). In Scott's essay, then, Poe found not only useful Gothic decor for "Metzengerstein" and "Usher," but also discussion of the insinuated supernatural, of the psychology of the supernatural, of eccentric and nervous (and drunken) Gothic heroes and narrators, of satiric and sportive Gothic, and, most importantly, of a special Gothic blend of the serious and the comic, based on overstrained emotions, that Scott called alternatively the "fantastic," the "grotesque," and the "arabesque."

Scott tended to dislike grotesque fantasy because he thought it was depressing and had little affinity with beauty. On this latter point at least, Poe thought otherwise. In an essay on N. P. Willis in the *Broadway Journal* (January 18, 1845), Poe defined "imagination," "fancy," "fantasy," and "humor" in a way that confirms his commitment to that Germanic fantasy which Scott identified with the grotesque. All four faculties have in common "the elements Combination and Novelty." The "Imagination," Poe says, is "the artist of the four": "From novel arrangements of old forms which present themselves to it, it selects only such as are harmonious;—the result, of course, is *beauty* itself— using the term in its most extended sense, and as inclusive of the sublime" (H 12:38).

Poe, we have seen before, considered the imagination as almost a divine power of man, a lesser power of God. The most perfect work of imagination would be God's universe (which just *may* be imperfect), a perfection the human artist obviously cannot hope to approach. Insofar as the imagination combines items in a truly novel form, it can be "said" to create, which the other faculties may do too, though not so well. True creation, however, is not within man's province (H 12:37–38). But the ultimate artistic beauty of "harmony," Poe says (like a Romantic Ironist), can be the result of the imagination transmuting the elements of *"either beauty or deformity"* (H 12:38): "The range

of the Imagination is . . . unlimited. Its materials extend throughout
the Universe. Even out of deformities it fabricates that *Beauty* which
is at once its sole object and its inevitable test" (H 12:39). The thoroughly or most purely imaginative work, argued Poe, has such a
"thorough harmony" that it is often "under valued by the undiscrim-
inating," since its combinations have a quality of the expected, the
smooth, the obviously appropriate. But when in a work "there is introduced the sub-element of *unexpectedness*" (matters never before
combined "brought into [a] combination" that "strikes us *as a difficulty
happily overcome*"), the result is a work of "fancy." A work of "fantasy"
carries these "enticing" imperfections of "difficulty overcome" to excess
and may result in painful incoherence instead of pleasurable harmony
if the writer, delighting in "novelty and unexpectedness of combination," avoids "proportion" (H 12:39–40). But there is, added Poe,
another, more harmonious, beautiful, and ultimately more truthful
kind of fantasy: "When, proceeding a step farther . . . Fantasy seeks
not merely disproportionate but incongruous or antagonistical elements, the effect is rendered more pleasurable from its greater posi-
tiveness . . ." (H 12:40). Into this kind of fantasy, which seeks the
incongruous and the antagonistical, "truth" makes a "merry effort" to
enter, and we recognize true "humor" (H 12:40).

Poe's identification of fantasy with, on the one hand, unexpectedness
and avoidance of proportion, and, on the other hand, with a work of
imagination that combines the beautiful and the deformed, the antagonistical and the incongruous, into a harmonious, truthful, beautiful
work of "humor," is most important. For it not only links Poe with
Scott's dubious review of Hoffmann's grotesques, but it also places him
deep within what he called the "vortex" of German theory from Tieck
and the Schlegels to Jean Paul.[8] And thus Poe's genre in his fiction is
just what he said it was in his first collection of tales: "grotesque and
arabesque." That by these terms Poe did not mean to split his work
in two but instead to emphasize its unity is further underscored by his
proposed title for an expanded collection two years later—the Germanic sounding "Phantasy-Pieces," tales of fearful humor, and of
ultimately harmonious irony.

III

The terms *grotesque* and *arabesque* frequently occur together in Poe's
writings in such a way as to suggest, predominantly, that they refer to
a single psychological effect or response having to do with ambiv-

alence, tension between opposites, and a sense of the transcendent ironic vision.[9] One senses the smile behind the phrasing of the statement in the preface to the 1840 collection of tales that the "epithets 'Grotesque' and 'Arabesque' will be found to indicate with sufficient precision the prevalent tenor of the tales here published" (H 1:150). While Poe does hint at the association of arabesque with Germanism and gloom, phantasy and horror, he refuses to be pinned down and in the next breath paradoxically denies Germanic horror in what he has just admitted are indeed Germanic horror tales. He writes in a subtle contradiction that "Germanism is 'the vein' for the time being. Tomorrow I may be anything but German, as yesterday I was everything else" (H 1:150).

Certainly, Poe's actual usage of *grotesque* does not have a simple comic or satiric quality. In the "Murders in the Rue Morgue," for example, Poe suggests in connection with the term *grotesque* a psychological sense of the weird. The unnamed narrator of the tale says that the common temper of Dupin and himself partakes of a "fantastic gloom," which is reflected in their inversion of night and day and in their choice of a "time-eaten and grotesque mansion" which had been "long deserted through superstitions into which we did not inquire . . ." (H 4:151). When the term *grotesque* comes up again toward the conclusion of the tale, Poe again links it with superstitious fear, but indirectly and with a number of ironic perspectives working on it. When the analytical Dupin reviews the circumstances of the murders (one woman's head is almost completely severed from her body, the other woman's corpse is "thrust up a chimney head downward," the locked chamber is in an "odd disorder"), he remarks almost comically that the extremity of the horror seems *"excessively outré"* (H 4:178). The whole situation seems, Dupin says, like a *"grotesquerie* in horror absolutely alien from humanity" (H 4:180). Moreover, the alien quality of the murders is intensified by the reports of the murderer's voice, which was "devoid of all distinct or intelligible syllabification." "What impression," Dupin asks the narrator, does the total pattern of these strange details make "upon your fancy?" The narrator, with "a creeping of the flesh," replies that some "madman . . . some raving maniac" must have committed the murders. But Dupin points out that madmen, "even in their wildest paroxysms" and "however incoherent" in their words, speak a human language; thus, their ravings have the "coherence of syllabification," which the overheard voice of the murderer did not. Dupin then shows the narrator a bit of hair "disentangled" from the "rigidly clutched fingers" of one of the murdered women. The narrator, "completely unnerved," remarks that "this is no *human* hair" (H 4:181). His horrified statement is the high point, emotively, of the tale, for the nonhuman quality of the hair suddenly, if briefly, brings the odd circumstances of the murders to a point of mystery and supernaturalism beyond the conventionally Gothic and into the realm of the inexplicably eerie and alien. Poe has here brought his tale to the point of the "estranged" world of the true grotesque, as Kayser defines it.[10]

That such estrangement is Poe's intention in this passage is confirmed by the emphasis on reactions of the narrator, which constitutes a pattern of dramatic irony in the tale. Significantly, however, there are two reactions to the strange circumstances of the murder, for Poe contrasts the "creeping flesh" of the narrator with the cold rationality of Dupin. Some critics have thought that Dupin is a symbolic projection of Poe's self-assumed superiority to the rest of mankind. Dupin's "superiority," however, contains at least two major ironies. First, regarding the relationship of the reader to the writer, we have seen that Poe commented in a letter to P. P. Cooke in 1846 that part of the "effect" of ratiocinative tales like "The Rue Morgue" consists in a hoax, in making the reader "confound the ingenuity of the supposititious Dupin with that of the writer of the story." Poe's mocking and self-deprecating irony regarding the relation of reader and writer is further revealed by his question, "where is the ingenuity of unravelling a web which you yourself have woven for the purpose of unravelling?" (O 2:328). Second, Dupin functions in the tale almost like the controlling ironic artist himself. After having "unnerved" the narrator by pointing out the grotesque details of the murders, Dupin calmly provides a realistic explanation which he has deduced from a number of small clues intricately related to the overall "outré" pattern of the situation. Through "deduction" and a leap of imagination, he sees through a chaos of bizarre appearances to the more pedestrian reality behind the deceptive "facts." The narrator's comment that "this is no *human* hair" epitomizes in its way Poe's ironic technique, since at the very instant that the narrator is duped into fancying some unnameable horror, the rational explanation begins. A nonhuman but humanlike animal, an escaped orangutan, has killed the two women, a rather disappointingly commonplace (certainly not grotesque) fusing of two different realms of existence, though doubtless satisfying on a detective-story level.

Dupin's phrase, "a *grotesquerie* in horror," suggests that the very extremity of the violence and of the unusual circumstances impresses him as some sort of "mocking" caricature of "ordinary" (Dupin uses the word) horror. Yet the sense of grotesque horror is momentarily increased by Dupin's matter-of-fact tone and then dissolved abruptly by the rational explanation. Moreover, the eerie in-between emotional state of the grotesque "ratiocination," in which the clues to the "solution" of a weird tale are ingeniously combined with Romantic-Ironic destruction of illusion, can be seen as the basic ironic technique of Poe's fiction. In the ratiocinative story proper, the reader is encouraged to try his wits against those of the writer in a search for clues within a rational pattern; the reader is encouraged to look for a realistic explanation from the very beginning. In the "Rue Morgue," however, when Poe's Dupin for all his rationality finally brings the reader to a flesh-creeping sense of the uncanny, then brings him up short again with the rational, the overall technique is much like the Romantic Irony at the conclusion of "The Premature Burial." Similarly, we have seen that in Gothic tales like "Ligeia" and "Usher," Poe constantly suggests the supernatural while carefully insinuating ratiocinative clues. He brings the reader to the edge of the supernatural, as it were, then leaves him confronting, through an "unnerved" narrator, the luminous eyes of Ligeia, or the pale figure of Madeline Usher returned from the grave. From the beginning, the reader is encouraged to doubt, although ambivalently, any rational explanation and instead to enjoy the luxury of a supernatural thrill, despite the psychological clues. But Poe also insinuates into his Gothic tales an absurd and mocking destruction of the spooky effect—such as the narrator's elaborate preparation in "Ligeia" of the bridal-funeral chamber, with its wind machine to animate the draperies, or the Gothic tale of the "Mad Trist of Sir Launcelot Canning" that the narrator of "Usher" finds in the library along with works not only by mystics but also by Ludwig Tieck.

Another example of the way he turns even the grotesque back on itself and its practitioners is found in the comic tale "Mystification," where Poe remarks of the hero that he was a "habitual mystific" who was "ever upon the look-out for the grotesque" (H 4:105, 106). Poe's narrator observes that the Baron Ritzner von Jung was one of those "anomalies now and then to be found, who make the science of *mystification* the study and the business of their lives" (H 4:104). As Harry Levin has suggested, the tale seems almost an analysis of Poe's own psychology. The narrator observes, "I truly think that no person at the university, with the exception of myself, ever suspected him to be capable of a joke, verbal or practical." For despite all the grotesque "drolleries" that he generated, Baron von Jung had the "consummate ability" to give the impression that everything happened in spite of his efforts to prevent them. He had, moreover, the "adroitness" to "shift the sense of the grotesque from the creator to the created." That is, he never came to be associated with the "absurdities" he produced but remained, incognito, detached from them. As the narrator says, "in no instance before that of which I speak [the ensuing tale], have I known the habitual mystific escape the natural consequences of his manoeuvers—an attachment of the ludicrous to his own character and person" (H 4:104–5).

Such multiple mocking irony, I suggest, is the basis of the "rare" and "glowing" humor that Poe saw in the grotesquerie of some of the writings of Tieck and Thomas Hood. Yet, though Poe uses the word *grotesquerie* in his *Marginalia* comment on Hood to indicate an area of extreme imaginativeness and wit, involving puns and an "ideal" but wild comic sense, the association of the grotesque with the uncanny psychological effect of superstition and terror on the fancy hovers over the surface. Of Hood, Poe writes:

. . . his true province was a very rare and ethereal *humor,* in which the mere pun was left out of sight, or took the character of the richest *grotesquerie;* impressing the imaginative reader with remarkable force, as if by a new phase of the ideal. It is in this species of brilliant, or, rather, *glowing* grotesquerie, uttered with a rushing *abandon* vastly heightening its effect, that Hood's marked originality mainly consisted:—and it is this which entitles him, at times, to the epithet "great." . . . (H 16:178)

Again, the "rushing *abandon*" suggests the overstrained emotions of a madman, forcibly recalling Poe's comment on the "wit and humor" of *The Doctor,* that seeming madman's "rhapsody" which yet did not have "the proper evidences of madness." The statement also is consistent with Walter Scott's association of the grotesque and arabesque with "overstrained" feelings tending toward pain and madness, which, to his disfavor, certain German writers favored. The psychological import of the term *grotesque,* then, should be clear; moreover, Poe uses the term in just that ambivalent way that the Romantic Ironists in Germany did to fuse ironically the sinister and the comic, the weird and the absurd.

The association of the grotesque with the odd, bizarre, eerie, and disturbing impression of things on the overstrained human mind Poe links with the term *arabesque* in "The Masque of the Red Death" (1842). The two terms are used together in such a way as to suggest a fusion of psychological meaning clearly connected with both sheer irony of events and with insinuated, mocking irony of tone and point of view. In an effort to escape the plague, Prince Prospero takes refuge with his guests in his country castle. He orders seven halls to be built according to a design which reflects his "love of the *bizarre*" (H 4:251). The apartments are irregularly laid out with sharp turns so that one's vision is focused and limited. Each room is decorated with different colors and lighted naturally from Gothic windows of the same color as the room. Otherwise, there are no lights, except from the flickering braziers in the connecting passageways that project glaring light through the windows, and produce a "multitude of gaudy and fantastic appearances." In the black chamber, "the effect of the fire-light that streamed upon the dark hangings through the blood-tinted panes, was ghastly in the extreme, and produced so wild a look upon the countenances of those who entered, that there were few of the company bold enough to set foot within its precincts at all" (H 4:252). The prince orders a ball to lighten the pervasive sense of death that oppressively hangs over everything. But a gigantic ebony clock, with its pendulum swinging monotonously, upon each hour utters from its "brazen lungs" a clear, loud, deep musical sound so peculiar that the musicians and dancers suddenly pause in their motions (like the performers of the *commedia dell'arte*) and listen: "the giddiest grew pale, and the more aged and sedate passed their hand over their brows as if in confused reverie or meditation" (H 4:253). When the echoes of the chiming clock die away, a light laughter follows and the musicians look at each other and smile as if at "their own nervousness and folly." Although this scene is repeated with each hour, the ball is "gay and magnificent." The guests are all masked in accordance with the instructions of their host. Poe writes that the guests' masks were "grotesque" and immediately proceeds to the "arabesque" decor:

There were much glare and glitter and piquancy and phantasm—much of what has been since seen in [Hugo's] "Hernani." There were arabesque figures with unsuited limbs and appointments. There were delirious fancies such as the madman fashions. There was much of the beautiful, much of the wanton, much of the *bizarre*, something of the terrible, and not a little of that which might have excited disgust. To and fro in the seven chambers there stalked, in fact, a multitude of dreams. And these—the dreams—writhed in and about, taking hue from the rooms, and causing the wild music of the orchestra to seem as the echo of their steps. And, anon, there strikes the ebony clock which stands in the hall of the velvet. And then, for a moment, all is still, and all is silent save the voice of the clock. The dreams are stiff-frozen as they stand. But the echoes of the chime die away . . . and a light, half-subdued laughter floats after them as they depart. (H 4:254)

This simultaneously grotesque and arabesque scene is strikingly akin to the grotesquerie of Hoffmann and Callot. But the important

point here is that Poe uses grotesque and arabesque together. Separately, he associates grotesque explicitly with glare and glitter,
piquancy and phantasm, and adds a half-satiric reference to Hugo's
play, all in all a kind of confusion of surface gaiety interrupted by a
weird sense of the ominous. The arabesque Poe associates more directly with Gothic figures, either disproportionate or disarrayed. Both
terms together, however, he connects with the delirious dreams of
madmen, in which are mixed the terrible, the disgusting, the beautiful,
the wanton, and the bizarre.

Moreover, in the midst of the revelry, a strange figure, dressed as
Death, appears, and the insulting "mockery" (H 4:256) of his costume
further defines the sinister "humor" of the true grotesque in its generic
sense: "Even with the utterly lost, to whom life and death are equally
jests, there are matters of which no jest can be made. The whole company, indeed, seemed now deeply to feel that in the costume and
bearing of the stranger neither wit nor propriety existed" (H 4:255–
56). That is, the costume seems now no joke, but the further point is
that the joke has become sinister, the humor ominous, the mockery
horrible. The stranger comes to seem like Death himself. Yet, while
the tale seems to tell of this supernatural visitation of Death, it can
also be read as an ironic tone poem about hysteria, engendered by
mood and setting, with a sarcastic concluding echo (as Levin seems
to have been the first to notice) from Pope's *Dunciad:*

And one by one dropped the revellers in the blood-bedewed halls of their
revel, and died each in the despairing posture of his fall. And the life of the
ebony clock went out with that of the last of the gay. And the flames of
the tripods expired. And Darkness and Decay and the Red Death held illim-
itable dominion over all. (H 4:258)

Such mocking irony reflects the larger jest of death and life basic to
the dramatic irony of the tale. Prince Prospero's sinister stronghold,
of course, contrasts directly with the enchanted island of his namesake,
Prospero, the magician in Shakespeare's *The Tempest.* The ironic
theme of Poe's tale focuses on the grimly perverse joke of Prospero's
having walled in death in a frenetic attempt to wall it out. While the
mocking undertone to all this may be described as that of the grotesque, the narrative point of view is that of the arabesque—of the
sardonically superior Romantic Ironist, who, after having evoked the
sinister scene from the well of subconscious (and metaphysical) fears,
at the end soars freely above it all.

IV

A striking feature of the grotesque and arabesque elements in both "Murders in the Rue Morgue" and in "The Masque of the Red Death" is that of the delusive or dreamlike effect of interior design.[11] And the close similarity of meaning of the two terms *grotesque* and *arabesque* as Poe uses them is further revealed in the wordplay of his satiric essay on interior design, "The Philosophy of Furniture" (1840), in which he ironically recommends an arabesque modification of the rather grotesque tastes of American "decorists." He ostensibly advises "median laws" in the patterns of carpeting, upholstery, curtains, and wallpaper. A carpet must have "distinct grounds"; the figures should be "vivid circular or cycloid" and "*of no meaning*": "The abomination of flowers, or representations of well-known objects of any kind, should not be endured within the limits of Christendom. Indeed, whether on carpets, or curtains, or tapestry, or ottoman covering, all upholstery of this nature should be rigidly Arabesque" (H 14:103–4). This usage of the term *arabesque* would seem to be a kind of Kantian conception, suggesting beauty of pure design, involving perspective against a distinct background, recalling the seventeenth-century distinction of perspective in scrollwork—except that Poe has here insinuated a punning contradiction that produces, at the least, a trace of doubt about the complete sincerity of his advice in the rest of the essay. Although the passage seems reasonable enough on the surface, Poe has turned the prejudices of two cultures topsy-turvy: Americans of taste will prefer Arab-esque patterns, reproducing no natural forms, and will not endure natural forms within the limits of "Christendom," especially on such items as "ottomans." Poe then goes on to describe perversions of taste that emphasize mere glare and glitter, glass and gaslight, "sprawling and radiating devises," "stripe interspersed and glorious with all hues, among which no ground is intelligible" (H 14:104). This perversion of quiet order into sprawling lines, glitter, and confusion is obviously like that grotesque confusion of Prince Prospero's halls in "The Masque of the Red Death" and gives another twist to the element of sardonic mockery we have just examined in that tale. Even the very title of the essay is a mock-serious device, the pretentiousness of which is undercut by the subject, and underscored by alliteration. The essay is always taken seriously, but its satiric level can be easily demonstrated. Published the same year as the *Tales of the Grotesque and Arabesque* (1840), the essay is contemporaneous with Poe's clearest formulation of his genre; and his satiric presentation of "decorist" theory makes for an illuminating comparison with the mocking decorist theory of the early tale "The Assignation."

A look at the opening of "The Philosophy of Furniture" clarifies the satiric irony of Poe's arabesque recommendations. Poe begins with vituperative comments on Romantic taste, accusing Americans of mere display. Since the well-furnished apartment in America is distinguished by lack of restraint and by general "want of keeping," he will recommend his own conception of the "ideal" room (H 14:101–3). But he gradually adds more and more "glitter" and "glare" and "picture" until he ironically produces his own perversion of quiet tastefulness. He suggests as "ideal" an oblong room, with crimson-paned windows (as in "The Masque of the Red Death"), curtained with airy silver curtains within the recess and with crimson silk curtains without. The curtains are drawn with ropes of thick gold; a rich giltwork ornaments the juncture of ceiling and walls; the walls themselves are "prepared with a glossy paper of silver gray tint, spotted with small Arabesque devices of a fainter hue of the prevalent crimson." Relieving the expanse of the paper are imaginative landscape paintings—such as Chapman's "Lake of the Dismal Swamp." The furniture is of crimson and rosewood; central in the room is an octagonal table formed of rich "gold-threaded marble" and a few "appurtenances" such as a candelabrum and a lamp with perfumed oil. The general similarity to the bridal chamber in "Ligeia" is easily seen, especially when Poe adds the final touch: all this quiet tastefulness surrounds a "sleeping" body (H 14:106–8).

In the context of Poe's career, suspicion of burlesque intent in this essay is confirmed by comparison of its "ideal" room with the room in the idyllic "Landor's Cottage" (1849), with the chamber of Prince Prospero, with the ghastly bridal chamber of Lady Rowena Trevanion (of Tremaine), and with the apartment of his Satanic Majesty the Devil in Poe's early satire, "The Duc de L'Omelette" (1832). Landor's room, set in a house itself set in a valley that is a kind of natural outdoor room or "amphitheatre," is similar in some respects to the ideal room of "The Philosophy of Furniture," but simpler, more realistic, less lurid in color; the design of the carpet, for example, consists merely of small circular green figures against a simple white background (H 6:270). In the "Duc de L'Omelette" the lighting arrangement of the Devil's apartment is almost precisely that recommended as ideal in "The Philosophy of Furniture." The last detail of the ideal room is "an Argand lamp, with a plain crimson-tinted ground-glass shade, which depends from the lofty vaulted ceiling by a single slender gold chain . . ." (H 14:109). In the earlier satiric tale, as we have seen, the

Devil's ruby lamp is suspended by a slender red-gold chain, the end of which is lost in the clouds like Coleridge, Carlyle, or the City of Boston. Similar "censers" in other tales are called "Saracenic" and "arabesque."

Thus Poe's earliest use of this setting and its fiery lamplight is blatantly comic and satiric, and it is such a setting in "The Philosophy of Furniture" that he associates with the ideal of the arabesque. But we have seen that the term is double-edged, employed as both design of no apparent natural meaning against the perspective of clear background and also as an ironic pun carrying one of the first clues to the hoaxing satire of the essay. The "pure beauty" of the arabesque pattern ostensibly connotes the opposite of the chaotic designs popular in America, but Poe's arabesque room reads like a grotesquerie of the ideal. We have seen also that in "The Masque of the Red Death" Poe associates arabesque clearly with gloomy Gothic figures in chaotic disarray and disproportion, suggesting the early eighteenth-century conception of the "Saracen" style of the Gothic. The word *arabesque* in "Red Death" suggests, in addition, an extreme psychological state as well as the merely weird, for the term is juxtaposed to the "delirious" "fancies" of a "madman." Moreover, there is in this tale an insinuated current of mockery at least as closely associated with arabesque as with grotesque.

Thus Poe uses what is basically a satiric decor, and a satiric lighting arrangement, ironically in Gothic tales like "The Assignation," "The Oval Portrait," "Ligeia," and "Usher." And he does so in connection with the word *arabesque* in such a way as to confirm absolutely the deceptive ambivalence of both his term and his "flawed" Gothic technique. The usual view of Poe's Gothic lighting and interior decor, when they are not considered merely melodramatic and tawdry, is that they are Gothic stage properties which suggest rather well the demonic and supernatural. Oliver Evans, for example, writes that Poe often carefully arranges his lighting so that it seems to well up from below, frequently connecting such light with the word *sulphurous*,[12] and thereby suggesting an "infernal illumination."

But on a level beyond the merely weird, though simultaneously with the weird, Poe's infernal lighting suggests, or is the objective correlative of, a tormented mind. The light it sees by wells up from the subconscious. Poe's characters often take a fiery "arabesque censer" as a symbol of their own state, as does the stranger in "The Assignation," an early tale as significant as "Metzengerstein" for seeing Poe's multiple levels of irony. The stranger characterizes his spirit as writhing, as though damned, in the fire of his lamp. As put bluntly here, the metaphor is a bit comic, rather like some imp in a bottle. The metaphor is comic in a less obvious way in Poe's tale itself, for Poe in "The Assignation" gives the surface story a surface reasonableness and effectiveness. But the tale is actually a satiric hoax, a pretended Romantic tale of passion which actually lampoons the type as well as the prototypes of its unnamed hero and unnamed narrator. The story is worth looking at in detail, for not only have its satiric butts been clearly identified, but Poe's technique of giving deceptive clues to the true insinuated meaning of the tale can also be clearly exemplified in connection with grotesque and arabesque decor.

The dramatic action of the tale is ostensibly serious and Gothic. An unnamed narrator, returning home at sunset in a gondola by way of the Grand Canal in Venice, hears a "wild, hysterical, and long continued shriek" (H 2:110), another of many such in Poe. Looking up, he sees a beautiful woman standing statuelike at an upper-story window, but in frozen horror, for her child has fallen into the black water of the canal. "Stupified and aghast," the narrator sees also the "Satyr-like figure" of old Mentoni, "thrumming a guitar" while desultorily giving "directions for the recovery of his child" (H 2:112). Suddenly a muffled figure steps out of a dark niche in the architecture of the building opposite and plunges into the water after the child. This strange figure "in an instant afterward" is standing "upon the marble flagstones" by the side of the Marchesa di Mentoni with "the still living and breathing child within his grasp." His cloak, drenched with water, falls about his feet and discovers "to the wonder-stricken spectators the graceful person of a very young man, with the sound of whose name the greater part of Europe was then ringing" (H 2:113). (The narrator does not give the stranger's name, but later reveals that he is an English poet.) The beautiful Marchesa Aphrodite, like a "statue that has started into life," then gratefully whispers to the handsome stranger that he has "conquered" and that "one hour after sunrise—we shall meet—so let it be!" (H 2:113–14). The narrator offers to take the dripping stranger home in his gondola, and the stranger (who has the mouth and chin of a deity, wild and full dark eyes, and a profusion of curling black hair over a broad ivory forehead) invites the narrator to come to his palace at sunrise. Early the next morning, the narrator is overwhelmed by the rich decor, especially the statuary, of the stranger's apartment, as well as by the stranger's somewhat mad behavior. About an hour after sunrise, the stranger shows the narrator a portrait of the Marchesa Aphrodite and calls the narrator to join him in drink. He then makes some remarks about life, death, and art, recites the lines "Stay for me there! I will not fail / To meet thee in that hollow vale," and seems to fall asleep. At this moment, a messenger brings news that the Marchesa has taken poison. The narrator tries to "arouse the sleeper," but the stranger's limbs are rigid and his eyes are riveted in death. As the narrator staggers back, he finds a "cracked and blackened goblet," and then "a consciousness of the entire and terrible truth" flashes over his "soul" (H2:124).

The melodramatic quality of the action and the language is given a quality of satiric exaggeration by the semicomic motif of statuary in the tale, including a reference to the survival of an altar to laughter, some banter about the *Apollo Belvedere*, as well as the statuelike appearances of the two major characters. The Marchesa is first seen in the niche of her window (looking like a statue of either Aphrodite or a Madonna) and the stranger seems to step from a dark architectural niche in the next building; in a moment they pose marblelike on the marble steps. The stranger's features are like those of the Apollo; his bearing recalls to the narrator's mind some words of *Bussy D'Ambois:* ". . . like a Roman statue! He will stand / Till Death hath made him marble!" (H 2:123). And when he dies his limbs become immediately rigid. It is as if Poe is suggesting, under the surface seriousness, that the characters of such tales are rigid and artificial, a satiric possibility that becomes more likely when the statue motif is seen in the context of Poe's use of *Childe Harold* and Thomas Moore's edition of the *Letters and Journals of Lord Byron* (1830).

Writing of his visit to the principal art galleries of Florence, Byron had mentioned, among other items, the Venus de Medici, Canova's Venus, the Antinous, and a work of Michael Angelo. Poe's unnamed stranger also alludes to these four figures. Further parallels in Poe's tale with Byron's affair with the Countess Guiccioli lie not only in the general setting, but also in specific details associated with Byron, the most obvious of which is perhaps the reference to the Bridge of Sighs, near a "palace and a prison." Richard P. Benton, in an article as significant for a just reassessment of Poe as Darrel Abel's on "Usher," has shown that while Byron's *Childe Harold* may have been the general or initial inspiration for Poe's story, two other references in "The Assignation" show not only that Thomas Moore's edition of Byron's letters was the immediate inspiration but also that Poe's narrator represents Moore himself. The tale is a kind of allegorical parody, Benton writes, in which Poe

played a joke on . . . [his] readers by presenting not only Byron, the Countess Guiccioli, and her old husband in the guises of his hero, heroine, and villain but also by presenting Byron's friend and confidant, the Irish poet

Thomas Moore, in the guise of the narrator of the story. And behind the mask of Tom Moore, of course, gleam the sparkling brown eyes of Poe himself.[13]

Moore's description of his 1819 visit to Byron's "palazzo on the Grand Canal," near the Rialto Bridge, is similar to the visit of Poe's narrator to the stranger's apartment. Moore was met by Byron who took him, in his gondola, to the palazzo. Then Byron led Moore "up the staircase" to his "spacious and elegant" rooms, where he expressed his unorthodox opinions on sculpture and painting. Poe's narrator says: "I found myself . . . at his Palazzo . . . [on] the Grand Canal in the vicinity of the Rialto," and was "shown up a broad winding staircase" into an apartment of "unparalleled splendor." Inside, the narrator is subjected to the stranger's unorthodox opinions on painting and sculpture. But the conclusive proof of the satiric "identity" of the narrator, is a pun. Benton explains:

"To die laughing," the stranger remarks to the narrator, "must be the most glorious of all glorious deaths! Sir Thomas More—a very fine man was Sir Thomas More—Sir Thomas More died laughing, you remember." There is no other reason for mentioning More in the story except to pun on the name Moore. Sir Thomas More did not die laughing; he was decapitated. (p. 197; see H 2:117)

Thomas O. Mabbott notes, however, that More's last words are supposed to have been a mild jest.[14] The reference then is doubly appropriate, and the real clue to the satiric suggestion of Tom Moore lies in the repetition. Benton, however, suggests that Poe is doing some decapitating of his own. Benton's concluding remarks regarding Poe's hoaxing irony are pertinent:

In sum, Poe's "The Assignation" was intended to be a hoax. Just as the joke perpetrated on the Parisian police in "The Purloined Letter" is based on the fact that the obvious is often overlooked, so Poe's hoax in "The Assignation" is based on the same fact. This time, however, Poe's joke . . . is on the vast majority of the readers of his own day, for no doubt only his more esoteric fans were in an intellectual position to appreciate his hoax. (p. 197)

More important here, perhaps, as far as clarifying Poe's conception of the ambivalent mockery of the grotesque and arabesque is what immediately precedes this passage. The narrator is overwhelmed by the dazzling decor of the stranger's apartment, which is distinguished by its want of "keeping" equally as much as by the magnificence of its treasures. "The eye wandered," the narrator says, "from object to object, and rested upon none—neither the *grotesques* of the Greek painters, nor the sculptures of the best Italian days, nor the huge carvings of untutored Egypt" (H 2:116). Somewhat as in "Ligeia," rich draperies tremble to a "low, melancholy music" and the "senses" are "oppressed by mingled and conflicting" perfumes from "strange convolute censers" which burn with "multitudinous flaring and flickering tongues of emerald and violet fire"—censers that are also called arabesque. The rays from the newly risen sun pour in through "windows formed each of a single pane of crimson-tinted glass," and the natural and artificial lights mingle and glance "to and fro, in a thousand reflections" (H 2:116), much as in the grotesque velvet chamber of "The Masque of the Red Death" and the "ideal" arabesque room of "The Philosophy of Furniture" (where such glitter and want of keeping are faults).

Laughing at the narrator's astonishment at the apartment and its art objects, the Byronic stranger comments that "some things are so completely ludicrous that a man *must* laugh or die" (H 2:117). He then makes the remark about Sir Thomas More and follows it with the intriguing comment that at Sparta there survives "among a chaos of scarcely visible ruins" an altar to laughter: "Now at Sparta were a thousand different temples and shrines to a thousand different divinities. How exceedingly strange that the altar of Laughter should have survived all the others!" (H 2:117). That this passage is an emblematic clue to the comic undertone and satiric point of the tale is corroborated by the stranger's exhibition of his art treasures. The stranger shows the narrator the *Madonna della Pieta* of Guido Reni, of which Mabbott observes (p. 416) "its presence even in a palace" is "amusing" for it is "over ten by twenty feet." Then the stranger expresses his preference for the Antinous over the Apollo; this, Benton suggests, is a comic rejection of the stranger's own image, for Moore had remarked on Byron's resemblance to the Apollo.

During and following this exhibition, the narrator observes that the Byronic stranger somehow seems "essentially apart from all other human beings." The narrator attributes the stranger's abstraction to a kind of "*habit* of intense and continual thought, pervading even his most trivial actions . . . and interweaving itself with his very flashes of merriment—*like adders which writhe from out the eyes of the grinning masks* in the cornices around the temples of Persepolis" (H 2:119; my italics). This striking fusion of the sinister and the comic announces an important psychological motif. The stranger's "mingled tone of levity and solemnity," his "nervous *unction*," his "excitability," and his frequent pauses in the middle of a sentence to listen to "sounds which must have had existence in his imagination alone" suggest madness. But this mingled tone of levity and solemnity, along with the excess of exclamation points, ineffables, tear-stained pages, huge art works, and submerged satiric puns, also becomes emblematic of the grotesquerie of the tale itself, culminating in a doctrine of incongruity associated with bizarre dreams, with death, and with arabesque censers. At the conclusion of the tale, the now drunken Byronic stranger says, ". . . to dream has been the business of my life. I have therefore framed for myself, as you see, a bower of dreams" (H 2:123). Commenting on the disorder, the want of keeping, in the decor of his "bower of dreams," he says: "Yet the effect is incongruous to the timid alone. Properties of place, and especially of time, are the bugbears which terrify mankind from the contemplation of the magnificent" (H 2:123). Once, he continues, he had been a "decorist," but now the incongruous mixture of his rooms is "the fitter" for him. "Like these arabesque censers," he adds, "my spirit is writhing in fire . . ." (H 2:124). Moreover, he suggests that the "delirium" produced by the decor of his apartment is the more valuable since it provides him with "wilder visions" of that "land of real dreams," death (H 2:124). The ostensible seriousness, the hoaxing satire, the altar to laughter, the doctrine of incongruity, the melodramatic death, the death jest and pun, the mingled tone of levity and seriousness which is like adders writhing from out the eyes of grinning masks, and the delirious dream of a spirit writhing in fire make "The Assignation" a synecdoche of the seriocomic, ironic ambivalence of Poe's arabesque tale.

V

The dreamlike delirium connected directly with the "writhing" light of the arabesque censer in "The Assignation" is consistent with Poe's association of the word with the dreams of the guilty and the insane in "The Masque of the Red Death." Grotesque and arabesque, then, seem, in addition to their other qualities, to be firmly connected in Poe's writings with the confusing and delirious influence of setting, of environment upon the overstrained human mind. As we have seen, Poe frequently links the terms with irregular, niched, multiform architecture, Gothic armorial trophies, flickering fiery light, the weird transformation of natural light through Gothic windows, and the like. But Poe also applies the word *arabesque* to a predominantly pleasant dreamlike vision of a natural paradise beyond or out of nature in "The Domain of Arnheim" (1847), but it too, like the other "landscape" tales Poe wrote in the 1840s, eventually comes to suggest something less "perfect" and more sinister than the surface "beauty" at first promised.

These landscape tales form a complement to the interiors we have just examined, though we should note again that each landscape, no matter how lush and expansive, also has an "architectural" feel, a sense of interior design. Moreover, each has a structure of dramatic irony that insinuates that man's feeble efforts to see harmonious permanence or to produce Godlike beauty in "natural" art are doomed to failure. In "The Island of the Fay" (1841), for example, which is a prose companion piece to an engraved plate in *Graham's Magazine,* the drowsy narrator comes upon a romanticized lake scene of a tiny fairy in a boat. But as her cyclical journey describes a series of concentric circles around an island in the lake, the little fay comes to seem to the narrator the last of her race, and she eventually draws nearer and nearer the shadows of the island and fades away into nothingness. This kind of dream vision, and arabesque pattern, we shall later see to be a major structural component of *Eureka,* in which the concentric circles of the pulsating cycles of creation and destruction that constitute the design of the entire universe also end in nothingness.

In "The Domain of Arnheim," Poe's use of the word *arabesque* in connection with a transcendent vision of ultimate beauty has also an "oppressive" and overly "dazzling" quality that "bewilders." In this tale, or essay, Poe indirectly connects the "arabesque devices in vivid scarlet" inscribed on an ivory canoe with the general form of an "irregular crescent," which is also the shape of the high-pointed canoe itself as it floats in a crystal river. Paradoxically, the river has etched a channel through hard granite so clearly that the "sharpness of outline . . . delighted while it bewildered the eye" (H 6:192). The devices on the canoe, the shape of the canoe itself, the winding cycles of the river, and the concentric circles of the great outdoor amphitheater that is Arnheim are all, clearly, conceived as an arabesque design governing the whole of the tale.

As the canoe approaches the paradise of Arnheim, the "visitor" is almost overwhelmed with a "gush" of "entrancing melody" and with a "strange sweet odor" that is yet "oppressive," as though of drugs. The vision of the visitor is then further bewildered by a

. . . dream-like intermingling to the eye of tall slender Eastern trees—bosky shrubberies—flocks of golden and crimson birds—lily-fringed lakes—meadows of violets, tulips, poppies, hyacinths and tuberoses—long intertangled lines of silver streamlets—and, upspringing confusedly from amid all, a mass of semi-Gothic, semi-Saracenic architecture, sustaining itself as if by miracle in mid-air, glittering in the red sunlight with a hundred oriels, minarets, and pinnacles; and seeming the phantom handiwork, conjointly, of the Sylphs, of the Fairies, of the Genii, and of the Gnomes. (H 6:196)

Again, overstrained feelings, confusion, and delirium are the constant qualities even in this basically pleasant description of an arabesque paradise, and in the tale as a whole death ironically makes a sinister intrusion. "Arnheim" is an extension of "The Landscape Garden" (1842), in which, as noted before, Poe uses rocky outcroppings and geological upheavals as symbolic, melancholy intimations of death amidst the ideal beauties of the natural world. "Arnheim" deals with the attempts of the wealthy Ellison to "improve" the landscaping concepts of the "grovelling herd" of men by constructing a fantastic, irregular, and unnatural paradise in the midst of a natural paradise, and, in so paralleling God's creation, to become Godlike himself. But he dies. The mockery of such simple dramatic irony is obvious once one steps back from the details of Ellison's "art work"; and in fact, similar dramatic irony informs each of the landscape tales Poe did in the 1840s, just as their physical settings tend to describe arabesque patterns of concentric circles and twistings and writhings, from which, implicitly, there is no exit. They are all deceptive, arabesque dreams.

But let us turn to another "interior" tale for one final example of the conjoining of semi-Saracenic Gothic beauty and delirium. For the arabesque dream also provides a major clue to the irony of "The Oval Portrait" (1842, 1845), a tale that is most significant for a clearer understanding of Poe's arabesque and his technique of hoaxlike dramatic irony. "The Oval Portrait" is ostensibly an occult tale of the metempsychosis of a young woman's soul into a painting, and the usual reading given it by critics focuses on its quality as a serious parable of the mysteriously ambivalent "moral" relationship of life and art.[15] The curious thing about such interpretations, however, is that they deal only with the last third of Poe's tale and virtually ignore the first two-thirds in which Poe focuses the reader's attention on the first-person narrator of the strange story. Even Poe's revisions, which are especially relevant to the character of this narrator, have been brought forward as evidence that Poe shifted his original intention. In his first version, titled "Life in Death" (1842), Poe seems to have intended a psychological study of the hypersensitive Romantic imagination. But in the second version, Seymour L. Gross suggests, Poe seems to have dispensed with "those macabre elements" which "threatened the thematic coherence and totality of impression in the story."[16] In the first version,

Gross writes, we find a passage that, "as do the opening paragraphs of several other of Poe's stories, sets out to delineate the neurotic imbalance of the narrator's mind"; but in the revised version the "narrator's mind is irrelevant, for once the story of the painter and his wife begins to emerge, the narrator is forgotten." Gross then considers the conclusion. In the second version, when the painter finishes the portrait, he exclaims: "This is indeed *Life* itself!" only to turn to a dead wife (H 4:249). "The tale ends, therefore," Gross remarks (with a pun I think would have amused Poe), "on thematic dead center." This thematic center is the moral blindness of the painter. In the original version of the tale, however, Poe had the painter add: "But is this indeed Death?" (H 4:318). This queer remark vitiates the proper effect of the story, Gross says, "for it takes it out of the realm of the moral and puts it into the realm of the psychological."

The fact that Poe's first intention clearly was to paint a portrait of a disturbed imagination does not, however, necessarily lead to the view that because Poe reduced the obviousness of his narrator's imbalance of mind he had shifted his intent from the psychological to the occult. "The Oval Portrait" may be read, just as it stands, as an ironic, fully dramatized, psychological portrait. What Poe did in revising "Life in Death" is what he consistently did in the revisions of all his Gothic works. In "The Oval Portrait" Poe's reduction of the obviousness of the narrator's imbalance of mind produces an ironic double effect. Simultaneously, while achieving a more authentic, realistic dramatization of a crazed mind from a first-person point of view, Poe also produces a spooky "Gothic" story that the majority of his nineteenth-century readers thrilled to. The revisions make the tale into another trap for "the unwary." "The Oval Portrait" remains what "Life in Death" was—a psychological study of the Romantic imagination— but with an added level of dramatic irony, and even, from the viewpoint of the hoaxer, a level of mockery aimed at the unwary reader who sees merely a story of the supernatural.

If the thematic center of the tale is the blindness of the painter, who, engrossed in his work, fails to see life fading from his model as it begins to glow in his painting, and if as the story develops the narrator of the tale is indeed forgotten in the latter part of the tale, then the "moral" reading naturally follows. But because the narrator is the focus of over half of "The Oval Portrait," his presence is still felt behind the concluding supernaturalism of the story. (Indeed, fewer than five hundred words are devoted to the painter and his wife.) If, then, we interpret the thematic center of the tale as a moral allegory, the work is incredibly flawed. Not only does the story, by this interpretation, lack the careful symmetry of most of Poe's other tales, but also the long first section of the tale (devoted entirely to introducing the narrator, setting the scene, and "finding" the "real" story in a mysterious book) has almost no relevance to the thematic center of the moral blindness of the painter. The coherence and totality of impression of the tale would be so badly flawed that we should hardly recognize the tale as Poe's were not his name appended to it.

Although Poe excised from "The Oval Portrait" many of the references to narcotics that are found in the earlier "Life in Death," he did not completely excise what he calls the "delirium" of the narrator. The narrator specifically mentions in the opening paragraph of "The Oval Portrait" that his immediate fascination with the richly framed paintings, which are hung in an eccentric manner in the niches of the weirdly constructed castle walls, is likely due to his "incipient delirium" (H 4:245). Moreover, the deceptive and confusing architecture of this Gothic chateau in the Apennines (one such as found in the "fancy of Mrs. Radcliffe") provides one of the major clues to the dramatic irony of the tale, for Poe associates a dreamlike atmosphere with the environment, and uses the word *arabesque* in connection with a setting full of odd twistings and turnings, with "manifold" and "multiform" armorial trophies, with sleep and dreams, and with the play of flickering light over the filigreed picture frames. By means of the eccentric setting and by carefully structured emphasis on the arabesque frames, Poe provides symbolic "clues" to the deceptive quality of the narrator's experience.

It is significant that Poe refers to the arabesque frames at two symmetrical points in the revised story: at the beginning of the narrator's "introduction" and at the end, just before he reads of the painter and his wife. Each time, the frames are mentioned in conjunction with the confusing architecture of the castle and with what the narrator is able to see from any one point of view. In the first paragraph, the narrator remarks on the "rich golden arabesque" frames of the many paintings which are hung not only from the "main surfaces" of the walls but also in the "very many nooks" of the "bizarre architecture" (H 4:245). Finding a small volume which describes the paintings, the narrator has his servant close the shutters and light the "tongues of a tall candelabrum" so that he may study the pictures more closely. After reading about the paintings for some time, he moves the candelabrum, carefully, so as not to wake his slumbering servant, in order to throw more light on the book. But "the rays of the numerous candles . . . now fell within a niche of the room which had hitherto been thrown into deep shade by one of the bed posts" to reveal a startlingly lifelike portrait of a "young girl just ripening into womanhood" (H 4:246). The narrator then shuts his eyes, for he fears that his vision has "deceived" him and that his "fancy" has run away with "sober" reason (H 4:246). Again looking at the portrait, however, he remarks that he could not and would not "doubt" that he "now saw aright" because the filigreed "Moresque" frame around the picture seems to provide conclusive evidence, to him, that he is not dreaming, for he sees that the picture is a picture. Moreover, the "first flashing of the candles upon that canvas" causes him now to become aware of a "dreamy stupor" that has been "stealing over" his "senses" (H 4:246). So much emphasis on shadow, drowsiness, and dreaming, however, produces not merely Romantic intensification of the strangeness of the experience but also an ambiguity, a suspicion, about the actuality of the events. And given Poe's normal use of the term *arabesque*, his pointed use of arabesque frames as evidence of the "reality" of what the narrator perceives is an ironic confirmation that the narrator is indeed dreaming the rest of the tale, including the story in the small volume which details the metempsychosis of the woman's soul into the lifelike painting.

Further supporting this reading of "The Oval Portrait" as a deceptive dream-experience, the reader will find that dream-imagery dominates the first two-thirds of the tale: the narrator is delirious and drowsy and his servant is slumbering; when the narrator shifts the candelabrum, the shadow of one of the bed posts shifts to reveal the recessed portrait which had been deeply submerged in the darkness; the small volume explaining the pictures is discovered mysteriously on the narrator's pillow. Moreover, Poe emphasizes the dreamy deceptive quality of the lighting through the eerie play of light and shadow from the numerous flickering candles over the multiform surfaces of the Gothic armor, the irregularities of the walls, and the filigree of the portrait frames, as well as through the reflected flashings of the oiled canvasses. Finally, we are given throughout the "introduction" a picture of the narrator falling asleep.

Thus, the discovery that the original version, "Life in Death," contained unequivocal evidence that Poe had first conceived of the work as a psychological portrait of a character in the throes of an opium dream tends to confirm the psychological interpretation of "The Oval Portrait" rather than to suggest Poe's complete shifting of his single preconceived effect.

Probably it is the length and the emphasis of the long passage in "Life in Death" which Poe omitted as a block from "The Oval Portrait," along with the omission of the clearly insane final remark of the painter, that deceives critics into thinking of Poe's second version of the tale as "moral." The emphasis on the delusiveness of the narrator's experience is so pronounced in the first version that it is quite natural (initially) to conclude that its relative de-emphasis in the second version indicates a shift of intent. The omitted portion, therefore, is worth a brief look. In the opening paragraphs of "Life in Death," Poe has his narrator explain his intrusion into the deserted chateau, commenting that he has lost so much blood in "an affray with the banditti" that he is delirious from pain and from lack of sleep. The narrator explains that in his weakened condition, rather than take a chance with being bled, he will rely on opium for relief from his pain. Poe then emphasizes the deceptive quality of things as the narrator sees them by devoting the bulk of the omitted passage to the narrator's hazy deliberations in judging the amount of opium he will swallow. In the "dull delirium" of his sleepless state, the narrator tries to judge the smallness of the dose of opium in terms of the whole piece which he holds in his hand. His "reeling senses" prevent him from "perceiving the incoherence of [his] reason" and he remarks that since he has always smoked opium before, never swallowed it, he has "no preconceived standard of comparison," nor the "faintest idea [then] that what I conceived to be an exceedingly small dose of solid opium might, in fact, be an excessively large one" (H 4:317). Next, as he gazes at the paintings in the bedroom, he remarks: "—I felt meantime, the voluptuous narcotic stealing its way to my brain, I felt that in its magical influence lay much of the gorgeous richness and variety of *the frames* —much of the *etherial hue that gleamed from the canvas*—and much of the *wild interest of the book* which I perused" (H 4:318; my italics). After this confession, the narrator shifts the candelabrum, sees the hidden painting, and reads the incredible story of the painter and his wife.

Thus, in the first version of the tale, Poe clearly set up the delusiveness of the experience as the narrator renders it. In the second version, three years later, Poe characteristically reduced the clear touches of psychological realism ("Romantic" on the surface as an opium-dream might seem) but without removing them altogether. In "The Oval Portrait" Poe makes the narrator less aware of his hallucinatory state. But by this maneuver Poe makes the general reader, too, less clearly aware of the narrator's state—thereby producing for the unwary a Gothic tale of the occult with a clear didactic point, but producing for the wary a multiform ironic tale, with no obtrusive didacticism, and with rather satisfying ratiocinative clues to a typical Poe hoax. Most telling of these clues is the subtly ironic paralleling of the narrative structure of the tale to its visual focal point: just as the strange portrait has an arabesque frame, so too does the painter's story have its arabesque frame. Here, then, the techniques of ambiguously explained psychological Gothic and of the grotesque and arabesque coalesce in a pattern emblematic of Poe's ironic consciousness.

Such arabesque construction reminds one strongly of A. W. Schlegel's remarks that the Romantic Ironist tacitly makes "a sort of secret understanding with the select circle of the more intelligent of his readers," that is, those who are able to see the "secret irony of characterization" in the arabesque design.[17] We have seen that such clues to the "secret irony"are carefully insinuated into the deceptively psychological Gothicism of "Usher" and "Ligeia" and, as well, carefully identified by Poe as arabesque. Poe's Gothic hoaxes probably reach a high point in the deceptive grotesquerie of "Ligeia" and "Usher," and we may recall here Poe's attitude in his letter to P. P. Cooke in 1838 regarding the technique and the reception of "Ligeia." "As for the mob," Poe writes, "let them talk on. I should be grieved if I thought they comprehended me here" (O 1:118). We should recall also the detailed description of the arabesque design of the tapestries in "Ligeia," wherein deceptiveness, confusion, point of view, and the subconscious are all associated with the arabesque pattern and effect.

The proposed Folio Club tales, and the publisher's rejection of them, have seemed to most critics important only for establishing some "point" to Poe's early satiric tales. But the burlesque, or ambivalently burlesque, intent is constant in Poe's fiction, and we may well note again Poe's early identification of the term *arabesque* with satire in his letter to Joseph and Edwin Buckingham, the editors of the *New England Magazine*, wherein he offered them a series of sequential satiric and burlesque stories as "Eleven Tales of the Arabesque (O 1:53). Poe's usage of *arabesque* here to mean burlesque not only strikingly confirms his conscious ambiguity in his use of the two terms, but also suggests that grotesque and arabesque together are meant to communicate a sense of overall irony.

The terms *grotesque* and *arabesque* recur again and again in his tales, and the basis of the later stories, equally as much as in the earlier stories, is some kind of ironic twist. Moreover, Poe's defense of the "Germanism" of his stories in the preface to the *Tales of the Grotesque and Arabesque* (1840) emphasizes the unity of the burlesque and the grotesque-arabesque point of view. He writes that he has written with "an eye to republication in volume form" and therefore desired "to preserve . . . a certain unity of design. . . . These many pieces are yet one book" (H 1:150). As late as 1846, three years before the end of his career, after writing about two dozen more "Gothic" tales and fourteen more comic tales, Poe notes: "In writing these Tales one by one, at long intervals, I have kept the book-unity always in mind—that is, each has been composed with reference to its effect as part of *a whole*" (O 2:328–29). It is true that Poe goes on to say that one of his chief aims "has been the widest diversity." But this diversity is within the limits of his chosen genre as he explained it in 1835: the ludicrous, grotesque, fearful, horrible, witty, burlesque, singular, and strange. "No two of these Tales," he claimed, "have the slightest resemblance one to the other either in matter or manner—still however preserving the character which I speak of" (O 1:57–58). This character, I submit, is that of Romantic Irony, as exemplified in Poe's *Tales of the Grotesque and Arabesque*.

6
The Nightside

*It is a translation . . . of an odd-looking MS. which I found,
about a year ago, tightly corked up in a jug floating in the
Mare Tenebrarum—a sea well described by the Nubian
geographer, but seldom visited, now-a-days, except by the
transcendentalists and divers for crotchets.*
          "Mellonta Tauta" (1849)

As THE NINETEENTH CENTURY wore on, Romantic writers tended to grow increasingly dark in their vision. Romantic Irony involved a recognition of the contrast between the inexplicable flux of life and vain efforts to impose pattern. It became therefore, Alan Reynolds Thompson suggests, a psychological way of avoiding spiritual self-destruction by laughing at the sources of one's own despair. (This is what I have suggested in Poe's structure of consciousness.) In Tieck's works, for example, experience constantly defeats romantic dreams, disillusion follows illusion, with sudden transitions from sentiment to self-mockery. All this was necessary if he was to maintain his mental balance, for as Tieck commented regarding his fiction, he was strangely frightened by the weird, subconscious "nightside" region he found he could tap.[1]

The compulsive literary explorations of Tieck and others, like Novalis, into the "nightside" of nature, along with Schelling's theories of the step-by-step development of inanimate nature toward animateness and conscious intelligence (compare "Usher" and *Eureka*), led to a fascination with the then apparently valid, mystical pseudosciences that arose around the end of the eighteenth century. Around 1790, for example, there loomed large in the field of natural sciences the concurrent and seemingly related investigations of gravitational attraction, acoustical vibrations, galvanic and voltaic electricity, and hypnotism. Oskar Walzel describes this activity as a

. . . movement which had had its inception approximately a generation earlier: the supplanting of the mechanistic conception of nature by the vital-istic-organic conception. . . . Mesmerism grew out of vitalism. In good faith and in accordance with his best judgment, Mesmer (1733–1815), by drawing false conclusions from perfectly correct observations, developed the doctrine of animal mesmerism. . . . The wealth of new discoveries in magnetism, elec-tricity, and galvanism, which had as yet by no means achieved summary order, opened wide the doors for false hypotheses and arbitrary analogies.[2]

Such fascination with pseudoscience was common among the German Romantics. Fichte (and Goethe) sought prototypes of life in scientific discoveries, as well as evidence in support of the psychological evolu-tion of spiritual processes. Schelling applied scientific discoveries to show the gradual assumption of consciousness in the universe, and wove a human element into nature. Novalis and Friedrich Schlegel transferred spiritual qualities to nature and tried to explain spiritual processes in terms of chemical reactions and electrical affinity. Johann Wilhelm Ritter sought the mystical bonds between nature and the human soul which were thought to exist in hypnotic sleep. Ritter and Novalis thought they had discovered a state of "involuntariness" (a "sleep-waking" state) in which the soul beholds the absolute; the con-sciousness of a human being in this state of involuntariness became a key to knowledge. Again Walzel's remarks are pertinent:

Here the line drawn from Fichte converges with the line which proceeds from the mysticism of the vitalists and from Mesmer. The marvelous results . . . expected from Novalis' "magic idealism," [and] the intensification of Fichte's "intellectual perception" to a magic power of self-enchantment and to occult control of nature . . . had their physical basis and their natural-philosophic probability . . . in animal magnetism, in hypnotic sleep . . . [and] in the involuntary "clairvoyance" of somnambulism. . . . (pp. 64–65)

From 1806 to 1830, G. H. Schubert undertook to investigate the sub-conscious seat of psychic disturbances and the mysterious phenomena of somnambulism as defining the place of man (with his "curious con-catenation of conscious and subconscious activity") on the "unstable fringe of the world of nature and reason" (Walzel, p. 245). In his *Views on the Nightside of Natural Science* (1808) and *The Symbolism of Dreams* (1814), Schubert attempted to show that phenomena inac-cessible to the waking consciousness are revealed in sleep, in dreams, in dreamlike states—an idea taken even further by Justinus Kerner (whom Poe seems to have read), in an effort to find new sources of knowledge in epilepsy, insanity, and catalepsy.

Poe, of course, reflects this interest in the subconscious and other nightside ideas extensively in his tales. As we approach this aspect of his work, however, we must put it in the context suggested by the preceding chapters and the first paragraph of this chapter. That is, these nightside materials are not only ideas—they imply a way of looking at ideas. They represent both a matter and a manner. Poe, with Tieck and the other Romantic Ironists, could work with these materials and see only in a doubling ironic mode. Thus Poe dealt with them more complexly than is usually assumed. He treated these "nightside" matters of the unconscious visionary, the sleep-waker, mesmerism, and other occult and pseudoscientific matters not just at face value, but ambiguously and ironically in his tales.

With reference to human magnetism, mesmerism, phrenology, sleep-waking, and the like, the real quality of Poe's seemingly serious advocation of the nightside may be seen as a touchstone symmetrically opposite the early tale "Metzengerstein" and the *Courier* satires with which this study began. For critics who advocate seeing Poe as a serious occultist, the most important stories besides "Usher" and "Ligeia" (and perhaps "Metzengerstein" and "The Oval Portrait") are likely to be "Eleonora," "A Tale of the Ragged Mountains," "The Facts in the Case of M. Valdemar," and "Mesmeric Revelation"—all of which deal with suspended animation or metempsychosis from one state of being to another.[3] It is principally these tales, and a few of Poe's critical comments in his letters and reviews, that we shall have reference to in this chapter in an attempt to answer the question of whether or not the same elements of mockery we have seen elsewhere manifest themselves in these nightside works. If the ironic vision is indeed integral to and coextensive with Poe's structure of consciousness, we should expect to find that ironic sensibility in these tales as well.

I

We may note, first of all, that Poe treated the occult sciences in a blatantly comic fashion too, as in "Some Words with a Mummy," in which the Egyptian nobleman, Count Allamistakeo, is resurrected (by means of the voltaic pile) in nineteenth-century America and confronted with modern invention, science, government, and culture. As the nineteenth-century gentlemen who have brought him to consciousness question him about Egyptian life, they find themselves rather hard put to find matters in which their own culture is superior; increasingly they ignore the implications of Allamistakeo's words, preferring to think him a bit addled. Finding him not quite well informed, after his long sleep, on modern advances, Mr. Silk Buckingham applies the "science" of phrenology, by "glancing slightly at the occiput and then at the sinciput of Allamistakeo." He then remarks:

"I presume . . . that we are to attribute the marked inferiority of the old Egyptians in all particulars of science, when compared with the moderns, and more especially with the Yankees, altogether to the superior solidity of the Egyptian skull."

"I confess again," replied the Count with much suavity, "that I am somewhat at a loss to comprehend you; pray, to what particulars of science do you allude?"

Here our whole party, joining voices, detailed, at great length, the assumptions of phrenology and the marvels of animal magnetism.

Having heard us to an end, the Count proceeded to relate a few anecdotes, which rendered it evident that prototypes of Gall and Spurzheim had flourished and faded in Egypt so long ago as to have been nearly forgotten, and that the manoeuvres of Mesmer were really very contemptible tricks when put in collation with the positive miracles of the Theban *savans*, who created lice and a great many other similar things.[4]

Similarly the Americans fail to triumph with questions of astronomy, optics, architecture, transportation, mechanics, steam power, metaphysics, or democracy. Regarding democracy, Count Allamistakeo observes that thirteen Egyptian provinces had tried it once but had consolidated into "the most odious and insupportable despotism that ever was heard of upon the face of the Earth," a state called "*Mob*" (H 6:136). Regarding metaphysics, the Americans present the Count with a selection from the *Dial*, the Concord transcendentalist journal. This turns out to be a "chapter or two about something which is not very clear, but which the Bostonians call the Great Movement or Progress." Of this the Count merely observes that "Great Movements were awfully common things in his day," and that the trouble with "Progress" is that it "never progressed" (H 6:136).

Finally, having failed on every count to demonstrate the superiority of nineteenth-century life, even in dress, the Americans confront Allamistakeo with "Ponnonner's lozenges" and "Brandreth's pills." At this:

The Egyptian blushed and hung down his head. Never was triumph more consummate; never was defeat borne with so ill a grace. Indeed, I could not endure the spectacle of the poor Mummy's mortification. . . .

Upon getting home I found it past four o'clock. . . . It is now ten, A.M. I have been up since seven, penning these memoranda for the benefit of my family and of mankind. The former I shall behold no more. My wife is a shrew. The truth is, I am heartily sick of this life and of the nineteenth century in general. I am convinced that every thing is going wrong. (H 6:137–38)

Surely the ironic satire of this tale should lead us to see that the "sincerity" of Poe's use of the occult sciences in his "serious" tales is questionable. That Poe did entertain the general Romantic yearnings of his times is obvious; but his attitudes are always presented as ambivalent, skeptical, detached; he uses the nightside as a maker of illusions, as a writer of fiction, as a "literary *histrio*," as he more than once characterized his kind (H 11:2).

One of Poe's most beautiful and poetic tales, according to Gothicist critics, is "Eleonora" (1841). It is also a remarkable example of Poe's purposely ambiguous treatment of Romantic interest in pseudoscience, the psychology of madness, the occult, and the sinister underside to things, and well illustrates Poe's simultaneous involvement in and detachment from the nightside. The tale seems quite serious in its opening gambit, which introduces the sleep-waking visionary who is the narrator of the tale.

I am come of a race noted for vigor of fancy and ardor of passion. Men have called me mad; but the question is not yet settled, whether madness is or is not the loftiest intelligence—whether much that is glorious—whether all that is profound—does not spring from disease of thought—from *moods* of mind exalted at the expense of the general intellect. They who dream by day are cognizant of many things which escape those who dream only by night. In their grey visions they obtain glimpses of eternity, and thrill, in awaking, to find that they have been upon the verge of the great secret. In snatches, they learn something of the wisdom which is of good, and more of the mere knowledge which is of evil. They penetrate, however rudderless or compassless, into the vast ocean of the "light ineffable" and again, like the adventurers of the Nubian geographer, "*agressi sunt mare tenebrarum, quid in eo esset exploraturi.*"[5]

To be sure, this passage has an occult, seemingly profound, and even a poetic surface; but it also is a passage likely to be quoted as an example of Poe's overdone Romanticism, with its dashes, its "ineffable," its climactic repetition, its piquant Latin phrase (which may be translated "penetrated into the Dark Sea, in which they were mere-

ly explorers"). The tale even has a Latin motto preceding this paragraph: *Sub conservatione formae specificae salva anima*: "Only in the
preservation of the specific form is the soul saved." We are set, then,
for a profound occult revelation.

In the first two-thirds of the tale, the narrator recalls the idyllic
days with his beloved Eleonora in the fantastically strange yet beautiful "Valley of the Many-Colored Grass." Yet the beauty of the valley
is suspiciously flawed, though the narrator seems not to notice. The
lovers' paradise is surrounded by precipitous mountains that shut out
the sunlight, while the winding river that circumscribes the valley in
an intricate twisting maze disappears into a shadowy gorge. To walk
anywhere requires "crushing to death . . . millions of fragrant flowers"
(H 4:237). The valley is eerily still, its river named "Silence," and its
tremulous rows of trees, reminiscent of "giant serpents of Syria," bow
undulantly in the barely perceptible wind (H 4:238). Even when a
cloud "all gorgeous in crimson and gold" (H 4:239) appears in the
sky, it gradually sinks lower and lower until it seems to imprison the
lovers (though in "grandeur," the narrator says) within the valley. It
is a setting much like that of the landscape tales we have looked at
earlier, where the overstrained mind refuses at first to see, amidst the
apparent beauty, the insinuated signs that are "prognostic of death."
Eleonora sickens, however, and the narrator rashly binds himself to a
promise not to remarry. The second part of his life he remembers as
a period of mourning, until beguiled by a second woman, the beautiful Ermengarde; he abruptly forgets Eleonora, remembering her only
when whispers out of the night tell him, as he sleeps (or sleep-wakes),
that for "reasons which shall be made known" to him "in Heaven" he
is absolved of his "vows unto Eleonora" (H 4:244).

The usual view of the tale (when it is not read as a dramatization
of Poe's love for Virginia, grief for her imminent death, and decision
to live on) is that Eleonora, with a dual personality, one melancholy,
one cheerful, returns as Ermengarde; and the husband, sensing her
return, has a dream-vision of his release from his former melancholy
vows.[6] And thus "Eleonora" is sometimes pointed to as the only tale
Poe wrote with a "happy" ending. The tale is rather more chilling and
double than this, however.

In the opening paragraph, Poe is careful to suggest the duality of
the sublime and the terrible that is possible for the sleep-explorer
lucky enough to achieve the thrilling glimpse of the great secret of
eternity. Poe then applies this double possibility, with some emphasis
on the sinister, to the veracity of the story, and begins to develop an

increasing ironic distance between the narrator and the reader. After all, the narrator in the first paragraph does tell us that he has a tendency to vigorous fancy and that he has even been regarded as mad. Indeed the rhythms and the subject matter of the paragraph are likely to suggest the rhapsody of a madman, and we have seen before, in "Ligeia" for example, with what subtle care Poe has his narrator reveal his madness in the opening paragraphs of a tale. The narrator of "Eleonora" says that (whether he is mad or not) there are "at least . . . two distinct conditions of my mental existence—the condition of a lucid reason, not to be disputed," which belongs to the first epoch of his life, and "a condition of shadow and doubt, appertaining to the present, and to the recollection of what constitutes the second great era of my being" (H 4:236–37). Obviously, a condition of shadow and doubt appertaining to his present state casts some doubt on his present memory of that past "not to be disputed" and the lucidity of his mind at that time—not to mention the efficacy of the forgiveness out of the night.

Moreover, the narrator is suspiciously emphatic as to the actuality of the earlier events. He says: ". . . what I shall tell of the earlier period, believe; and to what I may relate of the later time, give only such credit as may seem due; or doubt it altogether; or, if doubt it ye cannot, then play unto its riddle the Oedipus" (H 4:237). Poe thus sets up doubt and evokes some mystery about what has actually happened, recommending romantically and mysteriously that the reader doubt, ambivalently, the end of the tale. In a conventionally Romantic tale, this caution would serve to intensify the general indefiniteness and the actual (Romantic, transcendental, occult) truth of the metempsychosis of Eleonora into Ermengarde. But since it is put so oddly, with such emphasis on believing one part of the tale rather than the other, and with such emphasis on the uncertainty of good and evil, truth and actuality, the tale takes on an ambiguity that works against what is the final ostensibly "happy" resolution. If we believe one part of the tale, then we cannot believe the other; and if one part of what the narrator tells us is false, then how do we know how to take the other part? We are forced to consider the possibility that the narrator, half-mad, may have invented the first fantastic part about the Valley of Many-Colored Grass, with its absurdist landscape in which great Syrian serpent-plants do homage to a sun that never appears. He may have come up with the fantasy as a romantic escape from some dull reality; or he may have invented the absolving voice out of the night in order to forgive himself his lack of fidelity, or even to rationalize perhaps some deeper guilt regarding the dead Eleonora. (This is the only one of Poe's "marriage tales" in which the husband does not, apparently, somehow cause the death of the wife.)

Poe's revisions tend to support an ambiguously ironic reading of the tale. In the earlier version, the narrator says of Eleonora, "I could not but dream as I gazed, enrapt, upon her alternate moods of melancholy and mirth, that two separate souls were enshrined within her." Looking at Ermengarde, who has the same "auburn tresses" and "fantastic step" as Eleonora, the narrator says, ". . . there was a wild delirium in the love I bore her when I started to see upon her countenance the identical transition from tears to smiles that I had wondered at in the long-lost Eleonora" (H 4:314–15). Hardin Craig speculates that Poe took out both these passages in order to reduce obviousness and to experiment with "the indefinite," which Poe considered a major quality of Romantic poetry. But by reducing the narrator's identification of Ermengarde with Eleonora, Poe makes more reasonable the separate identities of the two women and strengthens his presentation of the real point of the tale: the narrator, fanciful and half-mad, has imposed his vigorous fancy on the flux of his idiosyncratic "reality." The clinching point is Poe's Latin motto to the story: "The safety of the soul lies in the preservation of the specific form." If Eleonora is now Ermengarde, the specific form has been violated. The sense of the motto, along with the narrator's remarks on his madness, confirms the delusiveness of the entire experience as he renders it.

Moreover, Poe twice remarks with approval, in a review and in a *Marginalia* note, upon De La Motte Fouqué's conviction in *Undine* that "the *mere death* of a beloved wife does not imply a final separation so complete as to justify an union with another!" (H 10:36; 16:49). "Eleonora" is ostensibly in the Gothic, sentimental Romantic mode and seems to suggest a weird, supernatural, but ideal love that endures beyond apparent earthly death. But the story may also be read as a dramatic presentation, within the context of Romantic materials, of the human mind refusing to see the sinister implication within the illusory, idyllic world of its own imagining, and then shifting the object of its passion and rationalizing its guilt—unless we are prepared to claim that Poe was a sincere believer in metempsychosis and sleep-waking revelations, and that the ambiguities of the tale are merely Poe's characteristic "flaws."

Contemporaneous proof of Poe's ambivalent skepticism concerning such occult matters is to be found in his *Marginalia* comment on a book on human magnetism by William Newnham. As remarked earlier, Poe here objects to Newnham's circular logic and points out the subjectivity of human belief: "That the belief in ghosts, or in a Deity, or in a future state, or in anything else credible or incredible—that any such belief is universal, demonstrates nothing more than . . . the identity of construction in the human brain . . ." (H 16:115; cf. 12:121–23). Further, Poe's final attitude toward mesmerism, magnetism, and the like is, like his initial one, sarcastically skeptical. In *Eureka* he wrote that although men have felt that there is some principle ordering the universe, something beyond the law of gravity, no one has really pointed out the particulars of such a principle, "if we except, perhaps, occasional fantastic efforts at referring it to Magnetism, or Mesmerism, or Swedenborgianism, or Transcendentalism, or some other equally delicious *ism* of the same species, and invariably patronized by one and the same species of people" (H 16:223).

II

Further use of occult dream-states, and of other occult materials, is found in "A Tale of the Ragged Mountains" (1844) which, significantly, makes specific reference to the German Romanticist Novalis, who not only entertained occult speculation of dream states but who also incorporated the theories of the Schlegels on irony into his aesthetics.[7] To a large extent, "Ragged Mountains" epitomizes Poe's fascination with but detached attitudes toward the pseudoscientific occultism of his age. The story ostensibly involves metempsychosis and supernatural revelation in a half-conscious sleep-state, though (as we should expect) Poe climaxed the tale with a disturbingly unsatisfactory gimmick. Indeed, "A Tale of the Ragged Mountains" (1844) is without doubt one of the least satisfying and most gimmicky of Poe's Gothic works if one takes it as straightforward, for Poe climaxes the story with the jarringly absurd device of having his narrator convinced by the accidental misspelling of a name that he has been a witness to metempsychosis, to sleep-waking revelation, to weird time displacement, and to the supernatural workings of a malignant fate. But Poe makes his narrator an unwitting dupe who misperceives the entire situation he has observed and who leads the unwitting reader to believe that his surface recounting of the circumstances of the death-dream of Mr. Augustus Bedloe comprises the whole of the story. "Ragged Mountains" is another of those tales in which, as Poe himself said, he wove a web for the purpose of unravelling (O 2:283). Poe carefully planted a number of clues to the real action of the story— only there is no Dupin to point them out. If, however, the reader will take the trouble to look for these ironic clues, he will find that under the supernatural tale lies, first, a "scientific" explanation of the apparently supernatural events, which leads, second, to a very different "psychological" explanation of the events, and, third, to an insinuated burlesque (under the whole structure of explanations) of a Gothic novel by Charles Brockden Brown.

There are only three main characters in Poe's tale: Bedloe, who suffers from a general degenerative neuralgic condition and is seeking help through mesmerism; Dr. Templeton, a practicing hypnotist; and an observing narrator. Bedloe one day goes out for a long walk; returning late, he tells Templeton and the narrator of having fallen into a realistic dreamlike state in which he felt himself transported to a distant place where he was surrounded by enemies. Bedloe pauses in his story to assure the narrator and Templeton that his experience had "nothing of the unmistakeable idiosyncrasy of the dream" but was "rigorously self-consistent" (H 5:170). Moreover, Bedloe says that "Novalis errs not in saying that 'we are near waking when we dream that we dream.' Had the vision occurred to me as I describe it, without my suspecting it as a dream, then a dream it might absolutely have been, but, occurring as it did, and suspected and tested as it was, I am forced to class it among other phenomena" (H 5:171). Bedloe's next sentence is then anticipated by Templeton. Although Bedloe is astonished, he continues telling the tale up to the point where he is killed by a poisoned arrow that strikes him in the right temple. The narrator suggests then that the "death" proves the experience to have been a dream, for here Bedloe is, alive. Templeton, however, is horrified and insists on hearing more. Bedloe tells him how he viewed his own corpse and then with unearthly lightness had "flitted" back to the Virginia mountains where he had been walking. Templeton then produces a miniature of his friend "Oldeb," points out the resemblance to Bedloe, and tells the tale of Oldeb's death nearly fifty years before. Oldeb had been killed in India by a poisoned arrow under the circumstances experienced by Bedloe; moreover, Templeton had been writing of these events this very afternoon. A week later, at the height of a fever brought on by his walk in the Ragged Mountains, Bedloe dies from the doctor's accidental application of a poisonous leech to his temple. At the end of the story, when the narrator complains that an *e* has been dropped from Bedloe's name in an obituary notice, it strikes him that this spelling is Oldeb reversed!

The tale on the surface seems to involve a combination of hypnosis, sleep-waking, and metempsychosis. But by placing the tale in its nineteenth-century context and reading it carefully, Sidney E. Lind in an article on "Poe and Mesmerism" has shown that "Ragged Mountains" (along with other Poe tales) is not a realistically handled tale of the supernatural, but is instead a psychological tale based on the possibilities of occult science—"a case study in mesmerism," as he says.[8] Poe actually uses only the "science" of mesmerism while, deceptively, suggesting supernatural events so forcibly that we tend at first to accept them and to mistake the real nature of the story. But Poe clearly emphasizes mesmerism in the opening portion of the tale; Templeton can put Bedloe into a hypnotic trance quite easily, "by mere volition" and over a distance, standard mesmeric procedure, according to Lind. Then Poe carefully makes clear that Templeton first became interested in Bedloe when he noticed a "miraculous similarity" to his friend Oldeb; subsequently, Templeton developed an "uneasy, and not altogether horrorless curiosity" about Bedloe (H 5:174). When Bedloe expresses his doubt that his experience in the mountains has been only a dream, Templeton agrees, "with an air of deep solemnity," and hints mysteriously that "the soul of the man of to-day is upon the verge of some stupendous psychal discoveries."

Templeton, therefore, is a believer in ghostly experiences, specifically in metempsychosis, and he has been preoccupied during his relationship with Bedloe with the idea that behind the likenesses of Bedloe and Oldeb there lurks, as Lind says, some deep and perhaps terrible significance; and as he listens to Bedloe's story he sits "erect and rigid in his chair," his teeth chattering and his eyes "starting from their sockets" (H 5:173). But although Bedloe often walked in the mountains, his experience occurred only on the day that Templeton was writing his recollections of Oldeb; this coincidence and Poe's early emphasizing of mesmerism clearly imply that the sympathetic and subdued will of Bedloe received the strongly emotional thoughts of Templeton through involuntary mesmeric transference and that he experienced them as a dreamlike actuality. But to Templeton, as Lind says, the experience is "a sudden and shocking revelation and confirmation of that in which he has hitherto half-believed—the actuality of metempsychosis." For Templeton, Oldeb's soul lives in Bedloe.

Lind leaves the matter here, essentially, reading the tale as an ambiguous but simple hoax, in which all the characters are duped, first Templeton, then Bedloe, and then the narrator, into believing the apparent metempsychosis. The reader, too, is duped or hoaxed if he misses the clues and takes the "psychological" tale as a supernatural one. There is, however, along with the absurd shattering of effect when the narrator is convinced by the typographical error, another major insinuated irony of plot. Lind argues that the tale would have been better constructed if Poe had made the credulous Templeton rather than the narrator mutter to himself at the end that *Oldeb* is the converse of *Bedloe*; but I think Poe had a slightly different point in mind. Templeton's "not altogether horrorless" fascination with Bedloe's resemblance to Oldeb, his uneasy "sentiment of horror" that causes him to keep it a secret, his teeth-chattering horror as he listens to Bedloe's tale, and his claim that he had tried to prevent the death of Oldeb are all ambiguous enough to provide one more psychological turn of the screw: horrified by Oldeb's "return," Templeton may have psychotically rekilled him in the person of Bedloe. (There is also an ambiguous financial arrangement between Bedloe and Templeton, enabling Templeton to give up his practice, thus providing an additional psychological twist to the real action of the tale.) An absurd corroboration, though less absurd than the typographical error and the backward spelling of Bedloe's name, is to be found in Templeton's name, for Oldeb is struck in the *temple* by a poison arrow, and Bedloe is poisoned by a leech attached to his *temple* by *Temple*ton. The submerged pun (which Lind notes also) I take to be a mocking challenge to the reader to see the further intricacies of the story: it links both the supernatural dream and Bedloe's death to the hypnotist. However, the pun suggests another, absurd but corroborating, pun: Templeton is like a leech on the wealthy Bedloe.

Further support for the "murder" of Bedloe is provided by the newspaper account:

. . . it appeared that, in the jar containing the leeches, had been introduced, by accident, one of the venomous vermicular sangsues which are now and then found in the neighboring ponds. This creature fastened itself upon a small artery in the right temple. Its close resemblance to the medicinal leech caused the mistake to be overlooked until too late.

N.B. The poisonous sangsue of Charlottesville may always be distinguished from the medicinal leech by its blackness, and especially by its writhing or vermicular motions, which very nearly resemble those of a snake. (H 5:176)

In the ostensibly Romantic and supernatural atmosphere of the tale, the serpentlike motions and blackness of the poison leech mysteriously correspond with the "writhing" Indian arrow, made in imitation of a creeping serpent, long and black and tipped with a poison barb, that struck Oldeb in the temple. But the account also contains a sign in capital letters asking the reader to mark well the fact that the poisonous leech may always be distinguished from the medicinal, a distinction we might well expect the physician to have been aware of.

Thus, Poe carefully planned the conclusion for ironic double effect:

for absurd Romantic corroboration of the supernatural and for absurd ironic corroboration of murder. If Templeton has murdered Bedloe, it is a far more effective gambit for Poe to have the narrator, rather than Templeton, conclude the tale as he does. The narrator, at first the only skeptic, is duped horribly and absurdly—as we are if we have not perceived the ironic distance Poe has interposed between his observing narrator and us.

Finally, there is one additional twisting that supports the hoaxing, half-bantering, half-satiric mood of the tale. Boyd Carter has pointed out that Poe seems to have borrowed a number of details in "Ragged Mountains" from Charles Brockden Brown's *Edgar Huntly* (1799).[9] Carter takes these "borrowings" seriously, even trying to exonerate Poe from the charge of plagiarism, but there is just enough distortion in Poe's twisting of *Edgar Huntly* to suggest a burlesque similar to his burlesque of Byron and Moore in "The Assignation."

The parallels between the two works do not form an allegorical pattern; but the general similarity is obvious, and two direct, though slightly askew, echoes in Poe's tale confirm, I think, a general burlesque intent. Of general similarities, Carter notes that: (1) Poe's Bedloe and Brown's Huntly and Clithero walk (or sleep-walk) in a mountain wilderness; (2) Poe's Templeton and Brown's Huntly are both preoccupied with the same problem, a friend murdered by Indians; (3) Poe's Templeton of Saratoga and Brown's Sarsefield are both physicians, have both been in Benares, where both had narrow escapes, and both have a soldier friend killed in India; (4) Poe's Bedloe, in his dream-experience, arms himself with the weapons of a fallen officer and engages in unequal combat, just as Brown's Huntly does; (5) Brown's Clithero speculates on the possibility of metempsychosis and thought transference, the apparent subjects of Poe's tale; (6) the real subject of *Edgar Huntly* is not the occult but murder, and Clithero, who has murdered a man in England, is attracted to the scene of Waldgrave's murder in America because of a "distant resemblance which the death of this man bore to that of which I was the perpetrator"—a parallel to Templeton's fascination with Bedloe's resemblance to the murdered Oldeb.[10]

In addition to these parallels, Carter notes that the descriptions of the setting and the incidents involve many similarities: the walks, the steep passes, the winding trails, the desolate solitude into which both Huntly and Bedloe penetrate with the feeling that each is the first civilized adventurer to do so, the majestic river, the fog, and the great precipice. Regarding the aborigines in both stories, Carter writes that "Poe's fierce inhabitants of the groves and caves of the Ragged Mountains all stem conceivably from Edgar Huntly's experiences with Clithero, panthers, and Indians in the Norwalk region." But Carter then makes this significant observation: the parallel characterization, description, and incidents in Poe's "Ragged Mountains"

. . . seem irrelevant to the story. Their introduction tends to divert attention from the themes of hypnosis, telepathy, and metempsychosis which apparently represent the author's principal preoccupation. . . . There is little in common between the oriental setting of Oldeb's murder and the Ragged Mountains. . . . *Why then does Poe fill up nearly one third of his story with descriptions and incidents which do not provide . . . even a convincing transition for Bedloe from the waking to hypnotic state?* (p. 195; my italics)

Carter's answer is that "the explanation probably lies in the fascination Brown's *Edgar Huntly* had for Poe." But the more satisfactory answer is that Poe was burlesquing, even parodying, *Edgar Huntly.*

As I have said, two rather direct echoes support such a reading. First, the solution to Waldgrave's murder in Brown's novel has a comic parallel in Poe's story: In *Edgar Huntly* an Indian woman named *Old Deb* provides the solution to Waldgrave's murder, and of course the name *Oldeb* provides the "solution" for the narrator in Poe's tale.[11] Second, one of the paralleled passages from *Edgar Huntly* involves Indians and Huntly's encounter with a panther. Poe emphasizes Bedloe's surprise at hearing a drum, in his "Indian" dream-experience, for "a drum in these hills was a thing unknown"; the sound of the drum is followed by "a rattling or jingling sound" as a half-naked man runs by him with a stick of steel rings (H 5:168). This scene, Carter points out, is "a corollary" to American Indians going to war in *Edgar Huntly.* Then Poe closes the passage with Bedloe's confrontation with a fierce beast—an indirect parallel with the famous panther scenes in *Edgar Huntly*—only Poe neatly, subtly, twists the point: ". . . panting after him, with open mouth and glaring eyes, there darted a huge beast. I could not be mistaken in its character. It was a hyena" (H 5: 168). The hyena, of course, as an eater of dead flesh, is an appropriate dream-symbol for Bedloe to see since he is a fated man. But the carrion-eater would seem appropriate also as a symbol of Poe's grotesquerie of a dead novel. Moreover, Poe's substitution of *hyena* for *panther* (actually an appropriation of a scene from Macaulay's 1841 review of G. R. Gleig's *Memoirs of the Life of Warren Hastings*) has yet another relevancy in the punning, hoaxing, burlesque atmosphere of the tale, for the voice of the hyena is well known for its resemblance to hysterical laughter.

III

The occult metaphysics of "Mesmeric Revelation" (1844) seems to be Poe's first formal presentation of the philosophy of *Eureka*, while at the same time the stylized rhapsody and logical gaps of the tale clearly show why serious critics like Woodberry call the philosophic Poe "his own dupe," and why modern critics so dislike Poe's "Romantic" style. But Poe here as everywhere else is not quite completely serious.[12]

The fictional frame for the philosophical dialog that forms the main part of the tale involves two characters, a hypnotist (P.) who puts Mr. Vankirk, a dying man in the last stages of consumption, into a mesmeric sleep in order to discuss the immortality of the soul. The rationale for this experiment is that deep mesmeric sleep closely resembles the "phenomena" of death, and the sleep-waker "perceives, with keenly refined perception . . . matters beyond the scope of the physical organs . . . moreover, his intellectual faculties are wonderfully exalted and invigorated . . ." (H 5:241). In this deep sleep Vankirk tells P. about the real nature of the universe until "with a bright smile irradiating all his features" he falls back upon his pillow and expires. His corpse then "had all the stern rigidity of stone" and "his brow was of the coldness of ice," suggesting phenomena of death that appear only after one has been dead for some time. The tale ends with the ostensibly unambiguous question (which if answered positively, from internal evidence, would "prove" the supernatural metaphysics of the tale): "Had the sleep-waker, indeed, during the latter portion of his discourse, been addressing me from out the region of the shadows?" (H 5:254).

Vankirk's revelations sound, on the surface, rapturously profound, but if we look at what he says very closely, and note some of the exchanges between him and P., Vankirk's unexplained assumptions, circular logic, metaphysical jargon, and mystic-poetic epigrams, paradoxes, and oxymorons begin to look suspiciously like a parody of occult metaphysics.[13] Typical of Vankirk's answers to P.'s questions is his paradox, "Your objection is answered with an ease which is nearly in the ratio of its apparent unanswerability," which is immediately followed by a dismissal of a difficulty by putting another paradox: "As regards the progress of the star [through the ether of space], it can make no difference whether the star passes through the ether *or the ether through it*" (H 5:248).

Vankirk's revelation begins with what would have been by Poe's time a conventionally topsy-turvy contention that the essence of the universe is matter. According to Vankirk, matter extends in "gradations" increasing in "rarity or fineness, until we arrive at a matter *unparticled*—without particles—indivisible—*one*. . . . This matter is God" (H 5:245–46). P. wonders if "in this identification of mere matter with God" there is "nothing of irreverence." Vankirk replies that there is no reason that "matter should be less reverenced than mind." God, it seems, is the "perfection of matter"; thought is "matter in motion"; motion is thought; thought in the "universal mind" of God creates material things; God's thoughts create "new individualities"—for which "*matter* is necessary" (H 5:246–49).

P., a bit confused, initiates a comic exchange by objecting that Vankirk now speaks of "mind" and "matter" "as do the metaphysicians." "To avoid confusion," Vankirk replies. He then explains that "mind, existing unincorporate" is "merely" God. God created "individual, thinking beings" and thus had to "incarnate portions" of his mind. "Thus man is individualized. Divested of corporate investiture, he were God."

P., to make sure he has heard right, asks if Vankirk has said "that divested of the body man will be God." Vankirk, "after much hesitation," replies, "I could not have said this; it is an absurdity." But P. refers to his notes. Vankirk then suggests that: ". . . man thus divested *would be* God—would be unindividualized. But he can never be thus divested—at least never *will be*—else we must imagine an action of God returning upon itself—a purposeless and futile action" (H 5:249). P. is again confused. Vankirk explains that man has: ". . . two bodies—the rudimental and the complete; corresponding with the two conditions of the worm and the butterfly. What we call 'death,' is but the painful metamorphosis. . . . The ultimate life is the full design" (H 5:250). We are not normally aware that this is the cycle of human existence, argues Vankirk, because: ". . . our rudimental organs are adapted to the matter of which is formed the rudimental body; but not to that of which the ultimate is composed . . . we perceive only the shell which falls, in decaying, from the inner form . . . but *this inner form as well as the shell, is appreciable by those who have already acquired the ultimate life*" (H 5:250; my italics).

This last statement is especially important since, as Vankirk's explanations get more rapturous and wild, he contradicts himself on this very point, which is supposed to provide a rationale for man's earthly existence. Vankirk explains that throughout the universe there is an "infinity" of "rudimental thinking beings" other than man, and that the "multitudinous conglomeration" of "rare matter" into "nebulae, planets, suns, and others" which are (naturally) "neither nebulae, suns, nor planets" is merely to supply "*pabulum*" for "an infinity of rudimental beings" (H 5:252). Thus, the stars that earthly man looks at with interest are not at all important; instead, what is truly important is the "substantive" space that "swallows up" the "star-shadows," "blotting them out as non-entities from the perception of angels" (H 5:252). Vankirk seems not to notice that if the rudimental material of the stars is, as he says, blotted out from the perception of the angels, then the "full design" of the two-body system of existence is violated (much as the "specific form" of Eleonora is violated) since both the "inner form" and "the shell" are supposed to be appreciable by the angelic beings now in their ultimate bodies.

Vankirk's dialog ends here in the earlier version of the tale, and he dies ecstatically (H 5:326). Apparently thinking that the tale was too ambiguous in this form, however, Poe in the later version inserted a long paragraph in which he has Vankirk repeat his self-contradiction and add a further rationale for earthly existence that becomes perhaps the major irony of the tale. P. does not ask Vankirk about his contradictory statement (perhaps he does not yet perceive it, for P. is the involved narrator-mesmerist of the tale). Instead, he wonders what the *"necessity"* of all this complex "rudimental" evolution into the "ultimate" could possibly be. Vankirk answers that "organic life and matter" were "contrived" with the "view of producing impediment." P., naturally enough, wonders why impediment was needed.

Vankirk's answer is roundabout: the "result of law inviolate is perfection—right—negative happiness"; but the "result of law violate is imperfection, wrong, positive pain"; through the "impediments afforded" by the "number, complexity, and substantiality" of matter, the "violation of law" is rendered "practicable" and thus pain is possible (H 5:253). P. then points out that Vankirk has still not told him what the point of all this complexity, impediment, and pain is. Vankirk answers that "all things are either good or bad by comparison," that pleasure "is but the contrast of pain. Positive pleasure is a mere idea." We must suffer in order to know bliss; and since in the inorganic, ultimate life we do not suffer, we have first to suffer the pain of organic life (Vankirk is dying from consumption) so that we shall know that we are experiencing "the bliss of the ultimate life in Heaven"; pain is "the sole basis" of bliss (H 5:253).

After this melancholy explanation of earthly life, which is painfully relevant to Vankirk's own condition, P. returns to the point on which Vankirk has contradicted himself, the "substantive vastness" of space and the unimportance (imperceptibleness) of the stars to the angelic beings. Vankirk's second rhapsody on the immaterial materiality of space begins with another blatant paradox. Infinity is substantive,

Vankirk says, because substance is a *"sentiment"* (H 5:253). He has an explanation for this paradox, however: substance is the "perception, in thinking beings, of the adaptation of matter to their organization." To "inorganic beings—to the angels—the whole of unparticled matter is substance . . . the whole of what we term 'space,' is to them truest substantiality." Just as we do not see the apparently immaterial material of the universe, angels do not see such material as the stars; it escapes "the angelic sense." Having thus unconsciously confirmed the purposeless creation of sentient beings and having characterized all human feeling as only "negative pleasure" and "positive pain," the mystic sleep-waker dies—the perception of the "full design" of the universe "irradiating his features" in a "bright smile."

Poe's revision a year later, in which he inserted Vankirk's long, melancholy recontradiction just before his beatific death, subtly emphasizes the irony and parody basic to this "philosophical" dialog. But there is also a good deal of external evidence for Poe's irony. One of Poe's favorite critical pastimes was the debunking of attempts at rhetorical persuasion through mere "epigrammatism," equivocation on words, and circular logic, as we have seen in his comments on William Newnham's *Human Magnetism.* "Mesmeric Revelation" begins with just such logic, and with an ironic clue. "Whatever doubt may still envelop the *rationale* of mesmerism, its startling *facts* are now almost universally admitted. Of these latter, those who doubt, are your mere doubters by profession—an unprofitable and disreputable tribe" (H 5:241). The "facts" of the tale are, of course, that Vankirk attained a state between life and death through mesmerism and thus proved the rationale of mesmerism and the mystic-metaphysics therein revealed. But in the *Marginalia* Poe gleefully complains about English commentaries and reprintings of "Mesmeric Revelation" and the significantly titled "The Facts in the Case of M. Valdemar." *The Popular Record of Modern Science* had claimed that the revelations in these tales bore *"internal evidence of authenticity!"* Poe's comment on the circular logic of this internal "evidence" (especially in "Valdemar," to be discussed momentarily) is sarcastic: ". . . all this rigmarole is what people call testing a thing by 'internal evidence.' The *Record* insists upon the truth of the story because of certain facts. . . . To be sure! The story is proved by these facts. . . . And now all we have to do is to prove these facts. Ah!—*they* are proved by the story."[14]

We have seen also that in *Eureka* the rationale of mesmerism is, for Poe, but a "delicious *ism*" of a certain "species" of people. In the middle of 1844 Poe is supposed to have attended lectures on "mesmerism, transcendental theories, and psychic phenomena" given in

New York by Andrew Jackson Davis, "a noted spiritualist and clair-voyant of that day."[15] Davis, in *The Magic Staff* (1857), wrote of a visit from Poe during which they discussed "Mesmeric Revelation." Davis had assured Poe that although Poe ". . . had poetically imag-ined the whole of his published article upon the answers of a clair-voyant, the main ideas conveyed by it concerning 'ultimates' were strictly and philosophically true. At the close of this interview he de-parted, and never came again" (p. 317). But Poe in No. 11 of "Fifty Suggestions" wrote of the "Poughkeepsie Clairvoyant": "There surely can*not* be 'more things in Heaven and Earth than are dreamt of' (oh, Andrew Jackson Davis!) 'in *your* philosophy'" (H 14:173). Moreover, to "Mellonta Tauta" (1849), a satire on logic, on culture, and on American concepts of progress (in great part adapted from a section of *Eureka*), Poe added a notation to the editors of *Godey's Lady's Book* (in which the tale appeared). He wrote that the article, which "I hope you will be able to comprehend rather more distinctly than I do myself," was (parodying a similar reference in "Eleonora"):

. . . a translation, by my friend Martin Van Buren Mavis, (sometimes called the "Toughkeepsie Seer") of an odd-looking MS. which I found, about a year ago, tightly corked up in a jug floating in the *Mare Tenebrarum*—a sea well described by the Nubian geographer, but seldom visited now-a-days, except for the transcendentalists and divers for crotchets.[16]

Perhaps the most direct external corroboration of Poe's ironic skepti-cism regarding the whole business of "Mesmeric Revelation" is pro-vided by his gleefully sarcastic response to being taken seriously by the occult mystics in general. In the *Marginalia* he wrote:

The Swedenborgians inform me that they have discovered all that I said in a magazine article, entitled "Mesmeric Revelation," to be absolutely true, although at first they were very strongly inclined to doubt my veracity—a thing which, in that particular instance, I never dreamed of not doubting myself. The story is a pure fiction from beginning to end. (H 16:71)

IV

In "The Facts in the Case of M. Valdemar" (1845) Poe explored, in a sense, the "opposite" possibilities of mesmerism and death-sleep, carry-ing the nightside writings of Justinus Kerner to an extremity of horror that yet suggests a comic grotesquerie, a weird combination of harmoniously blended contradictions.[17] M. Valdemar, like Vankirk, dying of consumption, agrees to summon the narrator when he knows that he is near death. In this instance, the narrator is supposed to arrest the "encroachments of Death" through mesmerism. The experiment is ambiguously successful, and Valdemar is suspended in a state of life-in-death sleep. When the narrator tries to communicate with him at the end of a seven-month period, Valdemar cries out in anguish, asking either to be put back into a deeper trance or to be "awakened" into final death (a piquant paradox). The narrator brings him out of the trance and watches with horror as Valdemar's body immediately crumbles and rots away into "a nearly liquid mass of loathsome—of detestable putridity" (H 6:166). Thus, even if "Mesmeric Revelation" is not read as a parody on the beatitudes of the psychal mystics, we are still faced with an apparent about-face on Poe's part the very next year in the horror of "Valdemar." Such a twist of apparent intent and belief, however, is characteristic of Poe's Romantic Irony.

One of the prominent features of "Valdemar" is its apparent verisimilitude, which caused the tale to be taken for a time as fact in both England and America. Poe describes the arrested death of Valdemar in grisly detail. As he slips into a deep trance, Valdemar's eyes roll upward to leave only the staring whites, his cadaverous skin takes on the hue of thin white paper, his upper lip writhes away from his teeth, his lower jaw falls with an audible jerk and locks, leaving the mouth widely extended and exhibiting a swollen and blackened tongue. From these gaping, motionless jaws comes (with a faint quiver of the swollen tongue) the harsh, broken, distantly hollow (as from a cavern deep in the earth), somehow "gelatinous" yet still distinct voice of Valdemar, claiming that he has died (H 6:160–63). Later, when Valdemar awakes, his rapid disintegration into a liquid mass on the bed is signaled by a yellow, pungent fluid issuing from his eyes (H 6:165).

Yet such horror has, nevertheless, touches of the comic, illustrative, presumably, of what Poe meant by the "ludicrous heightened into the grotesque." At the beginning of the tale, we are told that Valdemar is: ". . . particularly noticeable for the extreme spareness of his person— his lower limbs much resembling those of John Randolph; and, also, for the whiteness of his whiskers, in violent contrast to the blackness of his hair—the latter in consequence, being very generally mistaken for a wig" (H 6:155). Moreover, Valdemar is described as the "well-known compiler of the 'Bibliotheca Forensica,' and author (under the *nom de plume* of Issachar Marx) of the Polish versions of 'Wallenstein' and 'Gargantua'" (H 6:155). The exact point of the apparently satiric references to Randolph, Schiller, and Rabelais is a bit ambiguous. But to have labored like Issachar, described as an ass bowed down between two burdens (Gen. 49:14), in translating on the one hand Schiller's heroic play and on the other Rabelais's burlesque prose epic, and to have startling white whiskers in violent contrast to black hair, certainly suggest some kind of not completely serious symbolic doubleness.[18] Again, Poe is indulging in the hoaxer's jest, combining the comic with effective and apparently realistic grisly details—details which, if examined, are absurd.

Medical jargon, especially, serves Poe's double purpose of suggesting the real while actually writing absurdity. "The left lung had been for eighteen months in a semi-osseous or cartilaginous state, and was, of course, entirely useless for all purposes of vitality" (H 6:157). All but the lower half of the "right lobe" also exhibits this ossified state; and the small portion left is full of "extensive perforations" and has undergone "permanent adhesion to the ribs"; in fact, the whole of the functioning region of the right lung "was merely a mass of purulent tubercles, running one into another" (H 6:157). In addition to these difficulties, Valdemar apparently has "aneurism of the aorta," although the "osseous symptoms rendered an exact diagnosis impossible" (H 6:157). Not only has Poe's narrator given us an impossibly exact diagnosis of internal tissues in a still-living being, he has also made an impossible condition sound almost plausible: three-quarters of Valdemar's lungs has turned to bone, the other quarter (on which Valdemar relies for "purposes of vitality") is a mass of pus, adhesions, and holes —and he has a fatal aneurism. Despite this rather extreme condition, despite the fact that he has been given twenty-four hours to live, despite his ghastly appearance (his face "leaden" hued, his eyes "lustreless," the paperish skin of his face "broken through by the cheekbones," his "emaciation extreme," his "expectoration excessive," his "pulse barely perceptible"), Valdemar, when the narrator arrives, is sitting up in bed writing and conversing (H 6:157). Later (after Mr. L——l, a medical student, has swooned upon hearing the vibrating tongue quivering in the gaping jaws of Valdemar, and has been revived by several nurses), the narrator allows a grotesque pun (reminiscent of the Egyptian mummy's "mortification") to escape him as he shifts Valdemar's position on the bed in an attempt to "recompose" his patient, who momentarily begins to decompose.

Aside from the contrast between the horror of "Valdemar" and the "radiant" joy of almost the same situation in "Mesmeric Revelation," Poe's several comments about the two tales also put "Valdemar" into ironic perspective. We have already seen Poe's gleeful repudiation in the claim of the *Popular Record of Modern Science* that the two tales bore "internal evidence of authenticity!" In the same note, Poe also commented on the disbelief of the *Morning Post*. In insisting that the details of Valdemar's consumption are incredible and reveal the writer's ignorance, the *Post*, Poe said, missed the point of his verisimilitude, and displayed its own ignorance of pathology. Such symptoms, Poe continued, are plausible in the story and are based on actual diseases. Poe then pointed out that he had to "put an extreme case" lest the reader suspect that the victim survived without the help of the mesmerist.[19] Although by itself Poe's last comment is inconclusive, it does suggest Poe's awareness of multiple and deceptive meaning. In two letters, however, the point is clearer. Writing to Evert Duyckinck (March 8, 1849), Poe said that he thought the reason so many people believed in the reality of "Valdemar" was indeed the apparent "verisimilitude" of the tale (O 2:433). Moreover, Poe wrote, under the apparent verisimilitude of his Valdemar "hoax," there lay, as in Defoe, "a tone of banter." (This comment is surely reminiscent of A. W. Schlegel on verisimilitude in the "mixed" genre of the seriocomic.) In a letter replying to a query from one Arch Ramsay (December 30, 1846), Poe wrote: " 'Hoax' *is* precisely the word suited to M. Valdemar's case. The article was generally copied in England and is now circulating in France. Some few persons believe it—but *I* do not—and don't you" (O 2:337). Poe's skeptical attitude toward the nightside, despite his obsessive fascination with it, could hardly be clearer.

V

Human magnetism, mesmerism, metempsychosis, sleep-waking, electrical phenomena, spontaneous combustion, and the like figured prominently in the supernatural and horrifying tales of German, English, and American fiction writers in the late eighteenth and early nineteenth centuries and were staple elements in the pages of the influential *Blackwood's Edinburgh Magazine*. Reviewing the German literature at the end of the eighteenth century, Oskar Walzel remarks that the common trait of the flood of Gothic (as opposed to grotesque) tales of chivalry, robber knights, ghosts, and general horror is the entanglement of defenseless characters with an incomprehensible supernatural power. This is how Gothicist critics, who insist that a nineteenth-century tale, because it is weird, must be a supernatural tale and nothing else, would have us read Poe. But to read a Romantic Ironist this way is to miss half the point, and nearly all the fun. For the German Romantic Ironists, in contrast to more regular Romanticists and Gothicists, used these materials, as did Poe, for double effect, half-mocking and half-serious, to develop the theme of the deceptiveness of appearances. Writers like Tieck, von Arnim, Brentano, E. T. A. Hoffmann, and Jean Paul Friedrich Richter took from Kantian philosophy the central idea of the limitations of human sense perceptions and used the weird and terrifying aspects of "nature" and mental aberration ambiguously to suggest both a transcendental world beyond human ken and the invariable deceptiveness of any human perception or thought, especially since the human mind is readily subject to emotional stress. Although regular Gothic tales frequently made use of misperception, the grotesque tales of the Romantic Ironists normally were concerned with a weirder sensory deception, with some deeper psychological subjectivity. While they touched a deep level of irrational fear, they also gave rise to a high level of philosophical perception of the absurd. Tieck and Hoffmann especially showed the supernatural to be subjective inner experience—irrational fear welling up from a subconscious, timeless abyss of guilt and superstition.

This brings us, for a final point of reference, to a writer we have barely mentioned in connection with the nightside or Romantic Irony, Jean Paul Friedrich Richter, whose name is thoroughly associated with both. Jean Paul's comments on his own writing provide yet another dimension for approaching Poe's tales. Jean Paul has been taken as illustrative of one extreme of German nightside "depth-psychology," especially the development of the Romantic idea of myth into a conception of the subconscious archetype. Meyer H. Abrams writes: "Richter, building on earlier suggestions of the chaos, the darkness, and the mysterious depths in the creative mind, develops the nightside of the unconscious . . . in his writings we find ourselves half way from Leibniz to that later inheritor of the depth-psychology of German romanticism, Carl Jung."[20] Jean Paul, according to Abrams, clearly foreshadowed Jung's theories about man's collective unconscious and archetypal experience when he wrote of the unconscious realm of the mind as an "abyss" of which "we can hope to fix the existence, not the depth," and which "has a presentiment of . . . objects . . . beyond the reaches of time." This well of unconscious activity contains, says Abrams, "the common origins of dreams, the sense of terror and guilt, demonology, and myth." Although this realm of the subconscious and archetypal has many forms and names, its essential qualities are double, the terrifying and the sublime. Jean Paul wrote: "At one time it shows itself to men deeply involved in guilt . . . as a being before whose presence . . . we are terrified; this feeling we call the fear of ghosts. . . . Again the spirit shows itself as The Infinite, and man prays."[21]

More than one critic has intimated, as we have seen, that Poe pro-

jected from his subconscious mind the archetypal terrors of the race
and probably did not have full conscious artistic awareness of what
he had done. By this interpretation the ludicrous elements of Poe's
"tawdry" Gothic style are proof of his incomplete awareness and control. But it should be clear by now that such a view, if valid in one
dimension, is a distortion in another: it underestimates Poe's awareness of the literary ideas of his times, and also misconstrues the principal aim of Poe's kind of "serious" Romantic fiction, which is to explore,
ambivalently, the irrational sources of man's terror and despair in order to master them (as Fichte suggested) through a doubled vision,
through humor and irony.

Jean Paul's word, as mentioned in the preceding chapter, was *humor*
("annihilating" and "satanic") rather than *irony*. "Humor," according
to Jean Paul, is the "Romantic comic," the "sublime in reverse"; and
rational statements alone, without the simultaneous comic sense of the
irrational, are one-sided. "Annihilating" or "satanic" humor is in effect
both objective and subjective. On a grand scale, the comic is "intuited
infinite Unreason." More narrowly, the subjective element of comedy
lies in the contrast between the stupidity of the comic action and the
good sense of the spectator who lends or projects upon a comic character his own sense of incongruity. This neatly describes the reader-
character-author relationship we have seen in Poe. As Jean Paul puts
it, the objective element in the comic is our freedom of choice between
our own insight, and that of the comic figure, and that aspect of insight that we lend to the comic figure in his situation. The mind toys,
says Jean Paul, with various possibilities, plays, and dances in "freedom," and "genius" is the ability to harmonize contradictions and even
to "annihilate" them. Jean Paul's theory of comic contrasts in Chapter
IV of his *Introduction to Aesthetics* (1804, revised 1813) influenced
Hazlitt (whom Poe read) in his essay on "Wit and Humour" in the
Lectures on the Comic Writers (1819) and is perhaps indirectly the
source of Poe's definitions of fancy, imagination, humor, and fantasy.[22]
Moreover, like Schlegel, Jean Paul intruded songs and dreamlike or
absurd narrative intermezzos into his fiction, as Poe does for similar
reasons in tales like "Usher." Such practice was aimed at producing a
harmonious double effect of following "steam baths of emotion" with
"cold showers of satire."[23]

Reference to Jean Paul also brings us to yet one more aspect of the
nightside in Romantic literature, the recurrent figure of the "double"
or *Doppelgänger*. Insisting on a philosophical awareness of the doubleness of existence (especially the two extremes of the mind, conscious reflection and mysterious subconscious impulses), Jean Paul

made weirdly humorous use of the *Doppelgänger* to suggest a split, dissociated ego, one part usually acting, the other part observing, again a typical situation in Poe's fiction. Jean Paul's characters become terrified of their images in mirrors, or they meet their doubles on the street, or they compulsively make their own wax likenesses. Looking at his body, one of his characters remarks, "Somebody is sitting there and I am in him. Who is that?"[24] The artist himself also should have a sense of doubleness. "In my consciousness," Jean Paul wrote, "it is always as if I were doubled; as if there were two I's in me. Within I hear myself talking."[25] This sense of doubleness, of acting and observing or being observed, is like Tieck's irony in his early plays; and, as in Tieck, there is also a further doubleness: on the one hand there is something sinister and destructive about the feeling, and on the other hand it is absurd and laughable, and may be productive of "freedom." The motif of the double, or seeming double, thus has as its primary aim a suggested confrontation of the mind with itself, as we have seen in "Ligeia" and "Usher."

This has yet a further extension particularly relevant to reading Poe either as a craftsman or as a self-indulgent Romanticist. Jean Paul, echoing Friedrich Schlegel's concept of *Selbstparodie*, offers definitions of the artist's role in the production of "annihilating humor" that provide a further context for what has seemed to the Gothicist critics of Poe a particularly problematic idiosyncrasy. Poe has often been criticized for his sometimes startling intrusions of apparently autobiographical elements into a number of his wilder tales (like the date of William Wilson's birth and his name and the place of his education; or like the cousin-wife and her mother in "Eleonora"; or like the supposed similarity of the portrait of Usher to Poe's own face; not to mention the ever-present "I" of the tales). But the Romantic-Ironic point of such a technique is made clear in Article 34 of Jean Paul's *Aesthetics*:

. . . I divide my ego into two factors, the finite and the infinite, and I make the latter confront the former. People laugh at that, for they say, "Impossible! That is much too absurd!" To be sure! Hence in the humorist the ego plays the lead; *wherever possible he brings upon his comic stage his personal conditions, but only to annihilate them poetically.* For he is himself his own fool and the comic quartet of Italian masks, himself the manager and director. . . .[26]

Thus, through self-parody, annihilating humor, and doubleness, one can achieve freedom from the depressing conditions of earthly existence. Through humor man can look tolerantly at the whimsy and the horror, the eccentricity and the madness of the world with a self-preserving laughter "wherein is sorrow and greatness."[27] Jean Paul's concept of humor is essentially the same as Schlegel's concept of irony: the largest and freest view of the paradoxical and sinister world. And we may recall here that Friedrich Schlegel wrote of Jean Paul's "grotesques" that they were "the only romantic products of this unromantic age."

Thus, the thrust of the philosophy, the criticism, and the literature of German Romanticism was, for a while, toward an ultimate harmony involving a unification of opposites, an annihilation of apparent contradictions and earthly limitations, and a merging of the subjective human personality and objective rational understanding into a penetrating view of existence from the height of the ideal—but always with an eye to the terrors of an ultimately incomprehensible, disconnected, absurd, probably decaying, and possibly malevolent universe. The only attainable harmony out of all this deceptiveness and chaos was a double vision, a double awareness, a double emotion, culminating in an ambivalent joy of stoical self-possession—in irony. Irony thus becomes a double-edged pessimism and skepticism engendered by the self-awareness of the subjective human mind reaching out toward an illusive certainty. It is hard therefore to see comedy entering into Poe's writings by way of "hysteria," as previous critics have suggested, for humor, mockery, and irony were rationally planned elements in much of the best-known writing of the time. The comic rationale of Romantic literature had as its aim transcendence of self and self-generated fears through intellectual mastery of self. And comedy enters into Poe's "Gothic" writings not so much by way of hysteria as by way of a controlled, and therefore skeptical, philosophical despair.

7
Romantic Skepticism

It is laughable to observe how easily any system of
Philosophy can be proved false:—but then is it not mournful
to perceive the impossibility of even fancying any particular
system to be true? . . . only the philosophical lynxeye . . .
can discern the dignity of Man.
Marginalia (1849)

THE WHOLE of Poe's Gothic fiction can be read not only as an ambivalent parody of the world of Gothic horror tales, but also as an extended grotesquerie of the human condition. Nothing quite works out for his heroes, even though they sometimes make superhuman efforts, and even though they are occasionally rescued from their predicaments. They undergo extended series of ironic reverses in fictional structures so ironically twisted that the form itself, even the very plot, approaches an absurd hoax perpetrated on the characters. The universe created in Poe's fiction is one in which the human mind tries vainly to perceive order and meaning. The universe is deceptive; its basic mode seems almost to be a constant shifting of appearances; reality is a flux variously interpreted, or even created, by the individual human mind. In its deceptiveness, the universe of Poe's Gothic fiction seems not so much malevolent as mocking or "perverse." The universe is much like a gigantic hoax that God has played on man, an idea which is the major undercurrent of Poe's essay on the universe, *Eureka*.

Indeed, it is not too extravagant to claim that the basic structuring force of *Eureka* is an elaborate conceit on "nothing." In searching for the key to unlock the secrets that lie just beyond appearances, the "Poe" persona finds (just as do the characters in Poe's tales) that the great discovery is of nothingness, of illusion only. Thus, the hoaxlike irony of Poe's technique has its parallel in the dramatic world in which his characters move and in the overall philosophical vision that structures at every level all of Poe's fiction.

The ultimate irony of this universe, however, is the "perversity" of man's own mind. The mind, and the mind only, seems to sustain Poe's heroes in their most desperate predicaments; yet in an instant the mind is capable of slipping into confusion, hysteria, madness—even while it seems most rational. From a more Gothicist point of view, Edward H. Davidson, without using the term *irony*, and without reading Poe's Gothic tales ironically or satirically, comes to much the same conclusion regarding Poe's universe. "Poe's nightmare universe," Davidson writes, "is one in which . . . people . . . are condemned to live as if they are in some long after-time of belief and morality." The evildoer is driven by "some maggot in the brain" that leaves him a kind of "moral freak" in a universe that also has some fantastic defect in it. In Poe's universe, Davidson suggests, evil and suffering are "the capacity and measure of man to feel and to know"; pain is the basis of life, and death is the only release from his "grotesque condition of 'perversity.'"[1]

Poe's fiction developed from a basically satiric mode into an ironic mode in which a tragic response to the perversities of fortune and to the treacheries of one's own mind is contrasted by a near-comic perception of the absurdity of man's condition in the universe. Such a double perception, we have seen in Romantic theory, leads, through art, to a momentary transcendence of the dark chaos of the universe. If the artist (and through him the reader) can mock man's absurd condition at the same time that he feels it deeply, he transcends earthly or finite limits in an artistic paralleling of God's infinite perception. In Poe, however, such transcendence is always at the expense of the less perceptive mind. Poe plays a constant intellectual game with his readers; he tries to draw the reader into the "Gothic" world of the mind, but he is ready at any moment to mock the simplistic Gothic vision (under the trappings of which Poe saw man's real estrangement and isolation) that contemporary readers insisted on in the popular magazines.

In this concluding chapter, a brief chronological survey of Poe's Gothic works will help to suggest the basic ironic structures and tensions in each tale, with specific reference to the themes of perversity and nothingness as illustrative of the pervasiveness of the Romantic-Ironic consciousness in Poe. Three final works then will be examined in detail as touchstones of Poe's Romantic-Ironic skepticism. These are the novel *The Narrative of Arthur Gordon Pym* (1837–38), the tale "The Colloquy of Monos and Una" (1841), and the prose cosmogony

Eureka (1848), each of which critics have often placed at the "center" of Poe's philosophical vision.[2]

I

Under the Gothic surface of supernaturalism, Poe's major ironic themes of the perverse deceptiveness of experience, the propensity of the mind to abandon reason, the perverse impulse to act against oneself, and the absurdity of existence in a universe that does not provide for individual survival, appear with a remarkable consistency from his first "Gothic" tale in 1832 to his last in 1849. We have already seen that "Metzengerstein" (1832), which Poe intended to be a satiric parody of the supernatural horror tale, became his first Gothic hoax when his readers took the tale seriously. Its extended series of plot ironies, its caricatured fifteen-year-old Gothic villain, its dunderheaded Gothic narrator, and its melodramatic style all interweave to form a clear satiric pattern that mocks the few scenes of effective horror that Poe intrudes, as it were, into the satire. Moreover, the working out of an ominous prophecy is comically parodied by a confused curse, which also works out, ironically, in every detail, so that the plot as a whole becomes a kind of cosmic hoax, augmented by man's perverse propensity to act against his own best interests.

Poe's second "Gothic" tale, "MS. Found in a Bottle" (1833), on the surface a supernatural adventure story, not only parodies its literary type through blatant absurdities (such as the narrator's dabbing desultorily at a sail with a tarbrush only to discover that he has spelled out DISCOVERY) but also through the development of an ironic distance between narrator and reader that mocks the narrator's supercilious conception of his unshakable rationality.[3] At the beginning of the tale, the narrator, in a crisp and fact-filled style, insists on his unemotional and rational character. On a simple "Gothic" level, this emphasis seems to confirm the reality of the supernatural events to follow. But Poe immediately subjects his narrator to a terrifying storm; and in contrast to the stoicism of an old sailor whom he contemptuously calls "superstitious," the narrator himself becomes increasingly frenzied, and his style of narration highly cadenced and emotional. The machinations of fortune ironically preserve him from death at the very moment of apparent destruction by throwing him high into the air and into the rigging of a gigantic phantom ship, which we subsequently learn has been growing in the South Seas water like a living thing. The rest of the tale, in which the phantom ship with its silent statuelike crew sails into an opening at the pole and goes "down," is rendered with an atmosphere of dreaminess that, combined with the narrator's proven untrustworthiness, suggests that the incredible events are the delusions of a man driven mad. Seen as a voyage of "discovery," the ludicrous "supernatural" events act as a grotesquerie of the discovery of what lies beyond the normal world or beyond death, for the tale abruptly ends at the very verge of revelation in apparent final destruction and silence. Just as Arthur Gordon Pym journeys toward the great discovery of what lies "beyond" only to find the white blankness of nothingness, so the caricatured narrator of "MS. Found in a Bottle" discovers nothing. A further ironic twist is provided by the French motto to the tale, which insinuates that the narrator is a liar.

In "The Assignation" (1834), we have seen that it is the perverse fortune of the laughing and crying Byronic stranger to become united with his beloved only in death. The tale has seemed to most critics one of Poe's most intensely "Romantic" productions. But under its Romantic surface is presented a coded satiric allegory of burlesque parallels and contrasts to events in Lord Byron's life so that the tale is both a Romantic tale of dark passion and a burlesque of the genre. In "Berenice" (1835), another "serious" tale of compulsion which actually lampoons its literary type, it is the absurd obsession of the narrator with Berenice's teeth which leads to his grief, an obsession resulting from a temper of mind engendered by his grotesque birth and rearing. It has been his perverse misfortune to have been both born and brought up in a library, and thus he has become totally imbued with the Gothic horrors and weird philosophical (transcendental) mysticism of the day.[4] The major insinuated irony of the ostensibly supernatural "Morella" (1835) again lies in the suggested madness of the narrator, who, in a moment of perversity, names his daughter after her hated mother. Although the narrator tells us that through this error he had made it possible for the first Morella's spirit to take over the body of the second, Poe provides motive enough and ambiguity enough to suggest that the narrator may have murdered them both. External data surrounding the tale is especially suggestive. T. O. Mabbott writes that Poe probably got the name from some such current account as "Women Celebrated in Spain for the Extraordinary Powers of Mind," which appeared in *Godey's Lady's Book* in September 1834, a year before Poe's tale. Poe, he suggests, must have read of the great learning of Juliana Morella. But the important point is the corroboration of the psychological reading given by the fact that Juliana Morella's father left Spain because he was charged with homicide.[5]

"Shadow" (1835) and "Silence" (1837), under their mystic and "poetic" (and flawed) surfaces, in substance and style seem to be parodies of pseudopoetic transcendental fictions, especially those of Bulwer-Lytton, De Quincey, and the "psychological autobiographists" (Disraeli's *Contarini Fleming* was at first subtitled *A Psychological Auto-Biography*) indicated in Poe's subtitle to "Silence." "Shadow," after developing a sense of the finality of death, concludes with an ironic turn in which the chilling immortality of the "shadows" of the narrator's friends is revealed to him, though, since he and his companions are dead drunk, it is hard to tell how truly revealing the transcendental sleep-waking revelation is. "Silence" develops the theme of a deceptive and illusory world, with shrieking water lilies, lowing hippopotami, graven rocks whose letters change. At the end, a Demon laughs hysterically at a confused human being, while a lynx stares steadily at the Demon's face. That the lynx is a symbol of the ironic vision peering unflinchingly into the face of perversity is corroborated by Poe's lynx metaphor in *Marginalia*. Poe writes in *Marginalia*: "It is only the philosophical lynxeye that, through the indignity-mist of Man's life, can still discern the dignity of Man."[6] These, then, are the "Gothic" tales, published in the *Southern Literary Messenger* from 1835 to 1837, that Poe intended to include in the burlesque Folio Club series, tales he considered to be of a "bizarre and generally whimsical character" (O 1:103).

Between 1838 and 1840, the middle years of his career, Poe published, along with the *Narrative of Arthur Gordon Pym*, three of his most famous Gothic tales (as well as several counterpointed comic ones). "Ligeia" (1838), as we have seen, is only ostensibly a serious supernatural tale of metempsychosis; it can also be read as the story of the ambiguous delusions of a guilt-ridden madman who has probably murdered at least one wife and has hallucinated a weird rationalization of his crimes. "The Fall of the House of Usher" (1839), we have seen, is, despite the supernatural atmosphere, actually the tale of the frenzied fantasies of both the narrator and Usher, fantasies engendered by a vague fear that something ominous *may* happen and by the disconnected, weird environment. "William Wilson" (1839), though lacking the complexity of "Ligeia" and "Usher," exhibits Poe's continuing use not only of the double but also of double perspective. Although apparently a straight Romantic tale of a man's confrontation, supernaturally, with his own soul, the tale can be read as the delusive but perversely persistent confrontation of a guilt-ridden mind with itself. Whether the second Wilson, twin of the narrator, exists as a supernatural spirit or as a construct of the mind of the narrator remains ambiguous, as in other Poe tales, though the clues for a double reading are carefully planted. Again, the world that we perceive as readers is what is filtered through the subjective mind of the narrator, and it is this structure, along with some absurdist motifs (such as the precise timing of the second Wilson's entrances and his recurrent whisper), that gives rise to the dramatic irony of the tale. Certainly, if the second Wilson is the product of the imagination of the first Wilson, the first Wilson's behavior must seem to his companions, if not comic, very peculiar indeed. Ultimately, of course, the tale is a dramatization of the ultimate perversity of self-vexation and destruction; and the final emptiness of the mirror into which Wilson is left staring is a symbol of the illusory nothingness on the other side of appearances.[7] Each of these tales involves doubles and dramatizes a distorted universe as perceived by a totally subjective mind.

Of Poe's remaining fiction, nearly half (nineteen short tales of forty-two) are clearly comic; the twenty-three ostensibly Gothic and "philosophical" works, along with *Pym,* further extend the central theme of the subjective deceptiveness of the world in terms of nothingness and the perverse. "The Man of the Crowd" (1840), on the surface a tale about a lonely city wanderer who is weirdly suggestive of what Hawthorne called the Outcast of the Universe (in his own dark comedy, "Wakefield"), may be read also as the deluded romanticizing of the tipsy narrator, who perversely attributes a Romantic significance to an old drunk who wanders from bistro to bistro. Especially suggestive are the clues in the opening paragraphs and the misapplication of a quotation at the conclusion. The young man, after an entire night of following the old man from one crowded place to another, says that the old man is like the old German book which mysteriously would not "allow" itself to be read. T. O. Mabbott points out that it could not be read because it was so badly printed; thus, the allusion is a comic clue to the mocking irony under the Gothic surface. Mabbott also suggests parallels with two of Dickens's sketches by Boz, "Drunkard's Death" and "Gin Shops." A motif of clouded vision and smoky windows further suggests that in seeing the old man through the lens of the narrator, we are seeing "through a glass darkly."[8] We have seen that "Eleonora" (1841), ostensibly a story of metempsychosis, also suggests the Romantic imagination shifting the object of its passion or perhaps rationalizing a deep guilt; and we have seen that "The Oval Portrait" (1842), apparently a supernatural tale about the actual transfer of life from a living person to a painting, is also the delirious dream of a drug addict.

In "A Descent into the Maelström" (1841), Poe emphasizes the traditional Western themes of transcendence from a petty involvement with "self" to submission to a larger "design" of nature. Giving up all sense of mere individual importance, the narrator feels a positive wish to see what lies at the bottom of the whirlpool. Although he survives (probably by mere accident rather than by his careful observation of and submission to nature, since the mechanics of the hydraulic effect on geometric forms is false), his incomplete confrontation with nothingness at the center of the whirlpool (a "manifestation of God's power") yet turns his hair prematurely white. Thus the tale ironically inverts traditional Western belief: the narrator's mystical experience of the magnificence of God is one of horror rather than of beatitude. The design of the terrifying violence of the natural world (see the motto from Glanvill) becomes an object of contemplation, much as in "The Pit and the Pendulum," and, similarly, involves a contrapuntal mental regression and progression from the rational to the hysterical and then absurdly back again to the rational without cause. His new rational state, however, is forever, as in so many of Poe's tales, hovering on the edge of madness. At the point of apparent destruction, an ambiguous revelation of "pattern" reverses the narrator's mode of thought from the emotional to the rational; but he is plagued ever afterward by the "mystery" of the whirlpool, which becomes his monomaniacal obsession.[9]

"The Pit and the Pendulum" (1842) itself is one of Poe's clearest dramatizations of the futile efforts of man's will to survive the malevolent perversity of the world and to make order out of chaos. The tale has sometimes been read as the escape from madness through a descent into madness. Although the hero is mentally tortured until he confesses to himself that "all is madness" and that his mind has been "nearly annihilated," he learns to rely on primal cunning and an instinctive sense of danger. Under the razor-edge of the pendulum, he recovers his ratiocinative power: "For the first time during many hours —or perhaps days—I *thought*" (H 5:81). But the narrator thinks of his avoidance of the pit as "the merest of accidents, and I knew that surprise, or entrapment into torment, formed an important portion of all the grotesquerie of these dungeon deaths" (H 5:79). Under the pendulum he becomes "frantically mad" and strains to force himself against the slowly descending blade. The irony, the grotesquerie of human dignity and rationality, here lies in the narrator's ultimately futile efforts to change his basic condition. He cannot hurry destruction and thus avoid the torment allotted to him. His mind suffers another radical shock and hysterically shifts to an opposite mode, moving toward the rational only because of his helplessness in madness. Then, escaping from the pendulum, he is, ironically, again faced with the pit. The walls become heated, and for "a wild moment" the narrator's mind "refused to comprehend," although at length he says "it burned itself in upon my shuddering reason" (H 5:85). Thinking of the cooling waters of the pit he rushes to its edge, only to stop short, again in horror of such a death. Then as the walls begin to close in, he realizes that he had been destined by his tormentors for the pit in the first place (H 5:86) and that all his luck, all his cunning, and all his regained rationality have, ironically, trapped him into self-torment and increased his agony. The final irony comes with the sudden cessation of the movement of the walls, a rescue from outside that comes unexpectedly, independently, unconnected with his own personal fate at the last moment of his despair and defeat.[10] We shall have further reference to these two works momentarily.

"The Tell-Tale Heart" (1843), a study in obsessive paranoia, is yet another story of the mind watching itself disintegrate under the stress of delusion in an alienated world. It is the perverse fortune of the narrator to become fearful of the grotesque eye of a kindly old man, whom he says he loves. With a double perversity, he gives himself away to the police at the moment of success. Yet the narrator is caught in a weird world in which he loves the old man yet displays no real emotion toward him, in which he cannot let the "beloved" old man live and yet cannot kill him without remorse, in which he cannot expose his crime and yet must do so. The most blatant absurdist irony is that the apparent beating of his own heart which he mistakes, first, as the beating of the still-living heart of the old man, and which, second, seems to be an emblem of his own guilt (and which, finally, compels him to confess), may very well be initially the peculiar thumping of the wood beetles gnawing at the walls.[11] "The Black Cat" (1843) carries the same themes further and details more clearly the irrational desire, almost the ultimate irony, to act against oneself, with an ambiguous conclusion suggesting the agency of malevolent fortune at the same time that it suggests subconscious self-punishment. The major absurdist irony is similar to that of "The Tell-Tale Heart": the murder the narrator commits is the result of subconscious remorse over the cat he has previously mistreated and thus ultimately the device of his self-torture.[12] "A Tale of the Ragged Mountains" (1844), we have seen, is ostensibly a story of metempsychosis, but it is more probably a murder story in which all the characters (and possibly the murderer) are duped regarding the reality of events; and "The Premature Burial" (1844), though comically concluded, leaves us seriously entertaining the ghastly possibilities of an absurd situation.

One of Poe's less successful Gothic tales also fits this pattern of ironic mockery and perversity. "The Oblong Box" (1844), after a series of weird circumstances, concludes grotesquely with a commonplace explanation that is both absurd and upsetting. An artist brings aboard a ship a large, oddshaped box that contains, apparently, his paintings, but he is so vague and so melancholy in his replies to queries from the other passengers about the contents of the box that he and his wife become the center of quizzical and mildly malevolent gossip. His wife becomes the object of ridicule, because of her excessive chattiness, which strikingly contrasts with the excessive gloominess of the artist. The narrator conceives the idea that the artist is playing a pleasant joke on the passengers and in a bantering mood begins to insinuate to him that he knows what is in the box. But the artist reacts to his "witticisms" like a madman, laughing hysterically until he collapses. When the passengers are forced to abandon the ship in a storm, the artist insists that the oblong box be taken with them in the longboat. When the captain refuses, the artist lashes himself to the box and sinks with it into the sea. The captain gloomily comments that they will recover the box when the salt melts, thus mystifying everyone the more. Later the captain explains that the artist's wife had died; and, knowing the "superstitions" of the passengers, he and the artist had conveyed her corpse, packed in salt, aboard as merchandise. The woman's maid then acted the part of the artist's wife in order to forestall any suspicions about her absence and the presence of the box. But the deception ironically produced the unfortunate harassment of the artist, apparently driving him over the edge of madness. The grotesque effect of the whole tale is summed up in the final paragraph. The narrator concludes by saying: "My own mistakes arose, naturally enough, through too careless, too inquisitive, and too impulsive a temperament. But of late, it is a rare thing that I sleep soundly at night. . . . There is an hysterical laugh which will forever ring within my ears" (H 5:289).

Poe's vision of the perverse becomes codified in "The Imp of the Perverse" (1845), seemingly more an essay than a tale. It is another dark comedy of errors which clearly spells out Poe's fundamental conception that it is man's fate to act against his own best interests. But the dissertation on perversity has its dramatic irony, for the "rationality" of the narrator merely enmeshes him deeper in anxiety as he absurdly, helplessly, uses his imaginative intellect to will his own destruction by means of a mere whimsical thought. Having committed murder he reflects that he is "safe"—unless, of course, he be fool enough to confess. This foolish fancy immediately seizes him and he rushes out to confess his crime to passersby in the street. The recurrent confessional structure of other of Poe's tales is operative here too, for the narrator has apparently confessed to a priest in his cell the night

before his impending execution. In an attempt to explain his obsession with the possibilitiy that some "imp" in the structure of the universe has victimized him, the narrator succeeds in convincing us not
of his rationality but of his irrationality. The long prologue in its
"circumlocution" does not directly make his point but instead seems
to obscure the more direct and succinct conclusion. But the point of
this circumlocutious inventiveness becomes clear when the narrator
finally reveals to us his anxiety about his execution; his imagination
immediately foresees additional possibilities for perverse speculation:
in death he will be free of his physical chains and his cell—but what
new torments yet await him, he wonders, in what afterlife?[13]

We have seen that "Valdemar" (1845), ostensibly a serious Gothic
tale of the horror of prolonging life beyond the proper point of death,
not only is a "verisimilitudinous" hoax, but also contains absurd and
comic details suggesting satiric parody and mocking irony. Finally,
after Valdemar's "life" has been preserved by modern "technology" (in
this case, mesmerism), the last horrible details suggest the real, grisly
finality of death. "The Cask of Amontillado" (1846), on the surface
a tale of successful and remorseless revenge, we have seen to be
Montresor's deathbed confession, to an implied listener, of a crime
that has tortured him for fifty years. At the conclusion of the tale,
the apparently remorseless Montresor recounts the sudden sickening
of heart he felt at the end "—on account of the dampness of the cata-
combs," he hastily supplies. But, ironically his "revenge," as Montresor
himself defines it, has failed on every count. Two other darker tales
of the late forties have similar undercurrents of mockery. "The Sphinx"
(1846), comes quickly to a comic conclusion after a frightening and
weird but absurdly deceptive vision of a monster that turns out to be
a bug dangling only a fraction of an inch from the eye. "Hop-Frog"
(1849) is a compellingly ludicrous tale of horrible revenge told almost
sweetly in a fairy-tale style, at the conclusion of which the dwarf declares to the burning king and his ministers that their death is but his
last "jest."

Poe's six ratiocinative tales of the 1840s represent the few successes
of the acute mind in overcoming the bewildering deceptiveness of the
perverse world. Five of the tales are ostensibly serious ("Murders in
the Rue Morgue," "Marie Rogêt," "The Purloined Letter," "Gold-Bug,"
"Descent into the Maelström") and one is comic and suggests self-
parody ("'Thou Art the Man'"). The Dupin kind of mentality as-
sumes a godlike omniscience; the narrative "I" and the reader, the role
of dull-witted dupes. The major ironies of these tales are consistent
with Poe's more clearly Gothic tales: their basis is the discrepancy

between appearance and actuality; and the ease of Dupin's solutions contrasts with our mystification, as in the extravagant train of association in "Murders in The Rue Morgue" whereby Dupin guesses what his friend is thinking, or as in the absurdly simple irony in "The Purloined Letter" of hiding an object in plain sight where no one would think of looking for it. In "The Gold-Bug" we have yet another twist, for Legrand's ratiocination has nothing whatever to do with the final discovery of the treasure; instead a series of improbabilities and accidents lead to it, including such sardonic touches as having the weather-stained map specifically written in a water-soluble ink, pointing the telescope at the North Star instead of at the proper place on the cliff (if one checks the degree of angle carefully), and decoding a code riddled with errors in coding. Moreover, a coded allegorical burlesque of the alchemical tradition is interwoven with the main narrative so that it becomes, like "Von Kempelen and His Discovery" (1849), a satiric hoax aimed at men's dreams of getting rich quick, paralleling Poe's mockery of the landscape artists who sought to create the Earthly Paradise.[14]

The four poetic landscapes, "Island of the Fay" (1844), "Landscape Garden" (1842). "The Domain of Arnheim" (1847), and "Landor's Cottage" (1849), as we have already noted, ostensibly deal with the natural beauty God has created in the world but insinuate the melancholy facts of death, imperfection, purposelessness in contrast to man's futile imagining of an ideal state of harmony and beauty. Four philosophical dialogs, with and among bodiless spirits, "Monos and Una" (1841), "Mesmeric Revelation" (1844), "The Power of Words" (1845), and "Eiros and Charmion" (1839), deal with the philosophic problem of the artistic creation, projection, or imagining of the universe, which *Eureka* shows to be incomprehensible, death-ridden, and absurd in the limited perception of man. "Mesmeric Revelation," we have seen, is even a parody of occult metaphysics in its own terms. Each follows the same structural pattern of asserting some mystical meaning inherent in existence while quietly undercutting the assertion.

Poe's concept of the perverse functioning as both a world view and a psychology is, then, perhaps the ultimate grotesquerie to be found in his Gothic fiction. Poe's characters live in a cosmos where there are few certainties beyond that of individual annihilation. Indeed, in *Eureka*, Poe takes as his basic axiom the idea that the germ of "inevitable annihilation" is implicit in the original cause of existence. In a deceptive universe that does not provide for individual immortality, Poe's heroes and heroines struggle vainly to find order and to preserve their lives. Yet they are at the same time perversely fascinated with death as the ultimate fact of existence, and they yearn for knowledge of the secret that lies beyond death. But in Poe's universe, there is nothing beyond death, nothing beyond this life.

In a sense, the true horror, the true Gothic quality, of Poe's tales lies in their substantive irony, for Poe's tales are more than ironic in mode, more than supercilious hoaxes perpetrated on the unsuspecting devotees of the Gothic romance, though such mockery certainly looms large. The insinuated burlesque, the ironic modes of language, and the ironic themes merge with ironies of plot and characterization in the creation of an absurd universe. Poe's characters move in a world in which events are often disconnected and in which meaning is opaque. Although clear possibilities for "opposite" meanings are indicated to the perceptive reader, they are, for the most part, denied the characters.

If the reader is perceptive enough not to be taken quite all the way into the "subterrene night," he can achieve the same kind of sweeping and detached insight as that possessed by the "creator" of this fictional universe. The perceptive reader can, through a subjective involvement with the difficulties of the perverse creatures inhabiting the flawed and perverse universe, achieve an objectivity toward the perverse condition of man. This kind of ambivalent self-division and even self-parody is, of course, the philosophical irony of the German Romanticists—a sweeping, transcendental sense of the perverse duplicity of all things—and Poe's ironic rendering of the existential hoax that the perverse universe presents can be conclusively illustrated through three final works.

II

Certainly *The Narrative of Arthur Gordon Pym* (1837–38) is a clear example of the world view of the Romantic Ironist. The unifying theme of what seems to be a merely episodic narrative is the experience of the inner mind, the Romantic-Ironic theme of man's futile attempts to see through the deceptive illusoriness of the world and to discover the primal facts of existence and of the self. A perverse fate, augmented by man's own treachery and perverseness, repeatedly overtakes the characters in a series of plot ironies which progressively reveals that the assumed consistency and reality of the world are capable at any time of immediate disintegration.[15] Moreover, *Pym* is filled with comic exaggerations in the midst of a superabundance of prosaic facts about sailing, geography, and marine life. As always, Poe calcu-

lates his effects so as to deceive the reader at first and then to insinuate that he has been duped regarding the reality of events, and, in
fact, regarding the true action of the story.

The affinities of *Pym* with the techniques of Romantic Irony are
perhaps more obvious (though no deeper) than in any other story Poe
wrote, because they are on such a basic, indeed simple, level. Despite
the hoaxlike verisimilitude of the details, Poe ironically emphasizes
the fictionality of *Pym* while seeming to claim an "actuality," a "factual" truth for it. Harry Levin notes, for example, that the world of
Pym is, in the largest sense, a symbolic projection of the artist's mind
subjected to self-scrutiny, a theme signalled by Poe's introduction of
his hero as a man from "Edgar-town." [16] Moreover, the narrative is
prefaced by Arthur Gordon Pym's exposé of Edgar Allan Poe's fiction-
alizing of what were Pym's "true-life" adventures. Pym says in the
preface that he now offers the true narrative of what really happened,
though he professes to be content with Poe's rendering of the first part
of the adventure. Pym is, moreover, quite certain that the reader will
have no difficulty in perceiving, through the differences between
"Poe's" style and his own, where fiction leaves off and actuality begins
(H 3:2–3). In addition to these ironic frames, the narrative is concluded with an appendix (apparently the "publisher's") in which we
are informed that Pym's recent disappearance has prevented him from
telling the final truth about what happened and that "Poe," the original editor, has failed to see the true significance of the narrative (H
3:243–44). The Romantic-Ironic frames could hardly be clearer.

In the narrative itself, the plot, augmented and corroborated by
deception and perversity in the characters, moves through a symmetrical series of repeated ironies so extended that the perversity of
ironical fortune, as variously misperceived by man, becomes integral
to the central themes of man's futile quests for stable order and of his
discovery of the ultimate secret of existence. The easiest way to see
the extent of the deceptive quality of the perverse universe in *Pym* is
simply to note the sequence of ironical turns in fortune and the counterpoint, in the characters, of deception, treachery, and mutiny against
order or design. Perhaps no other story Poe wrote is so saturated with
ironic reversals of events.

In the first of the three principal episodes, two boyhood friends,
Pym and Augustus Barnard, slip out for a forbidden nighttime sail;
but the harmless sail on the calm sea ironically turns into a nightmare:
the boys drink too much, lose control of their boat, and are almost
capsized in a sudden storm. Then a ship bears down on them, seemingly determined to cut them in two, but at the last instant turns to

miss them. It sails away from them for a time, apparently abandoning them to the hostile elements. But at the moment of their greatest despair, the ship unexpectedly turns again and sends out a rescue party. Pym learns, however, that the mate had to threaten the captain with mutiny before he would put about. This first, very short, episode contains in small the themes and the types of the events that appear in the second episode. Deceptions, drunkenly erratic behavior, a sudden storm, a shipwreck, passing ships that promise rescue but bring only increased despair, and mutinies recur in the second part with a more intense sense of the perverse treacheries of man and the ironic twistings of an almost malevolent fortune.

In the second episode, Pym and Augustus decide to seek adventure on a real sailing ship, but to do so they must again deceive their families. Ironically, however, at the moment of apparently triumphant escape from parental control, they meet Pym's grandfather as they are about to board a ship called the *Grampus*. Pym manages to deceive his grandfather, however, by impersonating a drunken sailor, and the old man goes away convinced that appearances are indeed deceiving. Augustus is a member of the crew of the *Grampus*, but Pym must practice another deception. He stows away in an iron box in the hold to await the new freedom that will be his when Augustus can release him. But the perverse twistings of fortune transform Pym's hiding place into a prison, for the crew of the *Grampus* mutinies and imprisons Augustus.

Trapped in the hold, Pym becomes delirious under the influence of the foul air, the darkness, the lack of food and water, and the sense of confinement. He becomes increasingly subject to weird and terrifying dreams of death and burial alive. Unaccountably, his faithful dog, Tiger, appears in the dark hold. A double treachery occurs when the good dog, as though sensing the hungry Pym's treacherous thoughts, attacks him savagely. Pym manages to fight him off, however, and later the dog disappears as mysteriously as he appeared. During this period of hallucinatory imprisonment, Pym sinks into ever deeper despair as his rational mind fails again and again to conceive of a way of escape. Ironically, however, Pym for a long time never suspects that his apparent rationality has been distorted and decayed by the extremity of his predicament.

The clearest example of Pym's mental state is his discovery of a note that he is sure is from Augustus. Because of the darkness he cannot read it. The irony of his situation is obvious: he seems to hold the means of his escape in his hand, but cannot make use of it. Then his mind ingeniously devises a method of producing light; he rubs between his fingers some phosphoric dust that he has found in the hold. The feeble glow is enough to enable him to see the note. But there is nothing written on it. At this point the perverse fates of the universe seem to have mocked not only his predicament but also his almost superrational efforts to escape from it. But another, absurdist, irony is to come. Much later, it occurs to Pym that there are two sides to a piece of paper and that he has looked at only one. At this point Pym remarks that he found his "intellect . . . in a condition nearly bordering on idiocy" (H 3:38). Then at the deepest point of his despair, rescue ironically is made imminent through a series of mutinies above decks that shifts the newly established order of command.

Augustus's imprisonment by the original mutineers seems to make Pym's predicament hopeless; but, ironically, through Augustus's imprisonment the secretly imprisoned Pym escapes violent death; and eventually Pym's original deception, since he is not known to be aboard, leads to his escape through yet another overthrow of "established" order. The original mutineers find themselves in the ironic position of fending off a second "mutiny." But just as the second group of mutineers, under the leadership of Dirk Peters, seems about to wrest control of the ship from the "loyal" members of the first group, Peters is deserted by his followers in another perverse shift of loyalties. Peters then recruits Augustus to his side, and through him, Pym. Pym immediately decides to try another deception; he plans to work upon the "superstitions" of the leader of the original mutineers, the mate of the original crew. Pym's sudden emergence from the hold in the guise of the ghost of a man the mate has killed throws the mutineers into confusion; and Peters, Pym, and Augustus kill all but one of them, a man named Parker. But another perverse turn of fortune follows.

Although they now have human control of the ship, the actual control of the ship belongs to the elements. Damaged in the fighting and flooded in a storm, the ship is nothing more than a floating hulk. In the midst of a calm sea, Pym and his friends find themselves threatened with the perils of capsizing, not to mention thirst and hunger. Methodically, the now rational Pym explores the flooded hold in a series of dives that nets a bottle of wine. Pym continues his search but finds little; then when he asks for a drink from the wine bottle, he discovers to his outrage that his thirsty friends have treacherously drained it. But, ironically, Pym is thus spared the agonizing increase of thirst that the alcohol engenders.

The half-drunken state of Pym's "friends" is then echoed in the appearance of another ship. Rescue seems imminent, but the ship continually veers first away from them and then toward them again, as if the helmsman were drunk. As the ship comes closer, they see the passengers and crew standing at the rail; one of the figures nods at them and displays a brilliant smile. But the figures at the railing turn out to be a mockery of life. The men have died of some mysterious disease that has left them frozen in lifelike postures. The smiling figure is a grotesquerie of hope: "The eyes were gone," Pym says after a bitter remark on the deceptiveness of appearances, "and the whole flesh around the mouth, leaving the teeth utterly naked. This, then, was the smile which had cheered us on to hope!" (H 3:113).

From this figure, a seagull takes a piece of human flesh and drops it at Parker's feet, which causes the hysterical Parker to conceive of a perverse way to escape individual death through the deaths of one another, through cannibalism. But another ship is sighted a few miles away, and again rescue seems imminent. After watching it for a time, however, the four men realize it is sailing away in the opposite direction. Parker then suggests casting lots for the cannibalistic feast, and of course it is his perverse fortune to become the first victim.

When Augustus dies shortly after, Pym and Peters are overwhelmed with the realization of the hopelessness of their condition; only the uncontrollable hulk of their ship separates them from death. With an almost perverse precision of timing, the ballast then shifts and the ship overturns. Pym and Peters manage to climb up onto the hull, however, and in utter despair sit weeping; Pym remarks at this point that their "intellects were so entirely disordered by the long course of privation and terror" that they "could not justly be considered . . . in the light of rational beings." Pym further remarks that afterward their subsequent adversities, though more dangerous, were not to reduce them so thoroughly to a state of "supineness" and "imbecility," for it is the "mental condition" that makes "the difference" (H 3:144). But, again with absurd precision of timing, Pym discovers that the overturning of the ship is, ironically, "a benefit rather than an injury" (H 3:144), for they see that the hull is covered with enough barnacles to supply them with food for an inexhaustible period of time. But having seen this new possibility of survival, they are, of course, soon rescued by another ship, an "hermaphroditic brig," paradoxically named the *Jane Guy.*

Patrick F. Quinn writes, about the symmetrically repeated twistings of the first two episodes, that *Pym,* "which is so strongly marked by conflicts of a very evident sort . . . between man and man, and between man and nature" is also ". . . charged by an incessant struggle between reality and appearance. Pym is caught up in a life in which nothing is stable, in which nothing is ever really known; expectation and surmise can anticipate only false conclusions" (p. 181).

Certainly the deceptiveness of appearances and the inability of the mind to know, or even to surmise accurately, are points made abundantly clear in the third major episode, which repeats the thematic action of the first two, but with an ever-increasing intensity of the sense of ultimate "discovery" of a great secret. The captain of the *Jane Guy* sails farther and farther to the south, and Pym becomes progressively agitated. In fact, when the captain eventually decides to abandon his proposed polar explorations, Pym conducts a minor intellectual mutiny and persuades him to continue. In the white polar waters, teeming with pale white animals, the *Jane Guy* discovers, paradoxically, the black island of Tsalal, inhabited by black men, who, ironically (or perversely), have a morbid fear of the whiteness that surrounds them. An especially significant motif in this episode is that of reflection: the consternation of the white men over the nonreflecting water of Tsalal and the frenzy of Too-Wit when caught between two mirrors reflect the "fear of Nothing," toward which they are all journeying.[17] The natives are terrified of the white sailors, but they succeed in luring the crew to the land, where (in a kind of mutiny) they bury the hated white men in a landslide. Pym and Peters, however, have strayed from the main party and have become desperately lost in a gorge—a "misfortune" through which, ironically, they escape burial alive. Yet, in another way, they are still threatened with burial alive, for they wander deep into a labyrinth of caves and crevasses. Eventually, however, Pym and Peters emerge from the earth and set off to the south in a native canoe. At the end, they disappear into a cataract of whiteness falling on a warm and milky sea—but they see ahead of them a gigantic, shrouded, human form "of the perfect whiteness of the snow" (H 3:242). And the narrative abruptly ends, without detailing the final "discovery" that Pym had anticipated with such excitement, though presumably they would have penetrated the veil of water and been buried alive. Yet Pym seems to have escaped.

The "perversity" of Pym's excitement is not only confirmed by the eventual deaths of nearly all the characters, but also by the remarks Pym makes at the beginning of the third episode. The memories of shipwreck and mutiny aboard the *Grampus* seem to Pym and Peters to be only a "frightful dream," from which they have awakened, rather than "events which had taken place in sober and naked reality." Pym says: "I have since found that this species of partial oblivion is usually brought about by sudden transition, whether from joy to sorrow or from sorrow to joy—the degree of forgetfulness being proportioned to the degree of difference in the exchange" (H 3:150).

The perverse tendency of the human mind to misperceive, or to fail to learn from experience, or to be overcome with sudden irrational impulse is emphasized at two symmetrically located points in the novel. In both instances, Patrick Quinn notes, the explicit statement of the theme of perversity is associated with burial alive, a significant point in light of the ultimate theme of the book and of all of Poe's fiction: Poe's image of man is that of a forlorn, perverse sentient being buried alive in the incomprehensible tomb of the universe. Early in the tale, Pym, considering himself lost and buried alive in the hold of the *Grampus*, has only a gill of liqueur as food. Actuated by what Pym himself calls "one of those fits of perverseness which might be supposed to influence a spoiled child in similar circumstances," he drains the bottle at once and smashes it (H 3:44). Toward the end of the tale, descending the face of a canyon wall with Peters, Pym is possessed by what he calls *"a longing to fall"* that becomes "a passion utterly uncontrollable" and, swooning, he is saved only by Peters's quick action (H 3:230). Quinn notes also that Pym's concept of adventure is focused on images of shipwreck, desolation, and death. Pym's whole life pattern, Quinn writes (pp. 193–94), his flight from his family and an assured fortune, and his Romantic adolescent desires for shipwreck and famine, can be seen as a larger dramatization of the instinct of perverseness. But Pym's death impulse is also a Romantic desire to penetrate the ultimate secret; and the shipwreck image, Quinn notes, occurs with similar meanings in "Eleonora" and "MS. Found in a Bottle." In "Eleonora," as we have seen, the narrator writes that dream-explorers "penetrate however rudderless or compassless into the vast ocean of the 'light ineffable' and again like the adventurers of the Nubian geographer" into the sea of darkness. In "MS. Found in a Bottle," the narrator has a sense of "hurrying to some exciting knowledge—some never-to-be-imparted secret whose attainment is destruction."

Discovery of the great secret of the condition of the self in the universe is what Davidson, in what is probably the most insightful commentary of *Pym* we have had, suggests is the central subject of Pym's symbolic adventure back into time and timelessness. What Pym discovers at the pole, as he moves through a world before time, is a final deceptive perversity of fortune, the final grotesquerie in the journey toward "discovery" of the self. First, the journey from ignorance to knowledge involves an inversion of the usual concept of learning. Pym moves from "ignorance," away from his complex and sophisticated social world, to a "primal" knowledge that is increasingly simple. Pym learns that the mind is one with the body, with thirst and hunger. Near the pole, the colors of the world become simplistically bifurcated into white (the sea, the animals, the sky) and black (the natives, the land). The constantly increasing whiteness of everything begins to suggest an original unity to all things, but it is a unity that Davidson calls the "negation of fact and shape." Whiteness becomes a symbol of ultimate illumination: the primal quality of the universe is a chaotic fusion of Oneness and Nothingness. At the end of Pym's journey stands death, a gigantic figure in a shroud of blinding whiteness—an ironic inversion of the conventional metaphor of the blackness of death. The blinding "illumination" is the perception of the nothingness on the other side of death. "Nothing was all," writes Davidson; "there was no other word for it but 'white,'" followed by abrupt silence. The "search for the self's true center," Davidson continues, "ends in the death of the self"; for the ". . . hero finds himself only at the moment he loses himself; he dies the instant he is about to be born again; the blankness of eternal mystery engulfs him the moment he faces the white light of revelation" (pp. 174–77).

Pym's journey back into time also parallels an inversion of birth and maturation; as Pym sails the amniotic sea toward the warm and milky cataract of water at the pole, he is reabsorbed into the great womb of the world, buried alive as it were in eternal unbeing.[18] In this context, a peculiar quality to *Pym*, never adequately remarked by critics (though one, in his title at least, hints at the matter), is that thematically *Pym* also divides into two parts: the first part of the entire regressive journey takes place in what is apparently the waking state; then, in the middle journey, Pym climbs into his coffin (the "iron-bound box" in the hold of the *Grampus*); the troubled dreams he suffers during the "letting go" constitute the second half of the narrative, wherein he seems to undergo a resurrection but actually regresses further and further into unbeing. This deceptive hoaxical structure to the romance wraps one further layer of irony around the whole system of ironic structures; and the gigantic hoax thus played upon rational man is made quite clear in the curious and bitter appended "explanation" of the symbolic chasms and caves of Tsalal, seemingly written by a gigantic hand in the rock, in the most ancient of languages. Whatever God there may be in the universe, if any, has moved Pym from darkness to whiteness, from nothing to nothing, and mockingly exacted a perverse vengeance for some unknown offense: "*I have graven it within the hills, and my vengeance upon the dust within rock*" (H 3:245).

III

The tale "The Colloquy of Monos and Una" (1841) seems at first a radical modification of Poe's view of the grotesque vengeance of God upon his perverse creatures. Davidson, for example, sees the tale as Poe's development of the concept of the primal "nothingness" beyond death in *Pym* into a concept of harmonious and even "loving" primal order—a sense of God's beneficence that is supposedly given further elaboration in "Mesmeric Revelation" and *Eureka*.[19] "Monos and Una" Davidson describes as ". . . an account of the passage of human consciousness from life through death to the life-beyond-death on the other side where occurs a final 'merging' into 'Love' or the harmonious principle uniting all things in the mind of God or the One" (p. 133). Through submission to the natural laws of the universe, man may attain true contentment, the tale seems to say. But like "Mesmeric Revelation," "Monos and Una" and *Eureka* are deceptively ironic— and quite chilling.

Instead of "affirming" meaningful order, purpose, and love as basic principles in the universe, Poe insinuates into these works a quiet ironic despair. On the other side of death, there still remains the perverse whiteness of nothingness. The only real intimation in "Monos and Una" that there may be something beyond death lies in the initial dramatic situation. Two spirits, lovers, discuss the great cycle of being which moves from an original "unity" in God, through matter, to a dispersion in individualized material creatures and back to unity again in unparticled matter. But the rest of the tale progressively focuses on the horror of living-death.

That Poe's use of spiritualistic ideas in his "occult" tales of the 1840s is ironic we have already seen. And like the beatific "revelations" of Vankirk, the perception of the "unity" of Monos and Una with the "One" involves a number of ironies, some further clue to which the reader familiar with Poe's works first sees in the motto: "mellonta tauta," that which "is to come." "Mellonta Tauta" (1849), we should recall, is the title of Poe's satiric tale about "progress," the epigraph to which punctures Andrew Jackson Davis, the "Poughkeepsie Clairvoyant."[20]

As "Monos and Una" begins, both "spirits" remark on the grim phantasm, Death, which in life seemed always to act as "a check to human bliss—saying unto it 'thus far, and no farther!'" (H 4:200). Monos, apparently the "male" spirit, is asked by Una to recount "the incidents" of his "own passage through the dark Valley and Shadow." But Monos replies, "One word first, my Una, in regard to man's general condition at this epoch" (H 4:201). The suspicion that Poe's awkwardness in thus introducing "a philosophical" view of human existence is consciously comic finds immediate corroboration in the sarcastic comments that Monos next makes (in elevated "Romantic" language) about transcendentalism, art, the progress of culture, and—Jacksonian democracy. In vain had men of "poetic intellect" like Monos himself warned mankind of the "misrule" of the "utilitarians" and of the falsity of the progressive and optimistic transcendentalists. Although the arts, or art itself, "arose supreme," such men managed to "cast chains upon the intellect" which had first elevated art. Man failed to perceive that nature was his true teacher, and that submission to the great design of nature would save mankind from false philosophies. Instead, man

> ... grew infected with system, and with abstraction. He enwrapped himself in generalities. Among other odd ideas, that of universal equality gained ground; and in the face of analogy and of God—in despite of the loud warning voice of the laws of *gradation* so visibly pervading all things in Earth and Heaven—wild attempts at an omni-prevalent Democracy were made. (H 4:203)

After a lengthy description of similar perversions of nature, and some Vankirkian observations on the materiality of mankind, which should eventually be "Death-purged" (H 4:205), Monos finally gets around to Una's question—what his "sensations" of death had been—reminiscent, of course, of the *Blackwood's* style and Poe's early satires on sensation tales. After several days of "dreamy delirium," he says, "there came upon me . . . a breathless and motionless torpor" that "was termed *Death* by those who stood around me" (H 4:206). But he retained "sentience"; his senses were still "active, although eccentrically so—assuming each other's functions at random." The rosewater that Una applied to his lips, for example, affected him as a vision of flowers, more beautiful than those on earth, but whose "prototypes" now "bloom" around the two spirits (H 4:207).

After much detail about his rather grotesque synesthesia, and the gradual "wreck and chaos" of his senses, as well as his awareness of the weeping and the grief-stricken looks of Una, Monos comes to the matter of time. Time seemed to become a sixth sense, perfect and harmonious, a "mental pendulous pulsation" that seemed to be the very "moral embodiment of man's abstract idea of Time," attuned to the "cycles of the firmamental orbs themselves" (H 4:209). Monos became aware, as he lay dead upon the bed, of the "irregular" tickings of the clock on the mantel and of the watches of the attendants. They were "omni-prevalent" "deviations" from "the true proportion" of time and affected him just as "violations of abstract truth were wont, on earth, to affect the moral sense." He then realized, he says, that this grotesque experience of irregular tickings was the first step of his timeless soul upon the time-structured universe of eternity—a paradox to be horribly worked out and "affirmed."

Monos then describes his sensations at midnight in the coffin. A dull electrical sensation numbingly pervaded his body, a vague sensation which became a sense of the "loss of the idea of contact." All that was left was the sense of "duration"; and Monos realized that his body had begun to decay:

Yet had not all sentience departed; for the consciousness and the sentiment remaining supplied some of its functions by a lethargic intuition. I appreciated the direful change now in operation upon the flesh . . . when the noon of the second day came, I was not unconscious of those movements which displaced you from my side, which confined me within the coffin, which deposited me within the hearse, which bore me to the grave, which lowered me within it, which heaped heavily the mould upon me, and which left me, in blackness and corruption, to my sad and solemn slumbers with the worm. (H 4:210–11)

Surely Poe's ironic technique here is obvious. Poe begins the tale with Monos's denial of the ultimate grimness of death, which merely seems to check all human bliss, especially that of true love. Then, after Monos's awkward railing against any abstract systems not conjoined with "natural" processes, there follows a reverent abstract system based solely on the "natural" process of decay. The "sentience" of the dead body is thus the substance of over half the tale. Gradually, the sense of mystic unity with the great design of the universe is undercut by increasingly horrible details. The soul lying passive in its grave is aware only of decay and the gradual annihilation of itself in its only form, the material "sentience" of the body.

The seminothingness after death is in this tale something more horrible than mere nothingness—burial "alive" in which an eternity passes before the "peace" of nothingness comes. The final four paragraphs of the story deepen the contrast between upper and insinuated meaning, as we are led to suspect that the spiritual region from which the two spirits speak is still that of the mouldering grave itself, the "prototypes" of flowers around them mere seed and roots, the voices of the spirits perhaps the abstracted voices of the elements. Monos mentions the passing of a year, during which time his "consciousness of *being* had grown hourly more indistinct, and that of mere *locality* had, in great measure, usurped its position. The idea of entity was becoming merged in that of *place*" (H 4:211). This abstract "philosophical" language is immediately followed by connotatively contrasting details: "The narrow space immediately surrounding what had been the body, was now growing to be the body itself." If Poe had wanted to emphasize the true pleasure of unity with the material essence of the universe, he surely would not have chosen such details or such words as "blackness," "corruption," "sad," "worm," "darkling," "damp," and "mouldering."

But, vaguely stirred by a disturbance above his grave, Monos had briefly a sense of "nebulous light" amid the darkness, that of "Love." "Men toiled at the grave in which I lay darkling. They upthrew the damp earth. Upon my mouldering bones there descended the coffin of Una." But then the nebulous light faded, the "feeble thrill" of recognition "vibrated itself into quiesence"; and all became again "void." "The sense of being had at length utterly departed, and there reigned in its stead . . . dominant and perpetual—the autocrats *Place* and *Time*." Monos concludes with the observation that what he was then "*was not*," that he had "no form," had "no thought," had "no sentience," and was "soulless," though obviously he has regained sentience at the time of this colloquy. "For all this *nothingness*, yet for all this *immortality, the grave was still a home*, and the corrosive hours, comates" (H 4:211–12; my italics). To this Una does not reply. There is only silence. Thus ends Poe's tale of the "union" of true lovers, who need not have feared the grim finality and isolation of death. The silence of final nothingness is as central to the meaning of the tale as is the final discovery of the blankness of nothingness to *Pym*. The tale of "Monos and Una" is an about-face consideration of the perverse possibilities of immortality: here the eternal rotting away into "unity" with the essence of the universe—which is nothingness.

IV

We come now to our final major test case, Poe's long essay on the design of the universe, *Eureka*. Poe's ironic "philosophy" is nowhere more poignant than in his "affirmation" of order and purpose in the universe of *Eureka*. Despite the uppercurrent of hopefulness, however, the undercurrent of insinuated meaning is pessimistic. At one point, Poe argues that "the Universe is a plot of God" and that the "plots" of God must be perfect (H 16:292). Imperfections must only be seeming. Man's "finite intelligence" (though a reflection of the creative power of God) can construct only imperfectly. Obviously, therefore, man cannot construct perfect theories of the universe. Moreover, limited man is faced with an ultimate fact, his "inevitable annihilation."

Richard Wilbur has observed that Poe's basic thesis in *Eureka* is that the Universe is some kind of "a work of art . . . which men are intended to grasp esthetically rather than rationally." This thesis is, paradoxically, derived from Poe's first proposition in *Eureka* that inevitable annihilation is the basic fact of all existence. In the act of destroying, according to Wilbur's interpretation of Poe, man abets the destructive phase of the design of the pulsating universe, endlessly creating (in expanding) and destroying (in contracting).[21] Such a reading is, of course, another version of the shift toward harmonious "love" that Davidson sees in Poe's later works, and this reading has recently received further support.

Since the sublime symmetry of design thus makes conventional evils beautiful to contemplate as part of the cosmic pattern, and since a tendency toward destruction is evidence of a return to the original unity of all things in God, we can, according to Joseph Moldenhauer, understand Poe's ecstasy at the conclusion of *Eureka*. For we perceive the final aesthetic and moral vision implicit in Poe's fascination with death in the tales and poems. "Life, in Poe's value system, is inimical" to the "aesthetic bliss" of the ultimate unity of death, according to Moldenhauer; and he points out that most other critics have seen nature and death, as well as madness, perversity, and terror, in Poe's works as disharmonious rather than the harmonious elements in the grand design that they actually are. Previous critics, in reading man's condition as diametrically opposed to the harmonious condition of art, have, in Moldenhauer's view misread Poe's "transcendental" vision.[22] But Moldenhauer's view of Poe and his critics is surely but a partial truth. Partial too, I will agree, is the older view that nature for Poe is merely destructive. But one cannot claim for the fascinated vision of death and dissolution in Poe's writings a totally ecstatic and beatific vision. To claim such would be as serious a misreading of Poe as that of those critics Moldenhauer wishes to correct.

The problem for any critic who would deal with *Eureka* is its complexity of tones: for it is at times comic and satiric, at times melancholy, at times coldly and precisely rational, at times intuitional and ecstatic. Yet, oddly, no one but Patrick F. Quinn has ever given serious thought to the equivocal note of Poe's concluding "optimism."[23] And to those critics, like Davidson and T. S. Eliot, who have tried to confront *Eureka* in the context of Poe's career, the essay represents an inconsistent shift from the bleak world view informed by death, destruction, or burial alive to a vision of a universe informed by Divine Love—a vision that did not logically develop out of the life's work of the author.[24] And Quinn, too, finally sees *Eureka* as inconsistent, call-it an "unintentional poem of death," since it contains under the surface affirmations of Divine Love a consistent vision of horrible annihilation.

The difficulty is the word "unintentional," for *Eureka* presents the kind of ironic complexity, ambiguity, and ambivalence that is to be found in all of Poe's creative works: a tension between the creative and the destructive impulses of the universe as perceived (and misperceived) by the questing "philosophical lynxeye." And the ambiguities, the parody, the melancholy, the humor of *Eureka* are all part of a skeptical entertaining of ideas about the nature of the universe and about the methods of attaining knowledge. The tension between the sense of the creative and the sense of the destructive in *Eureka* and in Poe's other works results in what, I believe, cannot be called other than skepticism. Although assuredly Romantic in the quest for aesthetic consistency and design, *Eureka* presents a skepticism that results from the appalling possibility that the essence of the universe is neither creative nor destructive in any design—but simply void. Or to use the recurrent word of *Eureka*—nothingness.

Poe seems to believe finally in neither the creative nor the destructive *per se*, nor even in "design" (whether teleological or statically self-perpetuating). It is only in the vision of void that Poe comes close to "belief." It should be perfectly clear by now where all this is tending, for I have been insisting throughout that the vision of void—or rather its possibility—is at the bottom of all of Poe's fiction, and that this theme of nothingness needs to be more fully recognized for its true significance in such central works as "Ligeia," "The Fall of the House of Usher," and *The Narrative of Arthur Gordon Pym*.[25]

The scheme within which Poe believed man might reasonably think his existence purposeful involves a paradox that is partially reconciled by the Romantic theories of the aesthetic imagination to which Poe subscribed. It is important to emphasize, however, that Poe's Romantic conception of the imagination is characteristically melancholy: only through an artistic imaginative power can man, by perceiving some overall design, find any hope of purpose to his existence in the face of nearly overwhelming doubt. The perception of design in *Eureka* is a desperate, intuitive leap, the final act of the rational mind confronting horrible doubt—much like that of the narrator of "A Descent into the Maelström," who tries in his quiet desperation to perceive some design, or order, or Divine Will, in existence.

Because the basic proposition of *Eureka* declares that inevitable annihilation is built into the structure of the universe, man's belief in a designed universe has to be reconciled with ultimate annihilation. Poe claims in *Eureka* to have found in the universe a design both scientific and aesthetic. The current discoveries of astronomy (which are not our subject here) corroborated, in Poe's view, the current Romantic literary analogies of God as an Artist shaping the cosmos, with divine symmetry, to his own end. But Poe puts forward this argument with deceptive irony, especially when he writes in *Eureka* that the universe is a "plot of God" and that this plot consists of "cycles" of creation and annihilation. "Novel universes" swell into "objectless" existence, he says, and then subside into nothingness.

If it were not for this grand design, Poe suggests, seemingly with a straight face, if the whole structure of the larger Universe of universes actually had a "conceivable end," then existence would have to be regarded as a badly contrived romance: "We should have been forced to regard the Universe with some such sense of dissatisfaction as we experience in contemplating an unnecessarily complex work of human art. Creation would have affected us as an imperfect *plot* in a romance, where the *dénoûment* is awkwardly brought about by interposed incidents external and foreign to the main subject" (H 16:306). Poe raises the metaphor of the universe as an artistic creation to analogical "evidence," and it is the perception of some overall design that gives rise to his apparent ecstasy at *Eureka*'s end. But Poe makes the metaphor serve another function, for with it he has cast doubt upon the perfection of the universe as a work of art: the universe just may be an imperfect plot in an awkwardly designed romance.

Divorced from the apparently ecstatic (but ambivalent and possibly ironic) affirmations that mankind must trust in an animate God shaping the universe with love, Poe's logical argument is that even endlessly repeated cycles of creation, destruction, and re-creation make a design that provides mankind with some hope that the universe is not chaos. Only with some view of aesthetic design in the universe, Poe suggests, can we "comprehend the riddles of Divine Injustice." Only with some sense of aesthetic design does the "evil" manifest in the universe become "intelligible" and "endurable" (H 16:313).

These remarks have never been emphasized by critics of Poe's thought, with the result that the implicit melancholy skepticism of the essay has never been seriously considered. Despite the uppercurrent of ecstasy at the conclusion of *Eureka*, the moral undercurrent of meaning reaffirms the bleak world view that had been the consistent vision of his career—the vision of the appalling possibility of void at the bottom of existence.

The birth, death, and resurrection of the universe as stated in *Eureka* has a further (aesthetic) twist ignored by Poe's readers. The specific design that Poe sees is a melancholy symmetry of nothingness. According to Poe, the present material universe is an expression of God's original "nihility." When God's present expansiveness concentrates again into primal "unity," the universe will "sink at once into that Nothingness which, to all Finite Perception, Unity must be—into that Material Nihility" from which it was evoked (H 16:310–11). What will then remain will be God in his original state: nothingness.

The larger point, however, is that because the final nothingness is a return to the original state of the universe, the "end" of the universe is not a finite end. The grand aesthetic design to existence, then, is this cycle of nothingness. The origin of the universe lies in nothingness, its present material state is but a variation of the original nothingness, and its final end is a reconstitution of the original nothingness. It is in such a universe, rather than that informed by the conventionally benign oversoul of the transcendentalists (or unconventionally as interpreted by Moldenhauer as "blissful" aesthetic unity), that all sentient being finds itself buried alive.

The Romantic skepticism implicit in the pun-sprinkled, multitoned, and intricately ironical text of *Eureka* is perfectly caught by the first part of Poe's beautifully ambiguous sentence on consistency and symmetry (H 16:302): "A perfect *consistency*," he implies, "can be *nothing*. . . ." The perfect consistency of the design of the universe which Poe sets up in *Eureka* is its cycle of nothing: the absolute truth. The nihilism of this vision leads to the paradoxical creation of the elaborate form of words which (expressed unequivocally in the tale "The Power of Words") is the universe, the work of art which refers to nothing outside itself—indeed, which is a facade for the nothingness from which it is evoked. Poe's version of a single universal mind is solipsistic, and follows from his epistemological skepticism. Except by aesthetic analogy with creative imagination in man, we do not know what the universe is, nor do we know that we know anything. Seen whole, in its Romantic context of aesthetic analogy, the philosophical vision of *Eureka* presents the void, but expresses it as ambivalent skepticism, neither quite theistic nor quite atheistic. The canon of Poe's work is, I must emphasize, a literature of overwhelming negative possibility: the possibility that beyond the elaborate art of the game there is nothing.

V

We may recall again that ten years before *Eureka*, Poe sent Arthur Gordon Pym on a symbolic voyage that goes back in time toward the primal state of the world and ends in void. Pym's ultimate revelation about the structure of the world occurs with his disappearance at the pole before the strange figure in the white shroud. The enigmatic conclusion of the novel is itself emblematic of Poe's melancholy skepticism. Whiteness in *Pym*, we have seen, is an ironic, double symbol of both the white light of revelation and the blankness of nothingness. Pym moves from the complexity of the subjectively created world of men toward the simplicity of natural nothingness. Pym's final revelation is of nothingness; and it is at the moment of final knowledge that the main narrative breaks off—leaving the reader with the odd double sensation of having discovered something he has somehow missed.

That the possibility of an ultimate nothing is the consistent and conscious vision of Poe's writings is confirmed by journeys toward destruction (or perhaps unbeing) in other of Poe's works. Much as Pym does, the narrator of "MS. Found in a Bottle," we remember, disappears into the void at the pole just as he is on the verge of what he considers to be some fantastic "discovery" about the world. Similarly, the narrator of "A Descent into the Maelström" journeys into the void. In the vortex of the whirlpool, he sees the moon peering, like the eye of some inhuman god, down into the whirling funnel of waters which in turn seem to send up an eerie "yell . . . to the Heavens" (H 2:243). Yet it is clear that the objective correlative of his psychological state is still but a pathetic fallacy. He returns from the journey, but his "raven-black" hair has, significantly, turned an eerie white overnight.

The horror of horrors, which Poe leaves purposely unstated and which so appalls the narrator of "The Pit and the Pendulum," is the same unknown yet half-known nothingness, lurking at the bottom of the pit (like darkness over the waters in Genesis). The ultimate horror of nothingness is anticipated early in the story when the narrator, having just been cast into the dungeon, at first refuses to open his eyes for fear that "there should be *nothing* to see" (H 5:71). The full passage emphasizes the ultimate horror of the possibility of nothingness: "It was not that I feared to look upon things horrible, but that I grew aghast *lest* there should be *nothing* to see" (first italics mine).

This early incident in the tale is itself anticipated in the four opening paragraphs, wherein the narrator speculates on death and immortality in association not only with the conventional image of darkness, but also with nothingness, whiteness, blankness, and silence—the image system of *Pym, Eureka,* and other works. In the room of judgment, as the narrator begins to reconcile his spirit to what he hopes will be the "sweet rest" of the grave, he sees the white candles before him as white angels. Then as his spirit comes "at length properly to feel and entertain" the possibility of benign "rest," the opposite possibility overwhelms him, and the candles become to him "meaningless spectres" instead of saving angels. Then, the spectral candles sink "into nothingness" while the white-lipped, black-robed judges "vanish"—leaving "silence," "stillness," and the "blackness of darkness" (H 5:68–69).

The details of the story are worth yet a further look as corroborative imagery for the theme of the horrible possibility of nothingness. The original pronouncement of the priestlike, godlike, specterlike judges issues from their grotesque white lips as silence: "I saw [their lips] writhe with a deadly locution," the narrator remarks, "I saw them fashion the syllables of my name; and I shuddered because no sound succeeded" (H 5:68). The symbolic significance of a death sentence pronounced on a victim, the pronunciation of whose name by his judges yields no sound, can hardly be other than the theme of nothingness. When the narrator next loses consciousness, to awake in the dark dungeon, his "awakening" is so gradual that he seems to himself to be in a state of numbed sentience, or, in his exact words, in a "state of seeming nothingness" (H 5:69). The implicit theme of void is so nearly explicit as to leave no doubt of Poe's own clear-sighted vision. Particularly important to notice, however, is the precise phrasing— "seeming nothingness"—the true, recurrent, psychological horror of the tale.

Eureka represents not an inconsistent shift of Poe's bleak world view toward hope and a sense of Divine Love, but instead the further ambivalent, uncertain entertaining of the possibility that the design of the universe is but a symmetrical cycle of journeys out of, and back into, void. One needs, really, only to consider the number of Poe characters whose origins are unknown and who journey toward physical, mental, and spiritual destruction to realize how deep-seated an apprehension it was for Poe.

Paul Valéry saw long ago that the essence of Poe's dramatic and philosophical world view was this tension between nothingness and existence, partially reconciled by an aesthetic cosmogony. In a letter to Gide (June 13, 1892), Valéry praised Poe for his vision of *vertige* (void or vertigo) given *synthèse* (form or design) by the artist of the beautiful.[26] T. S. Eliot, in puzzlement over Valéry's admiration for Poe, tried to account for the phenomenon by declaring that Poe had the "powerful intellect" of a "highly gifted young person before puber-

ty," an intellect that delighted in "entertaining" ideas rather than believing them. Valéry, as a mature skeptic, had what Poe did not: a
"consistent view of life," for "Poe was no sceptic." It was, therefore,
Eliot said, probably the "contrast" between Poe's "entertained" ideas
and Valéry's mature skepticism that accounted for "Valéry's admiration for *Eureka*."[27] Eliot perhaps suspected more than he wanted to
admit. For these words echo a passage from *Eureka*, wherein Poe himself comments on the emotional difficulties of his speculation that the
symmetry of nothingness is the design of the annihilating universe:
although such speculation has the aesthetic consistency of truth, Poe
suggests, it is yet an idea so startling that even the most "powerful
intellect" cannot readily "entertain" it even on abstract grounds (H
16:309).

In Poe, murder is an aesthetic act beautiful to behold only in the
same sense that a desperate victim, confronting destruction, seeks solace in submitting to what he hopes is Divine Will—as does the desperately observant but submissive narrator of "A Descent into the
Maelström." But even if one survives for a time, his hair still turns
white from the confrontation. In Poe's tales, we feel a skeptical tension between disorder and hope, madness and rationality, uncertainty
and knowledge, despair and hope. It is this that animates all of Poe's
writings—from a single weird tale to a philosophical essay on the
universe.

For the Romantic Mr. Poe, the most "powerful intellect" was the
faculty of aesthetic imagination. And only the most "powerful intellect" has the stoic fortitude to "entertain" speculation on the melancholy symmetries of birth, death, and resurrection. But even the most
powerful of intellects can never know. At best, it can only guess, or
glimpse, or suspect. The undercurrent of argument in *Eureka* (a work
in which conventional humanistic assumptions are reversed) contradicts the uppercurrent of benign affirmation. The result is Poe's most
colossal hoax—just as the universe may be God's hoax on man (cf. H
16:306, 161; 7:16, 14:228). The aesthetic vision of *Eureka* easily translates into a solipsistic cosmogony of art for art's sake alone. Existence
is but a "poem" for the sake of the poem. The essay is itself an elaborate art structure, which, like the universe it describes, refers ultimately to nothing outside itself but the Nothing outside itself.

The quiet despair under the surface of *Eureka* thus mocks the poetic
affirmations of the yearning imagination at the same time that they are
asserted most emphatically. Seen in the general Romantic context we
have been examining in this study, Poe's point is clear; the "effect"

aimed at in *Eureka* is an almost mystical, poetic perception of and simultaneous transcendence of the absurd hoax of individual existence. Such self-division and self-parody the German Romanticists would have applauded as irony, the consummate fruit of the artistic and philosophical mind.

In Poe's world view, then, it is the perverse nature of things that man, as an individual, thinking creature, is subject to the "indignities" of ignorance and of ultimate annihilation of the self. But through a "lynxeyed" vision of the demonic (of the perversity of the universe and of one's own mind), man may still retain some of the dignity he feels in himself as a rational and feeling entity buried alive in the vast impersonal or malevolent system of the universe. This is the Romantic-Ironic vision. We have already noted the lynx image in the Folio Club tale, "Silence," and in the *Marginalia*. In "Silence" the Demon laughs hysterically at man's confusion in an absurd world of weird, shifting appearances. But the lynx comes out of the cave and stares steadily into the Demon's face. And in *Marginalia*, as we have seen, Poe calls what can only be the ironic vision of existence the "philosophical lynxeye that, through the indignity-mist of Man's life, can still discern the dignity of man."

Thematically, Poe's Gothic and philosophical works suggest that the deceptive perversity of the universe and of the mind can only be transcended by the godlike imagination of the ironic artist, who yokes together contrarieties and sees beyond hope and despair, beyond good and evil, by deceptively intruding the comic into the tragic, the satiric into the demonic. Through such simultaneous ironic detachment and involvement, the German ironists thought, the Romantic artist achieves a liberating transcendental perception of the dark paradox of human existence.

REFERENCE
MATTER

Notes

. . . when you let slip any thing a little too absurd, you
need not be at the trouble of scratching it out, but just add a
foot-note and say that you are indebted for the above
profound observation to the "Kritik der reinen Vernunft," *or*
to the "Metaphysische Anfangsgründe der Naturwissenschaft."
This will look erudite and—and—and frank.
　　　　　"How to Write a Blackwood Article" (1838)

Perspectives

1. See Henry James's comment in his essay on Baudelaire in *French Poets and Novelists* (London, 1878); D. H. Lawrence's chapter on Poe in *Studies in Classic American Literature* (1923; reprint ed., New York: Viking, 1964); Aldous Huxley's essay "Vulgarity in Literature" in *Music at Night and Other Essays* (London: Chatto & Windus, 1931); and especially Yvor Winters's "Edgar Allan Poe: A Crisis in the History of American Obscurantism" in *Maule's Curse: Seven Studies in the History of American Obscurantism* (1938; reprint ed., Denver: Alan Swallow, n.d., as part of *In Defense of Reason*); and T. S. Eliot's *From Poe to Valéry* (New York, 1948; reprinted in *To Criticize the Critic*, New York: Harcourt Brace, 1965). For a concise overview of the critical response to Poe, see Floyd Stovall, "The Conscious Art of Edgar Poe," Ch. VII of *Edgar Poe the Poet: Essays Old and New on the Man and His Work* (Charlottesville: University Press of Virginia, 1969), pp. 181–86. Stovall puts Poe's critics into six categories: (1) those who simply like to read Poe's poems, tales, and essays; (2) those who are content to analyze and interpret individual works without evaluating Poe as a writer; (3) those who dislike Poe's writings so thoroughly that they simply cannot see what other intelligent writers appear to see plainly; (4) those who use psychoanalysis (of the author) as a technique of criticism; (5) those who like Poe but feel as if they should not; (6) those who do not like Poe but feel as if they ought to because certain French writers and critics whom they admire have praised him. (Stovall emphasizes Poe's conscious control and intellectuality throughout the nine essays that

comprise what is the only respectable book-length study of Poe as a poet yet to appear.)

2. Allen Tate, "Our Cousin, Mr. Poe," given as a speech and published 1949; reprinted in *Collected Essays* (Denver: Alan Swallow, 1959); see especially pp. 455, 470–71.

3. See, most notably, Joseph Wood Krutch's "psychoanalytic" biography, *Edgar Allan Poe: A Study in Genius* (New York: Knopf, 1926), though a long list could be drawn up of those who, dissatisfied with Poe's humor, echo C. Alphonso Smith's judgment that Poe's laughter "is surely a falsetto cackle," in *Edgar Allan Poe: How to Know Him* (Garden City, N. Y.: Doubleday, 1921), p. 51. Smith was one of the first to try to take the humorous side of Poe seriously.

4. See N. Bryllion Fagin, *The Histrionic Mr. Poe* (Baltimore, Md.: The Johns Hopkins Press, 1949).

5. Leon Howard, *Literature and the American Tradition* (Garden City, N. Y.: Doubleday, 1960). Howard's conception of Poe is based on Fagin's. See also Killis Campbell, *The Mind of Poe and Other Studies* (1933; reprint ed., New York: Russell & Russell, 1962); Campbell was one of the first to suggest that Poe was essentially a "player." The best known "psychological" approaches to Poe, besides Krutch's, include nearly all the major French studies, such as those by Roger Asselineau, Gaston Bachelard, Jacques Bolle, Nicolas-Isidore Boussoulas, Jacques Castelau, Edmond Jaloux, Emile Lauvrière, Camille Mauclair, but especially Marie Bonaparte's *The Life and Works of Edgar Poe: A Psycho-Analytic Interpretation*, trans. John Rodker (1933; translated reprint ed., London: Imago Publishing Co., 1949). Poe's vogue in France is detailed in Patrick F. Quinn's *The French Face of Edgar Poe* (Carbondale: Southern Illinois University Press, 1957) and Célestin P. Cambiaire's earlier *The Influence of Edgar Allan Poe in France* (1927; reprint ed., New York: Haskell House, 1970). See also several studies by Léon Lemmonier, one by Louis Seylaz, and especially Joseph Chiari's *"Symbolisme" from Poe to Mallarmé: The Growth of a Myth* (London: Rockcliff, 1956).

Curiously, recent German interest in Poe (principally stylistic and metaphysical) has not been marked by an awareness of the importance of German Romantic theory for Poe's development. Besides a multivolumed translated edition of Poe's *Werke* now in progress, ed. Kuno Schuhmann and Hans Dieter Müller (Freiburg: Walter-Verlag, 1966– there have been three booklength critical studies within the last ten years: Franz H. Link, *Edgar Allan Poe: Ein Dichter zwischen Romantik und Moderne* (Frankfurt/Main: Athenäum, 1968), Klaus Lubbers, *Die Todesszene und ihre Funktion im Kurzgeschichtenwerk von Edgar Allan Poe* (München: Max Hueber, 1961), and Armin Staats, *Edgar Allan Poes symbolistische Erzählkunst* (Heidelberg: Carl Winter, 1967). (Mention may also be made here of Harro H. Kühnelt's earlier *Die Bedeu-*

tung von Edgar Allan Poe für die englische Literatur, Innsbruck: Wagner, 1949.) Of these, Staats's book is probably the most original and ambitious, for he seeks to tie Poe's theory of unity to his concept of the universe, to his concept of the sublime, to his dominant themes of identity, and to his theories of verisimilitude and symbolism, wherein the symbol fuses the abstract and the concrete, the conceptual, and the real.

Another side of Poe to receive recent serious attention, though much too long delayed, is that of the hard-working journalist confronted with the practical day-to-day concerns of editor and reviewer enmeshed in the literary warfare of his times. Arthur Hobson Quinn's *Edgar Allan Poe: A Critical Biography* (New York: Appleton-Century-Crofts, 1941) offers reliable data on this side of Poe's life, but further details and important insights are offered by: Perry Miller's *The Raven and the Whale: The War of Words and Wits in the Era of Poe and Melville* (New York: Harcourt, Brace & World, 1956), Sidney P. Moss's two studies, *Poe's Literary Battles: The Critic in the Context of His Literary Milieu* (Durham, N.C.: Duke University Press, 1963) and *Poe's Major Crisis: His Libel Suit and New York's Literary World* (Durham, N.C.: Duke University Press, 1970), Edd Winfield Parks's *Edgar Allan Poe as Literary Critic* (Athens: University of Georgia Press, 1964), Robert D. Jacobs's *Poe: Journalist & Critic* (Baton Rouge: Louisiana State University Press, 1969), John Walsh's *Poe the Detective: The Curious Circumstances Behind "The Mystery of Marie Rogêt"* (New Brunswick, N.J.: Rutgers University Press, 1968), and Michael Allen's *Poe and the British Magazine Tradition* (New York: Oxford University Press, 1969). A new work (too recent for me to deal with fairly) that attempts to deal with both the practical side of Poe and his "occultism" is Stuart G. Levine's *Edgar Allan Poe: Seer and Craftsman* (Deland, Fla.: Everett/Edwards, 1972). I take issue in this study with the traditional assumption that Poe was a serious occultist; see Chapter 6, "The Nightside."

6. Harry Levin, *The Power of Blackness: Hawthorne, Poe, Melville* (New York: Knopf, 1958), p. 163. Also see Richard Wilbur's brilliant speculation on the retreat into the "hypnagogic state" as the central theme of Poe's writings, "The House of Poe" (The Library of Congress Anniversary Lecture, May 4, 1959), reprinted in *The Recognition of Edgar Allan Poe: Selected Criticism Since 1829,* ed. Eric W. Carlson (Ann Arbor: The University of Michigan Press, 1966), pp. 255–77, and in the Introduction to the Laurel Poetry Series *Poe,* ed. Richard Wilbur (New York: Dell, 1959), pp. 7–39.

7. No one's definition of *irony* suits many others. Just as the term *Romanticism* becomes complicated and ambiguous under scrutiny, so the term *irony* becomes increasingly slippery under use, threatening to encompass everything, so that one finds it hard to see anything that is not ironic. In the ensuing discussion of *irony* as a term, I attempt to adhere to simple, pragmatic meanings; the involuted subtleties of Romantic

Irony soon to be detailed are complex enough without raising too many specters here. For general studies, see J. A. K. Thomson, *Irony: An Historical Introduction* (Cambridge, Mass.: Harvard University Press, 1927), pp. 2–38 in particular; G. G. Sedgwick, *Of Irony: Especially in the Drama* (Toronto: University of Toronto Press, 1948); Norman O. Knox, *The Word "Irony" and Its Context, 1500–1750* (Durham, N.C.: Duke University Press, 1961); Douglas C. Muecke, *The Compass of Irony* (London: Methuen, 1969). For satire, I cite only Robert C. Elliott, *The Power of Satire: Magic, Ritual, Art* (Princeton, N.J.: Princeton University Press, 1960), especially pp. 257–75. Finally, the seminal work in the understanding of irony and satire and humor is a book focused on none of them, Arthur Koestler's *The Act of Creation* (New York: Basic Books, 1964), a fine synthesis of philosophical, psychological, and physiological ideas on artistic creation, scientific discovery, and the logic of humor. The common denominator, Koestler suggests, is the simultaneous perception of a chain of logic applicable to two or more normally incompatible contexts. My basic assumptions about irony, satire, and humor follow Koestler, though at some distance.

8. Fuller documentation and discussion follows in Chapter 2, but here may be noted several works. William K. Wimsatt, Jr., and Cleanth Brooks in *Literary Criticism: A Short History* (New York: Knopf, 1957), especially p. 397, provide an initial starting point, to be followed by reference to Wellek (W 2:16 ff). Lawrance Thompson in *Melville's Quarrel with God* (Princeton, N.J.: Princeton University Press, 1952), comes close, in his analysis of Melville's "triple-talk" and of Melville's sense of the perverse duplicity of all things, to seeing "Romantic" irony as Melville's basic mode. Poe's "quarrel," however, was with an absurd universe, more than with an "evil God." John Seelye in *Melville: The Ironic Diagram* (Evanston, Ill.: Northwestern University Press, 1970), p. 2, mentions Melville's "sympathy with the forms and attitudes of romantic irony" derived from his reading of Coleridge and the Schlegels on Shakespeare; but Seelye drops the idea after this hint. Alfred A. Marks in "German Romantic Irony in Hawthorne's Tales," *Symposium* 7 (1953): 274–304, is the only other critic I am aware of who has seen the significance of Romantic Irony for American Romanticists. But see R. W. B. Lewis, *The American Adam: Innocence, Tragedy, and Tradition in the Nineteenth Century* (Chicago: The University of Chicago Press, 1955), pp. 6–8, for discussion of the "three voices" of American intellectual history: the party of Hope (who rejected inherited sin), the party of Memory (who embraced the idea of inherited sin) and the party of Irony, who (characterized in one sense by Hawthorne) "seemed skeptically sympathetic toward both parties and managed to be confined by neither" (p. 7). The best overall study of Poe's place in the Romantic era is Edward H. Davidson's *Poe: A Critical Study* (Cambridge, Mass.: Harvard University Press, 1957), one of the few important book-length

studies to deal fairly with Poe's humor. A new, but idiosyncratic, study of Poe that takes into account the hoaxical and comic aspect is Daniel G. Hoffman's *Poe Poe Poe Poe Poe Poe Poe* (Garden City, N.Y.: Doubleday, 1972), though the occultist and Gothic side of Poe still predominates.

9. See, first, J. A. K. Thomson, *Irony: An Historical Introduction*, p. 185. In a once famous essay, "On the Irony of Sophocles" (first published in the British periodical, *Philological Museum*, in 1833), Bishop Connop Thirwall gave real currency to the English phrase "irony of fate." He used it to mean a "mocking" discrepancy between appearance and reality. He associated "Sophoclean" irony with both irony of fate and with two-edged language—ultimately, then, a "dramatic irony" involving both author and spectator. In his preface to his translation of Ludwig Tieck's two novella *"The Pictures" and "The Betrothing"* (London: Whittaker, 1825), Thirwall showed caution in laying before English readers tales that had no obvious moral. He even comments on the "strange notions" of the Germans that "a tale may have high value, though its moral essence cannot be extracted in a precept or aphorism; they even think it better for having no didactic object . . ." (p. xxxviii). Thus the "undercurrent" of meaning is much like Muecke's basic definition of irony: ". . . the art of irony is the art of saying something without really saying it. It is an art that gets its effects from below the surface, and this gives it a quality that resembles the depth and resonance of great art triumphantly saying much more than it seems to be saying" (*Compass of Irony*, pp. 5–6). Although this is only a partial definition of an effect (but an important effect) of irony, it significantly parallels Schlegel's concept of *mystic*. Cf. Poe, H 8:126; 11:68; 10:61 ff.; 13:148.

10. Among the many discussions of "The Cask of Amontillado," only one, in a textbook for freshmen, has presented such an acute analysis: see Lynn Altenbernd and Leslie L. Lewis, "The Nature of Fiction," *Introduction to Literature: Stories* (New York: Macmillan, 1963), pp. 2–9.

11. See especially Darrel Abel's brilliant "A Key to the House of Usher," *University of Toronto Quarterly* 18 (1949): 176–85; see also Richard P. Benton, "Is Poe's 'The Assignation' a Hoax?" *Nineteenth Century Fiction* 18 (1963): 193–97; Roy P. Basler, "The Interpretation of 'Ligeia,'" *College English* 5 (1944): 363–72; three articles by James W. Gargano, "'The Black Cat': Perverseness Reconsidered," *Texas Studies in Literature and Language* 2 (1960): 172–78; "Poe's 'Ligeia': Dream and Destruction," *College English* 23 (1962): 337–42; and "The Question of Poe's Narrators," *College English* 25 (1963): 177–81; two articles by Clark Griffith, "Poe's 'Ligeia' and the English Romantics," *University of Toronto Quarterly* 24 (1954): 8–25; "Caves and Cave Dwellers: The Study of a Romantic Image," *Journal of English and Germanic Philology* 62 (1963): 551–68; Stephen Mooney, "Poe's Gothic Wasteland," *Sewanee Review* 70 (1962): 261–83; and, more recently, James M.

Cox, "Edgar Poe: Style as Pose," *Virginia Quarterly Review* 44 (1968): 67–89.

12. For useful or revealing general studies of Poe's humor, satire, and penchant for hoaxing, see (in addition to items cited in the preceding note) Robert Kierly, "The Comic Masks of Edgar Allan Poe," *Umane-simo* 1 (1967): 31–34; Terence Martin, "The Imagination at Play: Edgar Allan Poe," *Kenyon Review* 27 (1966): 194–209; two articles by Stephen L. Mooney, "Comic Intent in Poe's Tales: Five Criteria," *Modern Language Notes* 76 (1961): 432–34; "The Comic in Poe's Fiction," *American Literature* 33 (1962): 433–61; two articles by Claude Richard, "Les Contes du Folio Club et le vocation humoristique d'Edgar Allan Poe," in *Configuration Critique de Edgar Allan Poe* (Paris: Minard, 1969), pp. 79–94; "Poe and the Yankee Hero: An Interpretation of 'Diddling Considered as One of the Exact Sciences,'" *Mississippi Quarterly* 21 (1968): 93–109; J. Marshall Trieber, "The Scornful Grin: A Study of Poesque Humor," *Poe Studies* 4 (1971): 32–34; two articles by William Whipple, "Poe's Two-Edged Satiric Tale," *Nineteenth Century Fiction* 9 (1954): 121–33; "Poe's Political Satire," *University of Texas Studies in English* 35 (1956): 81–95; and James Southall Wilson, "The Devil Was In It," *American Mercury* 24 (1931): 215–20.

13. Edward Wagenknecht, *Edgar Allan Poe: The Man Behind the Legend* (New York: Oxford University Press, 1963), pp. 235, 248–49.

14. Michael Allen, *Poe and the British Magazine Tradition* (New York: Oxford University Press, 1969); Poe's satire on *Blackwood's* and the sensationist tale is a major topic of Chapter 3 of this study.

15. The conclusion of Clark Griffith in "Poe's 'Ligeia' and the English Romantics"; see Chapter 4 of this study.

16. K. W. F. Solger, *Erwin*, 2 vols. (Berlin, 1815), 2:286–87; passage translated in G. G. Sedgwick, *Of Irony*, p. 17; see W 2:300 ff.

NOTES TO CHAPTER TWO
Romantic Irony

1. Either Thomas W. White, owner, or James Heath, his short-term first editor, in "Editorial Remarks," *Southern Literary Messenger* 1, no. 7 (March 1835): 387. These remarks appeared at the end of the issue; Poe's story appeared on pp. 333–36.

2. Palmer Cobb, *The Influence of E. T. A. Hoffmann on the Tales of Edgar Allan Poe*, Studies in Philology 3 (1908): 1–104. See Cobb's third chapter, "Poe's Knowledge of the German Language and Literature," pp. 20–30, where he lists several of the German literary figures that Poe refers to from time to time, including Schelling, Kant, Fichte, Wieland, Tieck, Novalis, Fouqué, Musaeus, Chamisso, Körner, Uhland, the Schlegels, Winckelmann, and others. Although Cobb concludes that Poe

could read German with ease, he notes the great number of translations
and critical essays available in English during this period. For a full discussion of German literature then available in translation in America, as
well as for a full discussion (including the arguments of Cobb, Belden,
Gruener, and others) of Poe's ability to read German, see Henry A.
Pochmann, *German Culture in America: Philosophical and Literary Influences, 1600–1900* (Madison: University of Wisconsin Press, 1957),
pp. 388–408 (especially pp. 388–92), and 709–22; cf. 381–82. Pochmann's detailed discussion strongly points to Poe's ability to read German, but I base the case for Poe's knowledge of German literature and
German critical theory principally on translations and the "vast amount
of discussion—charges, countercharges, denunciations, and vindications
—of the Germans and Germanism" in American magazines during the
period 1810 to 1864 (Pochmann, *German Culture in America*, pp. 328–
29; on pp. 393 ff., Pochmann gives arithmetic frequency tables of translations, notices, reviews, critical articles, and biographical sketches).
Thus, if Poe did have a reading knowledge of German, as would seem
to be the case, the likelihood of such influence as I suggest here is redoubled.

Among the large number of translated collections of German prose
available to Poe, the following are representative. (Translators, com-
pilers, and publishers are given when known.) *Popular Tales of the
Germans* (London, 1791); H. Mackenzie, *Dramatic Pieces from the German* (Edinburgh: W. Creek, 1792; London: T. Cadell, 1792); W.
Tooke, *Varieties of Literature from Foreign Journals and Original
Manuscripts* (London: Debrett, 1795); A. Thompson, *The German
Miscellany* (Perth: Morison, 1796); *Interesting Tales, Selected and
Translated from the German* (London: Lane, 1798); *The German Nov-
ellist: A Choice Collection of Novels*, trans. "Miss Eliza C——" (Gör-
litz: Anton, c. 1800); M. G. Lewis's translations and adaptations incorporated into the 1796 and 1798 editions of *The Monk* (London: J.
Bell), his verse collection, *Tales of Terror & Wonder* (London: pri-
vately printed, 1801), his *Romantic Tales* (London: Longman, 1808),
and his *Life and Correspondences* (London: Coburn, 1839); *The German Museum; or, Monthly Repository of the Literature of Germany*, 3
vols. (London: M. Geisweiler, 1800–1801); *The Juvenile Dramatist*,
3 vols. (Hamburg: Bachmann and Gundermann, 1801); B. Thompson, *The German Theatre*, 6 vols. (London: Vernor and Hood, 1801–
1802); T. Holcroft, *The Theatrical Recorder*, 2 vols. (London: Mercier,
1805–1806); M. Taylor, *Tales of Yore* (London, 1810); S. H. Utter-
son's English version of the famous *Phantasmagoriana*, from J. B. B.
Eyriès's French version (Paris, 1812), published as *Tales of the Dead*
(London: White, Cochrane, 1813) [see the review in *Blackwood's* 3
(August 1818): 589–96]; *An Essay of Three Tales . . . from the German* (Ghent: W. de Busscher, 1820); *Popular Tales and Romances of*

the Northern Nations (London: Simpkin and Marshall, 1823); *German Popular Stories* (London, 1823–1824); *Specimens of the Novelists and Romancers, with Critical and Biographical Notices*, 2nd ed. (Glasgow: R. Griffin, 1826); R. Holcraft, *Tales from the German* (London: Edinburgh, and Glasgow, 1826), reprinted as *Tales of Humour and Romance* (London, 1829; New York: Francis, 1829); T. Roscoe, *The German Novelists*, 4 vols. (London: Colburn, 1826); G. Sloane, *Specimens of the German Romance* (London: Whitaker, 1826); R. P. Gillies, *German Stories*, 3 vols. (Edinburgh, 1826); *The Odd Volume*, 1st series, 2nd ed. (Edinburgh and London, 1826), 2nd series (London, 1827); Thomas Carlyle, *German Romance: Translations from the German with Biographical and Critical Notices* (Edinburgh and London: Tait, 1827); *Tales from the German. By a Lady* (London: Anderson, 1827); *German Prose Writers* (London: Hunt and Clarke, 1828); *Foreign Tales and Translations, Chiefly Selected from the Fugitive Literature of Germany* (Glasgow: Blackie, Fullerton, 1829); *Lights and Shadows of German Life*, 2 vols. (London: Bull, c. 1832); *Romances of Many Lands*, 3 vols. (London: R. Bentley, 1835); J. Strang, *Tales of Humour and Romance from the German . . .* (n.p., c. 1836); *Library of Romance. A Collection of Traditions, Poetical Legends, and Short Standard Tales of All Nations* (London, 1836); H. Bokum, *Translations in Poetry and Prose from Celebrated German Writers* (Boston: Munroe, 1836); *Gleanings from Germany; or, Selected Specimens of German Romance and History* (London: Hodson, 1839); Thomas Carlyle, *Critical and Miscellaneous Essays, Collected and Republished*, 2nd ed., 5 vols. (1840; reprint ed., New York: Carey and Hart, 1846); *A Present from Germany; or, the Christmas Tree* (London: C. Fox, 1840); J. H. L. Weiss, *Moral and Religious Selections from . . . Jacobi, Shubart, Schiller, Ewald, Richter, Gellert, Haug, and Others* (Boston: Peabody, 1841); T. Tracy, *Miniature Romances from the German, with Other Prolusions of Light Literature* (Boston: Little-Brown, 1841); Mrs. S. [Taylor] Austin, *Fragments from German Prose Writers* (New York: Appleton, 1841); H. Reeve and J. E. Taylor, *Translations from the German* (London: Murray, 1842); G. F. Crosswaite, *Stories from the German* (London: Ryde, 1842); *Fairy Tales, Translated from the German* (Salsford: J. Wilson, 1843); *Romantic Fiction: Selected Tales* (London: Burns, 1843); *Popular Tales* (London: Burns, 1844); J. Oxenford and C. A. Feiling, *Tales from the German* (New York: Harper, 1844); *"The Christmas Roses" and Other Tales. Chiefly Translated from the German* (London: Cundall, 1845); *The Diadem for MDCCCXLVI: A Present for All Occasions. Translations from Goethe, Schiller, Uhland, Richter, and Zschokke* (Philadelphia: Carey and Hart, 1846); C. Brooks, *Schiller's Homage to the Arts, and Other Translations* (Boston: Monroe, 1847); *Beauties of German Literature. Selected from Various Authors, with . . . Biographical Notices* (London: Burns, 1847); F. H.

Hedge, *Prose Writers of Germany* (Philadelphia: Carey and Hart, 1849).

See the following studies: Bayard Q. Morgan, *Bibliography of German Literature in English Translation* (Madison: University of Wisconsin Studies, 1922); Henry A. Pochmann and Arthur R. Schultz, *Bibliography of German Culture in America* (Madison: University of Wisconsin Press, 1953); Scott H. Goodnight, *German Literature in American Magazines Prior to 1846* (Madison: University of Wisconsin Studies, 1907); Martin H. Haertel, *German Literature in American Magazines, 1846–1880* (Madison: University of Wisconsin Studies, 1908); Percy Matenko, *Ludwig Tieck and America* (1954; reprint ed., New York: AMS, 1966); Frederick Henry Wilkens, *Early Influence of German Literature in America, 1762–1825* (New York: Macmillan, 1900); Stanley M. Vogel, *German Literary Influences on the American Transcendentalists* (New Haven: Yale University Press, 1955); René Wellek, *Confrontations: Studies in the Intellectual and Literary Relations Between Germany, England, and the United States During the Nineteenth Century* (Princeton: N. J.: Princeton University Press, 1965); René Wellek, *Immanuel Kant in England, 1793–1838* (Princeton, N. J.: Princeton University Press, 1931); Susanne Howe, *Wilhelm Meister and His English Kinsmen* (1930; reprint ed., New York: AMS, 1966); Bayard Q. Morgan and A. R. Hohlfeld, *German Literature in British Magazines, 1750–1860* (Madison: University of Wisconsin Press, 1949); V. Stockley, *German Literature as Known in England, 1750–1830* (London: George Routledge & Sons, 1929); F. W. Stokoe, *German Influence in the English Romantic Period, 1788–1818* (1926; reprint ed., New York: Russell & Russell, 1963). It may be noted here that Paul Wächtler's *Edgar Allan Poe und die deutsche Romantik,* Diss. Leipzig 1911, deals with the psychological and physical similarities between Poe and certain German writers, more than with literary relations (see Pochmann, *German Culture in America,* p. 709).

3. The following works contain discussions of Romantic Irony: W 2; Raymond Immerwahr, "Romantic Irony and Romantic Arabesque Prior to Romanticism," *German Quarterly* 42 (1969): 665–85; Morton L. Gurewitch, "European Romantic Irony," Diss. Columbia 1957; Ingrid Strohschneider-Kohrs, *Die Romantische Ironie in Theorie and Gestaltung* (Tübingen: M. Niemeyer, 1960), which synthesizes a number of previous studies in German; Irving Babbitt, *Rousseau and Romanticism* (1919; reprint ed., New York, 1955); M. H. Abrams, *The Mirror and the Lamp: Romantic Theory and the Critical Tradition* (1953; reprint ed., New York: Norton, 1958); Douglas C. Muecke, *The Compass of Irony* (London: Methuen, 1969); G. G. Sedgwick, *Of Irony, Especially in Drama* (Toronto: University of Toronto Press, 1948); A. R. Thompson, *The Dry Mock: A Study of Irony in Drama* (Berkeley and Los Angeles: University of California Press, 1948); Oskar Walzel, *German*

Romanticism, trans. Alma Elise Lussky (1932; reprint ed., New York: Putnam's, 1966); Robert M. Wernaer, *Romanticism and the Romantic School in Germany* (New York: Appleton, 1910); William K. Wimsatt, Jr., and Cleanth Brooks, *Literary Criticism: A Short History* (New York: Knopf, 1957); and several studies of Ludwig Tieck and the Schlegels, cited in subsequent notes. See also Ralph Tymms, *German Romantic Literature* (London: Methuen, 1955).

4. A. R. Thompson, *The Dry Mock,* pp. 51 ff., uses Tieck's plays to illustrate simple Romantic Irony, and I follow him, for the most part, in this brief discussion of the plays. Translated passages from Tieck's plays, unless otherwise cited, are his. Wellek observes that "Tieck is an eclectic who reflects, almost year by year, the aesthetic theories of his contemporaries . . ." (W 2:89). See the following for additional discussion of Tieck and Romantic Irony: Raymond Immerwahr, *The Esthetic Intent of Tieck's Fantastic Comedy* (St. Louis: Washington University Studies, 1953); A. E. Lussky, *Tieck's Romantic Irony* (Chapel Hill: University of North Carolina Press, 1932); Percy Matenko, *Tieck and Solger: The Complete Correspondence* (1933; revised ed., New York: Modern Language Association, 1937); E. H. Zeydel, *Ludwig Tieck and England* (Princeton, N.J.: Princeton University Press, 1931); E. H. Zeydel, *Ludwig Tieck the German Romanticist: A Critical Study* (Princeton, N.J.: Princeton University Press, 1935). Tieck was one of the most popular of the "new" generation of German writers after Schiller and Goethe; see the lists of translations in Matenko, *Tieck and America,* pp. 38–47; Zeydel, *Ludwig Tieck and England,* pp. 182–220; Stockley, *German Literature as Known in America,* p. 321; and Pochmann, *German Culture in America,* pp. 393 ff. For Carlyle's discussion, see *The Works of Thomas Carlyle,* Centenary Edition, 30 vols. (London: Chapman and Hall, 1907), 21: 259.

5. Walzel, *German Romanticism,* p. 226—an interesting metaphor that parallels Allen Tate's depiction of Poe's recurrent persona as a "forlorn demon" endlessly repeated in a series of mirrors—apparently derived from Schlegel: "Only Romantic poetry can . . . become a mirror of the whole world round about . . . and yet . . . being free from all commitment to the real and the ideal, hover on the wings of poetic reflection midway between the artist and the artefact, raising this reflection to a higher power and a higher still and multiplying it as in an endless series of mirrors" (*Athenäum,* Fragment 116; trans. by Muecke in *Compass of Irony,* p. 204).

6. Walzel, *German Romanticism,* pp. 245–54; Abrams, *Mirror and the Lamp,* pp. 211 ff.

7. Translated by A. R. Thompson, in *The Dry Mock,* pp. 58–59. *Puss in Boots* was translated during Poe's time. One such translation, by "Mrs. Osgood," was published in 1846. An article on *Puss,* signed "L.," appeared in *The Southern Quarterly Review* in Charleston, S. C., in 1846

(9:237–43); see Matenko, *Tieck and America*, pp. 21–22. The review-er mentions the striking effect of the simulated audience and how these "pit performers" proceeded to "vent their jests upon the play itself." In his essay on Tieck in *German Romance* (1827), Carlyle, as was men-tioned, refers specifically to *Puss*, *Topsy-Turvy*, and *Prince Zerbino*. We find, he says, that under the "grotesque masque" of the dramatized fairy tale of *Puss in Boots*, Tieck "laughed with his whole heart, in a true Aristophanic vein, at the actual aspect of literature. . . ." As read-ers, we find "a feast of broad joyous humour in this strange phantasma-goria, where pit and stage, and man and animal, and earth and air, are jumbled in confusion worse confounded" while the "copious, kind, rud-dy light of true mirth overshines and warms the whole" (Carlyle's *Works*, 21:259). Poe was acutely aware of Carlyle; his references to Carlyle include H 4: 218, 221; 11:22, 99, 114–15, 175–177; 13:195; 14:180; 15:78, 79, 260; 16:2, 7, 16, 74, 99–101, 122, 167, 175. In his review of Algernon Henry Perkins's *Ideals and Other Poems*, Poe writes (*Graham's*, April 1842) that the author seems to try "to render con-fusion worse confounded" by introducing into his poetry the "hyper-ridiculous elisions" of Carlyle's prose (H 11:114–15). This phrasing confirms Poe's careful reading of the very section of *German Romance* that deals with *Puss*, *Topsy-Turvy*, *Zerbino*, and Tieck's Romantic Iro-ny. It should be observed, however, that whatever debt Poe may have owed Carlyle for his translations and discussions of German literature, Poe did not much care for Carlyle's own writing; see especially refer-ences in H 11.

8. See A. R. Thompson, *The Dry Mock*, pp. 62–63; Lussky, "The Sources of Tieck's Romantic Irony," Chapter IV of *Tieck's Romantic Irony*, pp. 118–58.

9. See H 11:99; 16:161. Poe quotes the same passage twice from the same work, suggesting that the work had unusual impress on him. *Peregrinus Proteus* was translated (anonymously) into English as *Private History of Peregrinus Proteus the Philosopher* (London, 1749). *Agathon* had been translated by John Richardson in London, 1773. Wieland's most influential work in America, *Oberon*, was translated in London, 1778, and in New York, 1840. *Don Silvio* was translated by John Richardson as *Reason Triumphant over Fancy* in London, 1773, and a collection titled *Select Fairy Tales from the German of Wieland*, "By the translator of *The Sorceror*," appeared in London, 1796. See Werner P. Friedrich, *History of German Literature*, 2nd ed. (New York: Barnes & Noble, 1961), p. 72, and the lists of Stockley, *German Literature in England*, and Morgan, *Bibliography of German Literature in English Translation*.

10. See Lussky, *Tieck's Romantic Irony*, pp. 99–108; Sedgwick, *Of Irony*, p. 16. Also see Raymond Immerwahr, "Romantic Irony and Romantic Arabesque Prior to Romanticism," pp. 673–82, for discussion of the re-lation between the arabesque and the Quixotic tradition. *The Sorrows*

of Werter. A German Story appeared in English in London in 1779 and again in 1801. *Wilhem Meister's Apprenticeship* was translated by Carlyle (Edinburgh, 1824). *Poetry and Truth* appeared as *Memoirs of Goethe* in London in 1823. Poe's references to Goethe include H 2:392; 7:28; 8:42; 9:202; 10:57; 11:5, 114; 12:13–14; 16:117. The earliest reference dates from 1829.

11. Wimsatt and Brooks, *Literary Criticism*, p. 372. Poe would have had access to Leibnitz's thought in English not only in the many anthologies of German prose, but also in *A Collection of Papers . . . Relating to . . . Natural Philosophy and Religion* (London: J. Knapton, 1717). See Poe's humorous use of "Leibnitz's *Law of Continuity*—according to which nothing passes from one *state* to another without passing through all the intermediate states" (H 16:46). Other references to Leibnitz are: H 2:126; 4:134; 9:65; 12:165; 14:217; 16:25, 223–24. Many translations of Kant's works were available, though it should be noted that Poe refers to even lesser known works of Kant by the German titles (see H 2:276, for example). Among the better known translations and textbook discussions are: F. A. Nitsch's *A General and Introductory View of Professor Kant's Principles* (London, 1796); *Project for a Perpetual Peace: A Philosophical Essay* (London: Vernor and Hood, 1797); A. F. M. Willich's *Elements of the Critical Philosophy* (London, 1798); *Prolegomena to Every Future Metaphysic* (London: Simpkin and Marshall, 1819); *The Metaphysic of Morals*, 2 vols. (London: W. Richardson, 1779), and translated anew with an introduction and appendices, including part of the *Critique of Practical Reason* (Edinburgh: Clark, 1836), *Critik of Pure Reason* (London: Pickering, 1838); *An Analysis of the Critik of Pure Reason* by Francis Haywood (London: Pickering, 1844); and *Religion within the Boundary of Pure Reason* (Edinburgh: Clark, 1838). Poe's references to Kant include: H 2:126, 271, 276, 359, 392; 4:218; 6:201; 11:136, 235; 16:188. Earliest references to both Leibnitz and Kant date before 1832.

12. Abrams, *Mirror and the Lamp*, p. 208.

13. See Walzel, *German Romanticism*, p. 41. In Carlyle's essay on "The State of German Literature," first published in *Edinburgh Review*, no. 92 (1827), reprinted in *Critical and Miscellaneous Essays, Collected and Republished,* Fichte is quoted extensively and discussed in the context of the aesthetics of Lessing, Goethe, Schiller, the Schlegels, Winckelmann, and others, with special reference to those "chief mystics in Germany," the "Transcendental Philosophers, Kant, Fichte, and Schelling!" See *The Works of Thomas Carlyle*, 26:58–84, especially. Carlyle pairs with these German authors the British writers Blair, Johnson, and Kames. Cf. Poe, who writes that the "critiques raisonnées" of Winckelmann, Novalis, Schelling, Goethe, and the Schlegels "differ from those of Kames, of Johnson, and Blair, in principle not at all" (H 11:5). Selections from Fichte were also available to Poe in *German Prose*

Writers (1828) and Austin, *Fragments from German Prose Writers* (1841). Translations of Fichte available to Poe include: *The Characteristics of the Present Age* (London: Chapman, 1844); *The Way Towards the Blessed Life* (London: Chapman, 1844); *On the Nature of the Scholar* (London: Chapman, 1845); *The Destination of Man* (London: Chapman, 1846); *The Vocation of the Scholar* (London: Chapman, 1847); and *Popular Works*, 2 vols. (London: Chapman, 1848–49). For Poe's references to Fichte, see H 2:28, 359, 392; 11:136. The earliest reference dates from 1832.

14. Schiller argued that beauty and morality are inseparable, a view Poe seems to dispute, with his formulation of the "heresy of the Didactic"; but, as we have seen, Poe does not object to a moral as the "undercurrent of a poetical theme." See his reviews of Longfellow's *Ballads* (H 11:64–85) and of Thomas Moore's *Alciphron* (H 10:65), where he notes that the term *mystical* is associated with such an undercurrent of idealism by the Germans. Cf. his remarks on truth and beauty and "harmony" in his 1845 review of Nathaniel Parker Willis (H 12:37–39).

15. Wimsatt and Brooks, *Literary Criticism*, pp. 368–70; the section on satirical poetry is translated in *Theories of Comedy*, ed. Paul Lauter (Garden City, N. Y.: Doubleday, 1964), pp. 307–13. Schiller was available to Poe not only in journal extracts and discussions (Pochmann, pp. 343–47, notes 187 Schiller items in American periodicals before 1864), but also in translated editions of the *Philosophic and Aesthetic Letters* (1837; London: Chapman, 1844), and the *Correspondence with Goethe* (London, 1845). Schiller's fiction, poetry, and drama were even more readily available, of course (see Morgan, *Bibliography of German Literature in English Translation*). Poe's references to Schiller include: H 2:279, 295; 6:155; 8:138; 9:202, 204. The earliest references date from before 1838.

16. Wimsatt and Brooks, *Literary Criticism*, p. 368; W 2:74–76; Abrams, *Mirror and the Lamp*, pp. 209–10. For echoes of these ideas in Poe's *Eureka*, see his remarks on poetic intuition in relation to induction and deduction as follows: H 16:183, 187–98, 205–7, 214, 221–22, 260–61, 275–76, 293, 304, 306, 312–15, all of which, however, are complicated by possible ironies. Schelling's ideas on tragedy and comedy help clarify his basic views: in tragedy the subjective and free choice of a human being clashes with necessity, or the objective order of the universe; in comedy human choice and character are fixed and fated but the world is treated subjectively, freely, ironically (W 2:81). Schelling also investigated occult sciences in pursuit (in part) of the secrets of the unconscious, discussed later in this study with reference to the sinister nightside of nature which was made use of increasingly by the Romanticist fiction writers. Abrams calls Schelling's *Transcendental Idealism* (1800) the "characteristic document of romantic philosophy in Germany"; the "extraordinary importance attributed to esthetic invention

may be regarded as the climax of a general tendency of the time to exalt art over all human pursuits" (p. 209). Schelling was available in Austin, *Fragments from the German Prose Writers* (1841) and in a translation of his *Philosophy of Art* (London: Chapman, 1845). Poe's references to Schelling include H 2:29, 358, 392; 11:5, 136; the earliest references date before 1832.

17. See H 11:5; see also H 16:1–4, for Poe's attribution of his whole *Marginalia* series to the German critics and what they were calling "the 'brain-scattering' humor of the moment." Cf. H 16:304.

18. Wimsatt and Brooks, *Literary Criticism*, p. 379; W 2:16ff.; quotation translated in W 2:17. Cf. Muecke, *Compass of Irony*, p. 201. In his novel *Lucinde* (1799), Schlegel said he aimed at the interplay of imagination, illusion, moral responsibility, and subjectivity. Hans Eichner has edited Friedrich Schlegel's *Literary Notebooks, 1797–1801* (Toronto: University of Toronto Press, 1957); in Poe's era Friedrich Schlegel's *Aesthetic and Miscellaneous Works* were translated by E. J. Millington and published in London in 1849. This was too late, of course, for Poe to have made use of, but Friedrich Schlegel's *Lectures on the History of Literature* was translated by J. B. Lockhart and published in Edinburgh in 1818. Although I believe that Poe's general acquaintance with Friedrich Schlegel's thought probably determined his definition of *arabesque*, it should be noted that Schlegel was defining and labeling a body of literature with which Poe, too, was familiar. See Chapter 5 of this study. See also the following studies for discussion of Friedrich Schlegel: Hans Eichner, "Friedrich Schlegel's Theory of Romantic Poetry," *PMLA* 71 (1956): 1018–41; Raymond Immerwahr, "The Subjectivity or Objectivity of Friedrich Schlegel's Poetic Irony," *Germanic Review* 26 (1951): 173–91; Raymond Immerwahr, "Friedrich Schlegel's Essay *On Goethe's Meister*," *Monatshefte* 49 (1957): 1–22; Victor Lange, "Friedrich Schlegel's Literary Criticism," *Comparative Literature* 7 (1955): 289–305. Hanna-Beate Schilling, in "The Role of the Brothers Schlegel in American Literary Criticism . . . ," *American Literature* 43 (1972): 563–79, lists seventy-four periodical items from 1812 to 1833 in American magazines which dealt with the Schlegels.

19. See H 8:275–318; 12:36–40. Tate, *Collected Essays*, p. 44, suggests these ideas came to Poe directly from Coleridge, derived, of course, from the Germans. See, in this context, Margaret Alterton, *Origins of Poe's Critical Theory* (1925; reprint ed., New York: Russell & Russell, 1965), pp. 68–79.

20. See W 2:14 ff. The translation of this passage, a famous one among the ironists, is from Sedgwick, *Of Irony*, pp. 14–15; cf. Muecke, *Compass of Irony*, pp. 194–95. See Schilling, "Role of the Brothers Schlegel," p. 576, for two citations of Schlegel fragments from the *Athenäum* appearing in American periodicals in 1830. There are doubtless many more as

yet unidentified. Pochmann lists twenty-four Schlegel items before 1864 (p. 346).

21. See Michael Allen, *Poe and the British Magazine Tradition* (New York: Oxford University Press, 1969), passim, but especially pp. 16–40, 129–61; the concept of a select coterie of perceptive insiders is fundamental to the argument. An earlier, important study of this concept is Richard P. Benton, "Is Poe's 'The Assignation' a Hoax?" *Nineteenth Century Fiction* 18 (1963): 193–97.

22. See A. J. Lubell, "Poe and A. W. Schlegel," *Journal of English and Germanic Philology* 52 (1953): 1–12; and Alterton, *Origins of Poe's Critical Theory*, pp. 30–35 ff., 68–78 ff., and passim.

23. See H 8:46–47, 126; 9:202; 10:65, 116; 11:5, 79, 250; 12:131; 13:43; 14:62, 180; 16:117, 144, for Poe's main references to the Schlegels. Earliest reference dates from 1835.

24. See Lubell, "Poe and A. W. Schlegel," p. 11. Lubell, careful at first about charging Poe with plagiarism, is not quite as clear as he might be. He writes that Poe must have known Schlegel's work, because he praises R. H. Horne's introduction to a translation published in 1840 (H 11:244 ff.). But Lubell rightly concludes, after presenting parallel passages, that "it is quite obvious" that Poe stole from Schlegel (probably from the British translation of 1815 or the American edition printed in 1833), for Poe reproduces both the content and the order of Schlegel's argument. Schlegel writes that Greek drama is characterized by an "Ideality" linked with the "prevailing idea of Destiny." Euripides' work represents a degradation of this ideality, since in his works "fate is seldom the invisible spirit of the whole composition, the fundamental thought of the tragic world." The "terrors of destiny" may "brighten" into indications of a "beneficent Providence," but in Euripides this concept of fate degenerates into "the caprice of chance." Poe writes that two of the three essential qualities of Greek drama are "Destiny or Fate" and "Ideality." But in Euripides we see a "perversion" of the "terrible spirit of predestination," a mellowing of this concept into "a kind Providence" that becomes in Euripides "the capriciousness of chance." Schlegel then discusses the role of the Chorus as an "ideal spectator." Sophocles, Schlegel remarks, "wrote a Treatise on the Chorus . . . in opposition to the principles of other poets," and "was able to assign reasons" for his usage. Poe writes that "Sophocles wrote a treatise on the Chorus, and assigned his reasons for persisting in the practice." Poe adds that the Chorus "was, in a word, *the ideal spectator*." (See Lubell, pp. 8–10; there are further parallels.) Poe's review of Euripides is in H 8:43–47; eventual reference to Schlegel, H 8:47.

25. Søren Kierkegaard, *The Concept of Irony, with Constant Reference to Socrates* (1841), trans. Lee M. Capel (London: Collins, 1966), pp. 260–61.

26. Kierkegaard, *Concept of Irony*, pp. 260–61. For Hegel on the Schlegels and Tieck, see Matenko's edition of the *Complete Correspondence* between Tieck and Solger, especially the Introduction, pp. 43–61. For Poe on Hegel, see H 16:164. For Solger on Tieck, see Matenko, *Complete Correspondence*, pp. 6–16. Cf. W 2:301.

27. Schlegel's *Lectures* was translated repeatedly from 1815 on. My copy is *A Course of Lectures on Dramatic Art and Literature*, "by Augustus William Schlegel," trans. John Black, rev. A. J. W. Morrison (London: Henry G. Bond, 1846; reprint ed., New York: AMS Press, 1965). References are by chapter and page number in parentheses in the text.

28. This *Marginalia* reference is omitted without explanation from the Harrison edition, as are a number of others. The entry can be found in the edition of Richard Henry Stoddard, *The Works of Edgar Allan Poe*, 6 vols. (New York: A. C. Armstrong, 1895), 5:283. The work referred to was translated as *"The Old Man of the Mountain," "The Lovecharm,"* and *"Pietro of Abano." Tales from the German of Tieck* (London: Moxon, 1831; New York, 1831). See Matenko, *Tieck and America*, p. 108. Matenko's fifth chapter, "Tieck, Poe and Hawthorne," pp. 71–88, contains a discussion of Poe's knowledge of Tieck, pp. 71–75; cf. Pochmann, *German Culture in America*, pp. 381–84. Poe may have derived his association of Hawthorne with Tieck from an article on "American Humor" in the *Democratic Review* of April 1835; see Matenko's discussion of Poe's "third-hand" impression of the similarities of Hawthorne and Tieck. See also Edwin H. Zeydel, "Edgar Allan Poe's Contacts with German as Seen in His Relations with Ludwig Tieck," in *Studies in German Literature of the Nineteenth and Twentieth Centuries: Festschrift for Frederic C. Coenen*, ed. Siegfried Mews, University of North Carolina Studies in the Germanic Languages and Literatures, no. 67 (Chapel Hill, 1970), pp. 47–54, a corroborative article that came to my attention after the present study had been completed. The fact remains, however, that Poe's quotation from *The Old Man of the Mountain* indicates that he read the work and that it made a striking impression. With Tieck's *The Journey into the Blue Distance*, Poe does more than "mention" it; he quotes from it, praising Tieck's humorous technique of misquoting (H 16:42). Tieck's fiction was available in many translations. Representative are the following: "The Sorcerors," "The Enchanted Castle," "Wake Not the Dead," "Auburn Egbert," "Elfinland," in *Popular Tales and Romances of the Northern Nations; "The Pictures"* and *"The Betrothing,"* trans. Bishop Connop Thirwall (London: Whittaker, 1825); "Faithful Ekhart," "The Fair Egbert," "The Runenberg," "The Elves," "The Goblet," in Carlyle's *German Romance* (1827); *Tales from the Phantasus*, trans. J. C. Hare, J. A. Froude, and others (London: Burns, 1845), which includes in addition to tales cited above, three tales not part of the German *Phantasus*: "The Reconciliation," "The Friends," and "The Brothers."

29. Harry Levin, *Power of Blackness* (New York: Knopf, 1958), pp. 133–35.
30. See also *Marginalia* on the *under*-use of the dash for second thoughts and for a remark on an "inexcusable Gallicism" (H 16:130–32, 153).
31. H 3:287. Scholars have often pointed out that all the books in Usher's library are real except, apparently, for the *Vigils of the Dead* and *The Journey*. The difficulty in identifying the Tieck volume has been that Poe omits the first half of the title; the whole title is *"The Old Book" and "The Journey into the Blue Distance."* See T. O. Mabbott's notes in *Selected Poetry and Prose of Edgar Allan Poe* (New York: Modern Library, 1951), p. 419; see also Matenko, *Ludwig Tieck and America*, pp. 72–73, who was unable to find any English translation. The common denominator of the titles has also puzzled critics, who have suggested such motifs as the deathwatch, marriage, satiric utopias, and inorganic sentience.

NOTES TO CHAPTER THREE
Flawed Gothic

1. References to letters written to Poe are to Harrison or to A. H. Quinn, *Poe: A Critical Biography* (New York: Appleton-Century-Crofts, 1941); Quinn (p. 200) gives a facsimile of the letter and the succeeding first paragraphs of Poe's neat copying out of "Epimanes."
2. "Maelström," though published several years later in 1841, may be an early tale. But the evidence for this is suspect, being mainly the testimony of John Latrobe years later. Latrobe remembered that "Maelström" was one of the tales submitted to the *Visiter* prize contest, for which he served as judge, but Latrobe's other "recollections" of Poe seem to be somewhat inaccurate. For further discussion (beyond A. H. Quinn) and a summary of discussions by Jay B. Hubbell and J. O. Bailey, regarding Latrobe, see William H. Gravely, Jr., "A Note on the Composition of Poe's 'Hans Pfall,'" *Poe Newsletter* 3 (1970): 2–5.
3. See Harrison's commentary on "Poe's Introduction for 'The Tales of the Folio Club,'" H 2:xxxv–xxxvi. T. O. Mabbott, in "On Poe's Tales of the Folio Club,'" *Sewanee Review* 36 (1928): 171–76, focused critical attention on this Introduction and printed a newly found letter to the Philadelphia publisher Harrison Hall in which Poe further explains and expands his scheme. James Southall Wilson in "The Devil Was In It," *American Mercury*, 24 (1931): 215–20, discusses the burlesque quality of several of Poe's early "serious" tales, identifies satiric echoes from other writers, and suggests probable "Folio Club authors" for several tales. Alexander Hammond in "Poe's 'Lionizing' and the Design of *Tales of the Folio Club*," *ESQ* 18 (1972): 154–65, shows that "Lionizing," in addition to a burlesque of Edward Bulwer-Lytton, N. P. Willis, and

others, is primarily a satiric imitation of Benjamin Disraeli's novel *Vivian Grey* and a burlesque of his early literary career. Hammond argues convincingly that Poe intended "Lionizing" to be the capstone tale for "Tales of the Folio Club." (Hammond has an essay forthcoming, which I have seen in manuscript, reconstructing the sequence and the satiric targets of the Folio Club.)

4. See A. H. Quinn, *Poe: A Critical Biography*, p. 250, for a description of the exchanges.

5. Kennedy to Poe, 9 February 1836 (H 17:28). Poe to Kennedy, 11 February 1836 (H 17:30; and O 1:84).

6. June 1836; see A. H. Quinn, *Poe: A Critical Biography*, pp. 250–51.

7. The details of Willis's affectations are from Kenneth L. Daughrity, "Poe's 'Quiz on Willis,'" *American Literature* 5 (1933): 55–62. Poe apparently had Willis in mind, along with others, again three years later when he published "Lionizing" in the *Southern Literary Messenger* of May 1835. For commentary on the sources and meaning of "Lionizing," see Richard P. Benton, "Poe's 'Lionizing': A Quiz on Willis and Lady Blessington," *Studies in Short Fiction* 5 (1968): 239–44; G. R. Thompson, "On the Nose—Further Speculation on the Sources and Meaning of Poe's 'Lionizing,'" *Studies in Short Fiction* 6 (1968): 94–96; and Richard P. Benton's "Reply to Professor Thompson," *Studies in Short Fiction* 6 (1968): 97. John Arnold, "Poe's 'Lionizing': The Wound and the Bawdry," *Literature and Psychology* 18 (1967): 52–54, expands on the frequently observed sexual innuendo in the tale.

8. The story appeared in the *Courier* on 3 March 1832. The *Courier* versions of the five tales are reprinted in J. G. Varner's *Edgar Allan Poe and the Philadelphia Saturday Courier* (Charlottesville: University Press of Virginia, 1933), now out of print. Harrison in *Works* gives other variant readings of these early tales, but was unaware of their having been first published in the *Courier*.

9. David L. Carson in "Ortolans and Geese: The Origin of Poe's *Duc de L'Omelette*," *College Language Association Journal* 8 (1965): 277–83, objects to what he calls the "tenuous assumption" by William Bittner in *Poe: A Biography* (Boston: Little, Brown, 1962) that Willis "was the sort of dilettante who reclined on ottomans—while eating olives—and who was certain to have known all of the currently fashionable haberdashers" (p. 277). It is true that Poe uses "ottomans" in more than one story, but Carson is unaware of the detailed evidence in Daughrity's article, "Poe's 'Quiz on Willis,'" which Bittner merely summarizes. Carson goes on to make a much more "tenuous" conjecture that the tale is based on a practical joke Poe is supposed to have played while at West Point. Moreover, Carson also ignores the evidence of R. L. Hudson in "Poe and Disraeli," *American Literature* 8 (1937): 402–16; Hudson suggests that Disraeli's *The Young Duke* is the butt of the satire. Her parallels are convincing, but she misconstrues the primary

target; Poe uses the episode from Disraeli to satirize Willis, puncturing both at the same time. The Young Duke has a "pretty bird," prays to "die eating ortolans," owns an elegant apartment, and has trouble at écarté. (Hudson also points out that a description of May Dacre in *The Young Duke* bears a resemblance to Ligeia.) David H. Hirsch in "Another Source for Poe's 'The Duc de L'Omelette,'" *American Literature* 38 (1967): 532–36, points to a review of *The Young Duke* in the *Westminster Review* for October 1831, but, like Carson, he omits mention of Daughrity's findings.

10. A probable Folio Club author is Mr. Snap, an editor.

11. The story appeared in the *Courier* on 9 June 1832.

12. The *Courier* version was a little more blatantly satiric. To "Abel Shittim," for example, Simeon declares "Let me no longer be called Simeon . . . 'he who listens'—but rather Boanerges, 'the son of thunder'"— that is, he-who-sounds, or the son-of-farts, supposedly a condition resulting from the eating of pork. Edward H. Davidson discusses indelicate innuendo in Poe's early works in *Poe: A Critical Study* (Cambridge, Mass.: Harvard University Press, 1957), pp. 145–48. The likely Folio Club author for the tale is Chronologos Chronology, who admired Horace Smith, and had a very big nose which had been in Asia Minor.

13. See A. H. Quinn, *Poe: A Critical Biography*, p. 194, for comments on the satiric butt of the story. Quinn suggests, however, that Poe makes some "parade" of his own, which is no doubt true but is to miss the point and fun of the parade. A possible Folio Club author for "Bon-Bon" is De Rerum Natura since he and the Devil in the tale both wear green spectacles (cf. Bittner, p. 290) and since the name is appropriate to the "philosophizing" of the tale.

14. The *Courier* publication was 10 November 1832.

15. September 1835. The subtitle was amended in 1846 to "A Tale Neither In nor Out of Blackwood." In the 1836 letter to Kennedy mentioned earlier, Poe specifies "Loss of Breath" as a satire aimed at the "extravagancies of Blackwood" (O 1:84). The obvious Folio Club author is Mr. Blackwood Blackwood, who had written certain articles for foreign magazines.

16. See Stephen L. Mooney, "Poe's Grand Design: A Study of Theme and Unity in the Tales," Diss. Tennessee 1962, pp. 116–17; and Margaret Alterton, *Origins of Poe's Critical Theory* (1925; reprint ed., New York: Russell & Russell, 1965), p. 11.

17. "Perversity" thus makes its appearance in the earliest of Poe's fiction. The human propensity to act against one's own best interests, an ultimate irony or grotesquerie, is a major theme in "Metzengerstein" and became an increasingly major theme in Poe's work. "The Imp of the Perverse" (1845) is but a codification of the theme, rather than a new idea in Poe's thinking. The beginning of "Imp" is vigorously sarcastic about the "systems" that psychologists and phrenologists have tried to

impose on the mysterious realms of personality and subconscious motivation, suggesting a certain presumptuousness in trying "to dictate to God" (H 6:145–46). T. O. Mabbott suggests that the anonymous writer of *Ramblings and Reveries of an Art Student* is clearly right in attributing the immediate source of "Imp of the Perverse" to the "perverse" behavior of Lady Georgianna in Chapter XXII of Fullerton's *Ellen Middleton*, a book that Poe reviewed six months prior to the publication of "Imp" (H 16:34, from the *Democratic Review*, December 1844); but both the concept of "perversity" and the term *perverse* date from 1831 in Poe's works. See Mabbott's notes to the tale in his edition of the *Selected Poetry and Prose of Edgar Allan Poe* (New York: Modern Library, 1951).

18. See M. S. Allen, "Poe's Debt to Voltaire," *University of Texas Studies in English* 15 (1935): 70.

19. The later versions show reduction of obvious exaggeration and absurdity; two notable changes are emphasis on mock learning and, what is more reasonable in a first-person story, keeping the hero alive. All the later versions are titled "Loss of Breath," though there are variations in the subtitle, as noted earlier.

20. The first corpse is fat and bloated, whose terrible lot it has been not to walk but to waddle, "whose circumgyratory proceedings" have been a "palpable failure," for in "taking a step forward, it has been his misfortune to take two toward the right, and three toward the left." Stephen Mooney suggests ("Poe's Grand Design," pp. 116–17) that Poe's description recalls Hazlitt's description of Coleridge's method of walking in "My First Acquaintance with Poets" (1823); I find this rather strained. But W—— with his long nose does suggest Wordsworth when one considers the two corpses together, though Poe may have had almost anyone in mind, Emerson or Longfellow, for example, or possibly John Wilson.

21. Confirming the sly indecency of the real "loss"; see Marie Bonaparte *The Life and Works of Edgar Allan Poe: A Psycho-Analytic Interpretation,* trans. John Rodker (1933; translated reprint ed., London: Imago, 1949), pp. 373–410, for an application of "impotence" to Poe himself.

22. A. H. Quinn, *Poe: A Critical Biography*, pp. 192–93. "Metzengerstein" was the first of the five stories that the *Courier* published, 14 January 1832.

23. Davidson, *Poe: A Critical Study*, pp. 138, 142. Davidson does, however, offer "Metzengerstein" as a "lampoon" in his anthology of Poe, *Selected Writings* (Boston: Riverside Press, 1956), but he gives only brief comment. For an attempt to discredit any such burlesque reading of the tale, see Benjamin F. Fisher, "Poe's 'Metzengerstein': Not a Hoax," *American Literature* 42 (1971): 487–94.

24. Bittner, *Poe: A Biography*, pp. 85–87. Bittner follows Bonaparte in the view that Poe began to see the young Baron Metzengerstein as himself and the old Count as John Allan!

25. See discussion of Schlegel's *Lectures* in preceding chapter; cf. Michael Allen, *Poe and the British Magazine Tradition* (New York: Oxford University Press, 1969).

26. See Davidson's chapter on "Death, Eros, and Horror" in his *Poe: A Critical Study,* pp. 105–35, for comment on the Gothic fashion in the literature of the time. For detailed consideration of short American Gothic works, see Mary Mauritia Redden, *The Gothic Fiction in the American Magazines (1765–1800)* (Washington, D.C.: Catholic University of America, 1939). For more general discussion, see Oral S. Coad, "The Gothic Element in American Literature before 1835," *Journal of English and Germanic Philology* 24 (1925): 72–93; Chapters X and XI of Edith Birkhead's *The Tale of Terror: A Study of the Gothic Romance* (London: Constable & Co., 1921); and the next chapter of this study.

27. Published in January. Poe also italicizes the last word of the tale ("a *horse*"), apparently to emphasize the absurdity of the concluding event. He later removed the subtitle, apparently because his readers continued to take the tale seriously.

28. Hoffmann's works are repeatedly cited as the source of Poe's Gothic works and especially of "Metzengerstein" and "The Fall of the House of Usher." But similarities to Hoffmann in these may be through Scott: Hoffmann's "Das Majorat" makes use of a "dismal uninhabited castle tenanted by an eccentric hero, the last of his noble race," writes Palmer Cobb in *The Influence of E. T. A. Hoffmann on the Tales of Edgar Allan Poe, Studies in Philology* 3 (1908): 9. As noted before Cobb argues for Poe's knowledge of German, but G. P. Smith, in "Poe's 'Metzengerstein,'" *Modern Language Notes* 48 (1933): 356–59, writes that Poe had access to Hoffmann's works in translation in the Baltimore Public Library. Translations of Hoffmann's tales were available in J. Strang's *Tales of Humour and Romance from the German* . . . (before 1836); in R. P. Gillies's *German Stories,* 3 vols. (Edinburgh: Blackwood, 1826), including "Rolandsitten" ("The Entail") and "Mlle. de Scuderi"; and in Carlyle's *German Romance* (1827), including both "The Golden Pot" and an introduction to Hoffmann's life and works in which he mentions the *Fantasiestücke,* the *Elixiere des Teufels,* which had just been published (Edinburgh: Blackwood, 1824), Fouqué's versification of Hoffmann's opera of *Undine,* the *Nachtstücke, Klein Zaches,* the *Serapionsbrüder* (small tales based, writes Carlyle, on "a little club of friends, which for some time met weekly in Hoffmann's house"), *Prinzessin Brambilla, Kater Murr,* and *Meister Martin;* Carlyle observes of such writings that there is "something player-like" in Hoffmann's character. "Master Flea" appeared in G. Sloane's *Specimens of the German Romance* (London: Whitaker, 1826), and "The Datura Fastuosa: A Botanical Tale," in the *Dublin University Magazine* 13 (1839): 707. In 1844, "The Elementary Spirit," "The Jesuits' Church in G——," and "The Sandman" appeared in J. Oxenford and Feiling's

Tales from the German (New York: Harper, 1844). In 1845, *Signor Formica* appeared (New York: Taylor). And "Master Martin and his Workmen" appeared in *Beauties of German Literature* (London: Burns, 1847). See also Lieselotte Dieckmann, "E. T. A. Hoffmann und E. A. Poe: Verwandte Sensibilität bei verschiedenem Sprach- und Gesellschaftsraum," in *Dichtung, Sprache, Gesellschaft: Akten des IV. Internationalen Germanisten-Kongresses 1970*, ed. Victor Lange and Hans-Gert Roloff (Frankfurt/Main: Athenäum, 1971), pp. 273–80; and Gisela Vitt-Maucher, "E. T. A. Hoffmanns *Ritter Gluck* und E. A. Poes *The Man of the Crowd:* Eine Gegenüberstellung," *German Quarterly* 43 (1970): 35–46. See H 10:39 for Poe's reference to the "Phantasy Pieces of the Lorrainean Callôt." Actually, Poe could have gotten all the German decor he needed from Walter Scott's essay devoted to Hoffmann, "On the Supernatural in Fictitious Composition," *Foreign Quarterly Review* 1 (July 1827): 60–98, and current English Gothic novels.

29. See Mabbott's notes to the tale in his edition of the *Selected Poetry and Prose of Edgar Allan Poe* (New York: Modern Library, 1951), p. 414; the actual setting of "Metzengerstein" is Hungary, the land of black magic, as Mabbott points out.

30. Sidney P. Moss, *Poe's Literary Battles* (Durham, N.C.: Duke University Press, 1963), pp. 33, 73, 183n, 164, 167; Mabbott, *Selected Poetry and Prose*, p. 414. G. P. Smith, "Poe's 'Metzengerstein,'" p. 357, points out the motif of the animated portrait. Another interesting possibility for Poe's source, especially for the idea of a satiric hoax, is a mildly clumsy Gothic poem called "The Spectral Horseman," ostensibly by one Margaret Nicholson (*Posthumous Fragments*, Oxford, 1810, pp. 23–25) but actually by Shelley. Shelley and some friends intended the volume as a "practical joke," a Romantic hoax somewhat in the manner of Chatterton but with satiric overtones. Thus they invented a mad washerwoman, whose decayed mind not only led her to write poetry but also to attempt regicide.

31. The rooms and their furnishings in "A Bargain Lost" are similar to a description of Vivian Grey's rooms. In a version of "Loss of Breath," as we have seen, the half-dead hero thinks of "falsities in the Pelham novels—beauties in Vivian Grey—more than beauties in Vivian Grey—profundity in Vivian Grey—genius in Vivian Grey—every thing in Vivian Grey." J. S. Wilson, "The Devil Was In It" (p. 220), also notes the parody of *Vivian Grey* in Poe's "King Pest" (1835). See also Hudson, "Poe and Disraeli."

32. The text is that of *Tales of the Grotesque and Arabesque* (1840), which preserves the early satiric gibes.

33. Mabbott's translation and identification of source (Luther's letters), *Selected Poetry and Prose*, p. 414.

34. This passage may have a political or historical implication. Given the allusion to Ethan Allen in the footnote, the passage here suggests the

Vermont–New York controversy in which Allen was involved and which was interpreted with further suspicion by the Congress. This hint is strengthened in a moment by the statement that Metzengerstein's boundaries have never been clearly settled. Nothing more, however, is made of this in the story. But Allen was involved in what some considered "treasonable" correspondence with the British; see Stewart H. Holbrook, *Ethan Allen* (New York: Macmillan, 1940), pp. 181 ff.; also see pp. 231–33 for Allen's "religious" image.

NOTES TO CHAPTER FOUR
Explained Gothic

1. For useful general treatments of American Gothic fiction see: Oral Sumner Coad, "The Gothic Element in American Literature before 1835," *Journal of English and Germanic Philology* 24 (1925): 72–93; Alexander Cowie, *The Rise of the American Novel* (New York: American Book Co., 1951); David Brion Davis, *Homicide in American Fiction, 1798–1860* (Ithaca, N.Y.: Cornell University Press, 1957); Leslie Fiedler, *Love and Death in the American Novel*, rev. ed. (New York: Stein and Day, 1966); James H. Justus, "Beyond Gothicism: *Wuthering Heights* and the American Tradition," *Tennessee Studies in Literature* 5 (1960): 25–33; Harry Levin, *The Power of Blackness* (New York: Knopf, 1958); Henry Petter, *The Early American Novel* (Columbus: Ohio State University Press, 1971); and Mary Mauritia Redden, *The Gothic Fiction in the American Magazines (1765–1800)* (Washington, D.C.: Catholic University of America, 1939). See also D. E. S. Maxwell, *American Fiction: The Intellectual Background* (New York: Columbia University Press, 1963); Joel Porte, *The Romance in America: Studies in Cooper, Poe, Hawthorne, Melville, and James* (Middletown, Conn.: Wesleyan University Press, 1969); Daniel G. Hoffman, *Form and Fable in American Fiction* (New York: Oxford University Press, 1961); and Jane Lundblad, *Nathaniel Hawthorne and the European Literary Romance* (1947; reprint ed., New York: Russell & Russell, 1965).

   General studies of the Gothic before 1900 to be consulted include: Robert Aubin, "Grottoes, Geology, and the Gothic Revival," *Studies in Philology* 31 (1934): 408–16; E. A. Baker, *A History of the English Novel*, 10 vols. (1924–39; reprint ed., New York: Barnes & Noble, 1950), especially vols. 3–6; Edith Birkhead, *The Tale of Terror: A Study of the Gothic Romance* (London: Constable and Co., 1921); Kenneth Clark, *The Gothic Revival: An Essay on the History of Taste* (1928; rev. ed., London: Constable, 1950); Arthur Clayborough, *The Grotesque in English Literature* (Oxford: Clarendon Press, 1965); Arthur L. Cooke, "Some Side Lights on the Theory of the Gothic Romance," *Modern Language Quarterly* 12 (1951): 429–36, James R. Foster, *History of the Pre-Romantic Novel in England* (New York: Modern Language Association, 1949); Paul Frankl, *The Gothic: Literary Sources and Interpretations through Eight Centuries* (Princeton, N.J.: Princeton University Press, 1960); Robert D. Hume, "Gothic versus Romantic: A "Revaluation of the Gothic Novel," *PMLA* 84 (1969): 282–90; Robert L. Platzner and Robert D. Hume, " 'Gothic versus Romantic': A Rejoinder," *PMLA* 86 (1971): 266–74; Alice M. Killen, *Le Roman "Terrifiant"* (Paris: Librarie Ancienne Edouard Campion, 1923); Maurice Lévy, *Le Roman "Gothique" Anglais, 1764–1824* (Toulouse: Assc. des Pubs. de la Facultés des Lettres et Sciences Humaines de Toulouse, 1968); Alfred E. Longeuil, "The Word 'Gothic' in Eighteenth Century Criticism," *Modern Language Notes* 38 (1923): 453–60; H. P. Lovecraft, *Supernatural Horror in Literature* (New York: World, 1945); Arthur O. Lovejoy, "The First Gothic Revival," in *Essays in the History of Ideas* (1948; reprint ed., New York: Putnam's, 1960); Robert D. Mayo, "How Long Was Gothic Fiction in Vogue?" *Modern Language Notes* 67 (1943): 58–64; Clara F. McIntyre, "Were the 'Gothic Novels' Gothic?" *PMLA* 35 (1921): 644–47; Masao Miyoshi, *The Divided Self: A Perspective on the Literature of the Victorians* (New York: New York University Press, 1969); Lowry Nelson, Jr., "Night Thoughts on the Gothic Novel," *Yale Review* 52 (1963): 236–57; Marjorie Hope Nicholson, *Mountain Gloom and Mountain Glory: The Development of the Aesthetics of the Infinite* (Ithaca, N.Y.: Cornell University Press, 1959); Peter Penzoldt, *The Supernatural in Fiction* (London: Peter Nevill, 1952); Mario Praz, *The Romantic Agony*, trans. Angus Davidson (1933; 2d ed., Oxford University Press, 1951; reprint ed., New York: World Publishing Co., 1956); Eino Railo, *The Haunted Castle: A Study in the Elements of English Romanticism* (London: George Routledge & Sons, 1927); W. D. Robson-Scott, *The Literary Background of the Gothic Revival in Germany* (Oxford: Clarendon Press, 1965); Montague Summers, *The Gothic Quest: A History of the Gothic Novel* (1938; reprint ed., New York: Russell & Russell, 1964); Peter L. Thorslev, Jr., *The Byronic Hero: Type and Prototype* (Minneapolis: University of Minnesota Press, 1962); J. M. S. Tompkins, *The Popular Novel in England, 1770–1800* (1932; reprint ed., Lincoln: University of Nebraska Press, 1961); D. P. Varma, *The Gothic Flame* (1957; reprint ed., New York: Russell & Russell, 1966). Richard P. Benton has edited "The Gothic Tradition in Nineteenth-Century American Literature: A Symposium," *ESQ* 18 (1972) : 5–123, which presents ten essays and includes a highly useful introduction by Benton, "The Problems of Literary Gothicism," pp. 5–9.

2. The word *Gothic* is found in the translators' preface to the Authorized Version of the Bible in 1611 to indicate the peoples of Eastern Europe

(those who speak the "Gothicke tongue"). See Redden, *Gothic Fiction in American Magazines*, p. 11; Lovejoy, "The First Gothic Revival," pp. 136–65.

3. Quoted in Lovejoy, "First Gothic Revival," pp. 137–39.

4. *Parentalia*, pub. 1750; Lovejoy, "The First Gothic Revival," p. 139.

5. See Arthur Hobson Quinn, *Edgar Allan Poe: A Critical Biography* (New York: Appleton-Century-Crofts, 1941), p. 289: "He [Poe] eluded a definition of the terms . . . but generally speaking, the Arabesques are the product of powerful imagination and the Grotesques have a burlesque or satirical quality." This bifurcation has persisted despite occasional attempts to modify it. L. Moffitt Cecil, in "Poe's 'Arabesque,'" *Comparative Literature* 18 (1966): 55–70, points out the meaning of "Eastern" or "Near Eastern" in Poe's usage of "arabesque" but neglects to mention the German Romanticists' transmutation of the Oriental tale and the term *arabesque* into a genre of and term for Gothic irony. Similarly, Lewis A. Lawson, in "Poe's Conception of The Grotesque," *Mississippi Quarterly* 19 (1966): 200–205, neglects the European uses of grotesque. For discussion of the German conception of tales of the grotesque and arabesque, see Kayser and Wellek as cited in Chapter 5.

6. See Lovejoy, "The First Gothic Revival," pp. 153–56; cf. W. D. Robson-Scott, *Literary Background of the Gothic Revival*, and Kenneth Clarke, *The Gothic Revival*.

7. The phrase is W. P. Ker's, *Cambridge History of English Literature*, 10: 217; see Lovejoy, "The First Gothic Revival," p. 164; cf. Nicholson, *Mountain Gloom and Mountain Glory*.

8. Clara F. McIntyre, "The Later Career of the Elizabethan Villain-Hero," *PMLA* 40 (1925): 874–80. Cf. Bertrand Evans, *Gothic Drama from Walpole to Shelley*, University of California Publications in English, no. 13 (Berkeley and Los Angeles, 1947). Cf. Coad, "Gothic Element in American Literature," p. 72. Lionel Stevenson notes in *The English Novel: A Panorama* (Boston: Houghton Mifflin, 1960) that elements of "mystery and terror" appear in the novel at least as early as 1753 in Smollett's *Ferdinand Count Fathom*.

9. Horace Walpole, *"The Castle of Otranto," "The Mysteries of Udolpho," "Northanger Abbey,"* ed. Andrew Wright (New York: Holt, Rinehart, 1963), pp. 3–4.

10. See Kayser, *The Grotesque*, passim. Fuller discussion follows in Chapter 5.

11. See Birkhead's seventh chapter in *The Tale of Terror* (pp. 128–44), George Kitchin, *A Survey of Burlesque and Parody in English* (Edinburgh: Oliver and Boyd, 1931), and Redden, *Gothic Fiction in American Magazines*, pp. 19–67.

12. Nathan Drake, "On Gothic Superstitions," reprinted in *Literary Hours* (London, 1804).

13. Tompkins, *The Popular Novel*, p. 263.

14. Arthur Ransome, *Edgar Allan Poe: A Critical Study* (1910; reprint ed., Folcroft, Pa., 1970), pp. 109–11.

15. Coleridge, *Monthly Review* (November 1794); Tompkins, *The Popular Novel*, p. 291. Although Tompkins's treatment of Radcliffe is not extensive, her observations on Radcliffe and on the English and German styles of Gothic stand almost alone in critical and historical insight. It is surprising that no one has followed up her perceptive analysis of the development of the Gothic romance—or her insightful suggestions about Mrs. Radcliffe.

16. See Coad, "The Gothic Element in American Literature," pp. 91–92, where he also comments on the American predilection for "sportive" Gothic and on the failure of American writers to make use of new sources of terror in Indian demonology and New England witchcraft.

17. William B. Cairns, *On the Development of American Literature from 1815 to 1833, with Especial Reference to Periodicals* (Madison: University of Wisconsin Publications, 1898), p. 64.

18. See O 2:433. Cf. James K. Paulding and John P. Kennedy on Poe's first satires (see Chapter 3 of this study); cf. Schlegel (see Chapter 2 of this study). Poe, in "Letter to B——" (1831), comments on the "old Goths of Germany" most provocatively, given the context suggested here. Judgment can be "too correct," he writes, an idea the Goths "would have understood [for they] used to debate matters of importance to their State twice, once when drunk, and once when sober . . ." (H 7:xi).

19. Roy P. Basler, "The Interpretation of 'Ligeia,'" *College English* 5 (1944): 363–72.

20. Cooke's letter is given complete, H 17:49–51. See James Schroeter's "A Misreading of Poe's 'Ligeia,'" *PMLA* 76 (1961): 397–406. In his denunciation of a psychological reading of the tale (and of such misguided critics), Schroeter is vigorously seconded by Edward Wagenknecht, *Edgar Allan Poe: The Man Behind the Legend* (New York: Oxford University Press, 1963), pp. 248–49.

21. See "Notes" to "Ligeia," H 2:388, 390, for the variant readings.

22. Willis is a butt of "The Duke de L'Omelette" and "Lionizing"; and Disraeli figures in "Lionizing," "Loss of Breath," "Silence," and "King Pest." See Chapter 3. But Poe seems to have been, in general, friendly towards Cooke even though he may have occasionally pulled his leg; see references to Cooke in Ostrom, *Letters of Edgar Allan Poe*.

23. Griffith, "Poe's 'Ligeia' and the English Romantics," *University of Toronto Quarterly* 24 (1954) 8–25.

24. See Richard Wilbur's Introduction to the Laurel Poetry Series of *Poe* (New York: Dell, 1959) and his "The House of Poe" (The Library of Congress Anniversary Lecture, May 4, 1959), reprinted in *The Recognition of Edgar Allan Poe: Selected Criticism Since 1829*, ed. Eric W.

Carlson (Ann Arbor: The University of Michigan Press, 1966), pp. 255–77, for comments on "Ligeia." William Whipple in "Poe's Political Satire," *University of Texas Studies in English* 35 (1956): 81–95, convincingly shows that "The Man That Was Used Up" is aimed principally at Johnson.

25. Edward Hungerford, "Poe and Phrenology," *American Literature* 2 (1930): 209–31.

26. See John E. Wilson, "Phrenology and the Transcendentalists," *American Literature* 28 (1956): 220–25.

27. See, in addition to those essays by Basler, Schroeter, Griffith, and Hungerford that I have already cited, the following. John Lauber, " 'Ligeia' and Its Critics: A Plea for Literalism," *Studies in Short Fiction* 4 (1966): 28–32, states clearly the desire of one critical group to see Poe interpreted "simply," but he is so resistant to seeing Poe's narrators as anything but straightforward and "simple" that he really does not engage the issue. James W. Gargano in "The Question of Poe's Narrators," *College English* 25 (1963): 177–81, briefly summarizes the case for the unreliability of Poe's first-person narrators in a handful of stories; and in "Poe's 'Ligeia': Dream and Destruction," *College English* 23 (1962): 335–42, Gargano emphasizes Poe's conception of the "Romantic" personality as unstable and furthers Basler's interpretation by detailing the mad narrator's attempt to "possess" a mere "dream." See, for similar interpretations, Jack L. Davis and June Davis, "Poe's Ethereal Ligeia," *Bulletin of the Rocky Mountain Modern Language Association* 24 (1970): 170–76; James M. Cox, "Edgar Poe: Style as Pose," *Virginia Quarterly Review* 44 (1968): 67–89. Joel Porte in *The Romance in America*, adopting a Freudian stance that becomes unusually productive, suggests that the narrator conjures up the "voluptuous Ligeia" as the consummation of "erotic dreaming" (pp. 70–76).

28. The double, the skull motif, and theme of mental and moral collapse are the most obvious similarities, and I propose here the further similarity of the conception of the meaning of a narrative. See Joseph Conrad, *Heart of Darkness* (New York: New American Library, 1950), p. 68.

29. Several studies of "The Fall of the House of Usher" may be mentioned here. Darrel Abel in "A Key to the House of Usher," *University of Toronto Quarterly* 18 (1949): 176–85, shows how the environment and Usher's fear terrorize the narrator to the point of hallucination. Abel's essay, a pioneering statement on the issue of the supernatural *vs.* the psychological reading of "Usher," has for twenty years almost never been given due acknowledgment. Leo Spitzer's often cited "A Reinterpretation of 'The Fall of the House of Usher,' " *Comparative Literature* 4 (1952): 351–63, for example, essentially repeats and finally obfuscates what Abel pointed out four years earlier. J. O. Bailey, "What Happens in 'The Fall of the House of Usher'?" *American Literature* 35

(1964): 445–66, argues for a supernatural interpretation based on vampire lore but clearly sets up the ironic dramatic tension between the two points of view of the tale. Also pertinent here is Maurice Lévy's "Poe et la tradition 'gothique,'" *Caliban: Annales de la Faculté des Lettres de Toulouse* 4 (1968): 35–51; translated and revised in *ESQ* 18 (1972): 19–29; Lévy rejects certain biographical Freudian interpretations of Poe's Gothic tales, and suggests instead that Poe was perfectly aware of a variety of Gothic techniques and that his imagery reflects a psychological archetype that the Gothic embodies. Thus we have three kinds of "psychological" approaches which must be carefully differentiated: (1) a biographical, "psychoanalytic" approach in which Poe himself is the subject; (2) a "psychological" interpretation of the characters and their actions and perceptions in the dramatic world of the tale; (3) an "archetypal" approach, which sees certain universal human responses deeply embedded in the works.

30. See Jean Ricardou, "L'Histoire dans l'histoire; La Mise en abyme . . . ," in *Problèmes du Nouveau Roman* (Paris: Let Seuil, 1968), pp. 171–76, for a slightly different discussion of the "Mad Trist" as a synecdoche of the story itself, and as representing a kind of preknowledge for the narrator of the inevitable outcome of the main narrative. See Claude Richard, "Poe Studies in Europe: France," *Poe Newsletter* 2 (1969): 22.

31. See H 14:167 for Poe's comment on miasmata; although he says that "injury" to the public from miasmata is questionable, his comment shows his awareness of the *supposed* properties of such gas (cf. H 14:168), thus making it a proper device for a fictional narrative. See I. M. Walker "The 'Legitimate Sources' of Terror in 'The Fall of the House of Usher,'" *Modern Language Review* 61 (1966): 585–92, for discussion of this and for a lucid "psychological" analysis of the dramatic action.

32. See in particular Maurice Beebe, "The Fall of the House of Pyncheon," *Nineteenth Century Fiction* 11 (1956): 1–17, and "The Universe of Roderick Usher," *Personalist* 37 (1956): 146–60; Joseph Gold, "Reconstructing the 'House of Usher,'" *Emerson Society Quarterly*, no. 38 (1964), pp. 74–76; John S. Hill, "The Dual Hallucination in 'The Fall of the House of Usher,'" *Southwest Review* 48 (1963): 396–402; Lyle Kendall, "The Vampire Motif in 'The Fall of the House of Usher,'" *College English* 24 (1963): 450–53; D. H. Lawrence, Chapter VI of *Studies in Classic American Literature* (1923; reprint ed., New York: Viking, 1964); Bruce Olson, "Poe's Strategy in 'The Fall of the House of Usher,'" *Modern Language Notes* 75 (1960): 556–59; Patrick F. Quinn, "That Spectre in My Path," Chapter VII of *The French Face of Edgar Poe* (Carbondale: Southern Illinois University Press, 1957); Paul Ramsey, Jr., "Poe and Modern Art: An Essay on Correspondence," *College Art Journal* 18 (1959): 210–15; E. Arthur Robinson, "Order and Sentience in 'The Fall of the House of Usher,'" *PMLA* 76 (1961):

68–81; William B. Stein, "The Twin Motif in 'The Fall of the House of Usher,'" *Modern Language Notes* 75 (1960): 109–11; Allen Tate, "Our Cousin Mr. Poe" in *Collected Essays* (Denver: Alan Swallow, 1959); Richard Wilbur, "The House of Poe," pp. 255–77. A symposium on "Usher," including six essays, a review-essay on three recent case-books on "Usher," and a "Checklist of Criticism Since 1960," appeared in *Poe Studies* 5 (1972): 1–23.

33. See Richard P. Benton, "The Mystery of Marie Rogêt—A Defense," *Studies in Short Fiction* 6 (1969): 144–51; and John Walsh, *Poe the Detective: The Curious Circumstances Behind "The Mystery of Marie Rogêt"* (New Brunswick, N.J.: Rutgers University Press, 1968) for two recent analyses of this work.

34. *Hawthorne's Works*, ed. George Parsons Lathrop, 15 vols. (Boston: Houghton Mifflin Riverside Press, 1882–1891), 1:52. For an interesting speculation on Poe's hoaxing in his review of *Twice-Told Tales*, see Robert Regan, "Hawthorne's 'Plagiary'; Poe's Duplicity," *Nineteenth Century Fiction* 25 (1970): 281–98; see also Alfred H. Mark's "Two Rodericks and Two Worms: 'Egotism; or, The Bosom Serpent,'" *PMLA* 74 (1959): 607–12, for speculation on the Poe-Hawthorne relationship.

NOTES TO CHAPTER FIVE
Grotesque and Arabesque

1. John Ruskin, *The Complete Works of John Ruskin*, ed. E. T. Cook and Alexander Wedderburn, vol. 2, *The Stones of Venice*, Chapter IV, "The Nature of Gothic" (London: G. Allen, 1904).

2. The discussion that follows relies heavily on K. Other studies I find much less useful. Arthur Clayborough, for example, in *The Grotesque in English Literature* (Oxford: Clarendon Press, 1965) spends too much time trying to find fault with Kayser without really offering much that is new—nor are his reservations about Kayser's work compelling. What I hope to show in this chapter is the close connection of Romantic Irony and the grotesque in terms of a "transcendental" vision generated by an almost Hegelian dialectic resolving contradictions. See also Lewis A. Lawson's "Poe's Conception of the Grotesque," *Mississippi Quarterly* 19 (1966): 200–205; and "Poe and the Grotesque: A Bibliography, 1695–1965," *Poe Newsletter* 1 (1968): 9–10. Another interesting but incomplete study relevant here is L. Moffitt Cecil's "Poe's 'Arabesque,'" *Comparative Literature* 18 (1966): 55–70, which suggests that Poe used the word *arabesque* as a counter to the word *Germanism*, details the many Near Eastern allusions and settings in Poe's tales, and rein-forces the idea that arabesque means primarily Arabian and "patterned strangeness" in the manner of abstract pictorial design reproducing no natural forms (proscribed by the Koran), as in an arabesque screen.

But Cecil neglects the European parallels we have seen—namely, the conception of the arabesque as an intricate design of ironies and tensions. See also Michael Steig, "Defining the Grotesque: An Attempt at Synthesis," *Journal of Aesthetics and Art Criticism* 29 (1970): 253–60; Donald H. Ross, "The Grotesque: A Speculation," *Poe Studies* 4 (1971): 10–11; Lee Byron Jennings, *The Ludicrous Demon: Aspects of the Grotesque in Post-Romantic German Prose* (Berkeley and Los Angeles: University of California Press, 1963). For expert corroboration of the generalizations about the arabesque and its relation to Romantic Irony, see Raymond Immerwahr, "Romantic Irony and Romantic Arabesque Prior to Romanticism," *German Quarterly* 42 (1969): 655–86.

3. That bifurcation between grotesque and arabesque mentioned earlier; see A. H. Quinn, *Poe: A Critical Biography* (New York: Appleton-Century-Crofts, 1941), p. 289. See K 24–27. Kayser points out that, despite this tendency to emphasize the comic from the seventeenth century on (in French usage), Larousse's *Grand Dictionnaire Universal* of 1872 mentioned a deeper and more sinister meaning prominent in the age of Romanticism.

4. Burton R. Pollin, "Victor Hugo and Poe," in *Discoveries in Poe* (Notre Dame, Ind., and London: University of Notre Dame Press, 1970), pp. 3–5; see *Foreign Quarterly Review* 2 (June 1828): 715–18. See W 2:255 and K 58–59. For further comment on Poe and Hugo and Poe's acquaintance with French Romantic writers in general, see Charles Lombard, "Poe and French Romanticism," *Poe Newsletter* 3 (1970): 30–35.

5. Hoffmann changed his third Christian name from Wilhelm to Amadeus, thus E. T. A., and thus the discrepancy between the standard appellation and Scott's title.

6. Pollin's attitude is curious. Noting Scott's "strong disapproval of Hoffmann's style," Pollin seems to think that Poe could not have read the review without adopting Scott's own views and therefore could not have been much influenced by Scott's own discussion of Gothic, grotesque, and arabesque effects. This is a bit condescending toward Poe. As Scott's title indicates, his dual concern is with Hoffmann in particular but with the "supernatural in fictitious composition" generally. See Paul A. Newlin's "Scott's Influence on Poe's Grotesque and Arabesque Tales," *American Transcendental Quarterly*, no. 2 (1969): 9–12. Scott's article appeared in *Foreign Quarterly Review* 1 (July 1827): 61–93.

7. For a relevant and illuminating discussion of Poe's "mysterious" effects, see S. K. Wertz and Linda L. Wertz, "On Poe's Use of 'Mystery,'" *Poe Studies* 4 (1971): 7–10.

8. In the *Marginalia* series in *Graham's Magazine* for December 1846, Poe accused "German criticism" in general of abounding in "brilliant bubbles of *suggestion*" that "rise and sink and jostle each other, until the whole vortex of thought in which they originate is one indistinguishable

chaos of froth." He concludes with an offhand attack on the Schlegels, which, given his thefts from them, reflects ironically on the whole note (H 16:115–17). For an interesting reference to Jean Paul, see H 11:185–86.

9. See K, passim, and Lawson, "Poe and the Grotesque: A Bibliography," pp. 9–10.

10. In addition to previous references, see Kayser's last chapter, "An Attempt to Define the Nature of the Grotesque," pp. 179–89.

11. On this complex matter of interior design and landscape aesthetics as manifest in "The Masque of the Red Death," "The Philosophy of Furniture," "Eleonora," "The Assignation," "The Island of the Fay," "The Domain of Arnheim," "The Landscape Garden," "Landor's Cottage," "The Oval Portrait," and other tales, the following works are relevant: Sam S. Basket, "A Damsel with a Dulcimer: An Interpretation of Poe's 'Eleonora,'" *Modern Language Notes* 73 (1958): 332–38; Cleanth Brooks, "Edgar Allan Poe as Interior Decorator," *Ventures* 8 (1968): 41–46; Jeffrey Hess, "Sources and Aesthetics of Poe's Landscape Fiction," *American Quarterly* 22 (1970): 177–89; Robert D. Jacobs, "Poe's Earthly Paradise," *American Quarterly* 12 (1960): 404–13; F. DeWolfe Miller, "The Basis for Poe's 'The Island of the Fay,'" *American Literature* 14 (1942): 135–40; Joseph P. Roppolo, "Meaning and 'The Masque of the Red Death,'" *Tulane Studies in English* 13 (1963): 59–69; Alvin Rosenfeld, "Description in Poe's 'Landor's Cottage,'" *Studies in Short Fiction* 4 (1967): 264–66; Georges Poulet, "Edgar Poe," in *The Metamorphoses of the Circle*, trans. Carley Dawson and Elliott Coleman (Baltimore, Md.: Johns Hopkins Press, 1966), pp. 182–202; Kermit Vanderbilt, "Art and Nature in 'The Masque of the Red Death,'" *Nineteenth Century Fiction* 22 (1968): 379–89. See also works by Evans, Benton, and Mabbott cited subsequently in this chapter.

12. Oliver Evans, "Infernal Illumination in Poe," *Modern Language Notes* 75 (1960): 295–97.

13. Richard P. Benton, "Is Poe's 'The Assignation' a Hoax?" *Nineteenth Century Fiction* 18 (1963): 193–94.

14. T. O. Mabbott, Notes to *Selected Poetry and Prose of Edgar Allan Poe* (New York: Modern Library, 1951), p. 415.

15. See, for example, Patrick F. Quinn, *The French Face of Edgar Poe* (Carbondale: Southern Illinois University Press, 1957), pp. 257–75; James Hafley, "Malice in Wonderland," *Arizona Quarterly* 15 (1959): 5–12. See also Richard W. Dowell, "The Ironic History of Poe's 'Life in Death': A Literary Skeleton in the Closet," *American Literature* 42 (1971): 478–86, for an unconvincing negative discussion of the unity of the tale, which nevertheless reveals some interesting facts about its publication history.

16. Seymour L. Gross, "Poe's Revision of 'The Oval Portrait,'" *Modern Language Notes* 74 (1959): 16–20.

17. *Dramatic Lectures,* Lecture XXIII, pp. 369–70. See Chapter 2, Section III, this study.

NOTES TO CHAPTER SIX
The Nightside

1. A. R. Thompson, *The Dry Mock* (Berkeley and Los Angeles: University of California Press, 1948), pp. 78–79; W 2:98–100.
2. Oskar Walzel, *German Romanticism,* trans. Alma Elsie Lussky (New York: Putnam's, 1966), pp. 60–61, 245.
3. See Henry Pochmann, *German Culture in America* (Madison: University of Wisconsin Press, 1957), pp. 394–97, for a consideration of these tales as derived from German sources. Doris Falk in "Poe and the Power of Animal Magnetism," *PMLA* 84 (1969): 536–46, discusses the theoretical conception of mesmerism and animal magnetism as Poe must have understood these ideas and deals with three "mesmeric" tales, but she betrays no sense of irony.
4. H 6:132–33. Gall and Spurzheim were the founders, more or less, of phrenology. Poe reviews an American edition of *Phrenology, and the Moral Influence of Phrenology . . . from the First Published Works of Gall and Spurzheim, to the Latest Discoveries of the Present Period* in the March 1836 *Southern Literary Messenger.* He seems on the surface to be serious—but it is hard to tell: "Phrenology is no longer to be laughed at. . . . It is assumed the majesty of a science . . . " (H 8:252). See also Burton R. Pollin, "Poe's 'Some Words With a Mummy' Reconsidered," *Emerson Society Quarterly,* no. 60 Suppl. (1970), pp. 60–67.
5. H 4:236. R. A. Stewart in his notes to "Eleonora" in the Harrison edition remarks that "adventures" for "adventurers" is a "bad error" of the Griswold edition (1857–58) which has been perpetuated.
6. See Hardin Craig, Introduction, *Edgar Allan Poe: Representative Selections,* ed. Margaret Alterton and Hardin Craig (1935; reprint ed., New York: Hill and Wang, 1962), pp. cii–ciii. Quinn and O'Neill (B 2:1079), following long established tradition, comment that Poe's relations with Virginia are obviously the basis of the tale. It is true that Eleonora is the narrator's cousin and that her mother figures shadowily in the story. But then we are faced with the curious implications that Virginia was two-soulled and that Poe came to love one part of her better than the other. Autobiographical allegory seems rather doubtful to me. But such autobiographical presentation of the author's personal conditions fits well with Jean Paul's conception of the ironic annihilation of mere selfness, as noted at the end of this chapter. See also Richard P. Benton, "Platonic Allegory in Poe's 'Eleonora,'" *Nineteenth Century Fiction* 22 (1967): 293–97; and Sam S. Basket, "A Damsel with a Dulcimer: An Interpretation of Poe's 'Eleonora,'" *Modern Language Notes* 73 (1958): 332–38.

7. Novalis, at the same time that he thought poetry should be the musical rendering of subconscious dreams, also called for a conscious irony. Poetry, according to Novalis, is the "truly, absolutely real"; it is thought, play, truth, aspiration—in short, all of man's volitional, "free" activity. Novalis thought language to be a system of hieroglyphics wherewith we are able to read the natural world. True poetry, then, is symbolic and, as such, partly conscious thought and partly subconscious (reflecting the real). Poetry, according to Novalis, is, or should be, dreamlike, making use of free association and wordplay; there might even be a poetry "without connection, but with association, like dreams—poems merely euphonious and full of beautiful words, but without sense or connection" (W 2:84). The supremacy of poetry, the insistence on symbol and dreamy, associative verbal music are all obviously relevant to Poe's concepts of poetry. Regarding fiction, however, and regarding conscious craftsmanship in general, Poe's evaluation of Novalis's ideas is ambivalent. Novalis claimed that the greatest freedom for the literary artist lies in fiction, and especially in the fairy tale since it deals with the world before and beyond time and history. The novel should be but a variant of the fairy tale, making use of an "irony" that aims at the "annihilation" of apparent contradictions and the attainment of a harmonious concept of wholeness. Irony, Novalis wrote, involves the union in the human being of both the conscious and the subconscious facets of the mind. Irony records an illumination through a double-vision; it reveals a true presence of mind attained through the ego's having passed through the subconscious realm. Poe was interested in the fictional uses of "perception" through the subconscious, through half-conscious sleep-states, through mesmeric trances, and the like. But Poe the craftsman could not accept Novalis's ideas about the artist's reliance on the subconscious mind. Poe quoted in the *Marginalia* Novalis's aphorism that "the artist belongs to his work, not the work to the artist," and commented that: ". . . in nine cases out of ten it is pure waste of time to attempt extorting sense from a German apothegm;— or rather, any sense and every sense may be extorted from all of them" (H 16:98–99). Poe then said that if the meaning of the aphorism is that the artist is a slave to his materials, to his theme, Novalis is wrong; for the true artist selects his materials according to the impression he wants to convey, although he must conform to whatever inner logic the materials selected may possess. Poe characteristically, and shrewdly, has it both ways. He calls for both conscious craftsmanship and intuitive recognition of the essence of the object, and he also both attacks another writer and yet partially accepts his ideas. Cf. his comments on Montaigne in the *Marginalia* (H 16:87–90). See the ironic application of a passage from Novalis's *Moral Opinions* (about coincidence and the imperfection of real events as modified from the ideal realm) in the motto to "Marie Rogêt" (1842). Novalis's prose was available in translation in *Fragments from the German Prose Writers* (1841); Carlyle's

Critical and Miscellaneous Essays (London, 1840); *Translations from the German,* by H. Reeve and J. E. Taylor (London: Murray, 1842); *Christianity or Europe,* trans. J. Dalton (London: Chapman, 1844); *Henry of Ofterdingen,* with Tieck's "Life of Novalis" (Cambridge, Mass.: Owen, 1842). The poems were available in numerous translated collections of German writing, and in several book-length collections of Novalis's songs and hymns. Poe's references to Novalis include H 5:2, 171; 9:202; 11:5; 16:98–99. The earliest reference dates from 1836. Carlyle's essay on Novalis, with selected *Fragments,* first appeared in the *Foreign Review,* no. 7 (1829).

8. Sidney E. Lind, "Poe and Mesmerism," *PMLA* 62 (1947): 1078–85.

9. Boyd Carter, "Poe's Debt to Charles Brockden Brown, *Prairie Schooner,* 27 (1953): 190–96.

10. See Carter, "Poe's Debt to Charles Brockden Brown," pp. 191–93, where the material is presented somewhat differently. Mukhtar Ali Isani in a forthcoming essay, which I have seen in manuscript, discusses Poe's borrowings from Macaulay and others for the Orientalism of the tale.

11. Old Deb is introduced as such in Chapter XIX. See Charles Brockden Brown, *Edgar Huntly* (1799; reprint ed., Port Washington, New York, 1963), p. 197; the name is also remarked by Carter as a noncomic parallel. Burton R. Pollin speculates on the influence of Victor Hugo on this tale in *Discoveries in Poe* (Notre Dame, Ind., and London: University of Notre Dame Press, 1970), pp. 24–28.

12. In two letters written in July 1844, just before the publication of "Mesmeric Revelation," Poe wrote James Russell Lowell and Thomas Holley Chivers brief summaries of his alternative to believing in "spirituality" that are parallel in phrasing to the tale (O 1:256–60). But, as always, it is hard to tell how serious Poe was. At this time Poe was trying, without luck, to get Lowell to join him in a magazine venture, and one year afterward in a note on Lowell's latest "farce" of a book Poe called him "the Anacharsis Clootz of American Letters" (H 16:69–70). In his letter to Chivers, Poe did write that his "own faith" was indeed his "own," and that Chivers would "find it, somewhat detailed, in a forthcoming number of the 'Columbian Magazine', published here [New York]. I have written for it an article headed 'Mesmeric Revelation,' which see" (O 1:259). But in "A Chapter on Autography," Poe called Chivers "at the same time one of best and one of the worst poets in America" for "even his worst nonsense (and some of it is horrible) has an indefinite charm of sentiment and melody," but "we can never be sure that there is *any* meaning in his words . . ." (H 15:241–42). Thus, Poe may well have been contemptuously hoaxing both of them. That Poe was hoaxing them seems to be borne out also by his telling Chivers that "Mesmeric Revelation" was a philosophical "article" and then exuberantly proclaiming in print that the article was "pure fiction" (H 16:71). Al-

though such usage is not everywhere consistent in Poe, the context tips the balance: the Swedenborgians, he said, had found everything he said to be true, though they initially doubted his veracity—"a thing which, in that particular instance, I never dreamed of not doubting myself" (H 16:71), as he remarked later. See also the letter (January 4, 1845) to George Bush (O 1:273), which seems to me primarily an attempt (as always with Poe) to gain wider recognition.

13. N. Bryllion Fagin remarks that the tale is rather like a "deadpan cartoon" of a sententious pedant; *Histrionic Mr. Poe* (Baltimore, Md.: Johns Hopkins Press, 1949), p. 73. The object of such satire would be an amalgam of a contemporary occultist and some more commanding theological figure; the name "Vankirk" suggests "of the church" (*van* + *kirk*) and a Scandinavian, possibly, then, Swedenborg (who spent much of his last years in Amsterdam). See H 16:71 and the conclusion to Section III of this chapter.

14. Omitted from Harrison; see Richard H. Stoddard, *The Works of Edgar Allan Poe*, 6 vols. (New York: A. C. Armstrong, 1895), 5:179–82; also see O 2:336.

15. See Lind, "Poe and Mesmerism," pp. 1086–87; the quotation from Davis is given by Lind.

16. See B 2:683 for the correct version. H 6:295 gives "Poughkeepsie Seer" (Davis's actual label) for Poe's "Toughkeepsie."

17. Kerner, as already noted, sought the "truth" about human existence and the nature of the universe in epilepsy, madness, and the like, as well as in mesmeric sleep. His *Seeress of Prevorst* was translated by Mrs. Catherine Crowe (London: Moore, 1845; New York: Harper, 1845) the year "Valdemar" was published. The death of Mrs. H——, the seeress, is similar to Valdemar's, although she dies joyfully. The similarity was first pointed out by the anonymous work, *Ramblings and Reveries of an Art Student in Europe* (1855); see Lind, "Poe and Mesmerism," pp. 1091–92. Also see Pochmann, *German Culture in America*, p. 396, for a standard comment on the connection between the two tales. Kerner's works were also available in many English collections of German writing (see B. Q. Morgan, *Bibliography of German Literature in English Translation*, Madison: University of Wisconsin Studies, 1922, p. 265).

18. The languages may be important too, for Poe once found a translation of the Book of Jonah into German hexameters comic, though he said he did not know why (H 16:40). See T. O. Mabbott's notes to "Valdemar" in *Selected Poetry and Prose of Edgar Allan Poe* (New York: Modern Library, 1951), p. 424, for a comment on Issachar, Schiller, and Rabelais; Mabbott thinks Poe did not care for Schiller or Rabelais, but the thrust is clearly at Valdemar rather than at them, and an intended comic clue to the qualities of the hoax, satire, or parody in the tale. A. H. Quinn, in *Edgar Allan Poe: A Critical Biography* (New York: Appleton-Century-Crofts, 1941), p. 330, seems so puzzled by the

humor-horror of the story that he calls "Valdemar" a "lapse from artistic sanity."

19. Omitted in Harrison; see Stoddard, *The Works of Edgar Allan Poe*, 5:183.

20. Abrams, *The Mirror and the Lamp* (New York: Norton, 1958), p. 211.

21. Quoted by Abrams in *The Mirror and the Lamp*, p. 212.

22. According to William K. Wimsatt, Jr., and Cleanth Brooks, *Literary Criticism* (New York: Knopf, 1957), pp. 378 ff., Jean Paul's concept of humor evolved from the English concept of "humours" associated with character types and especially with exaggerations and oddities, and developed into a philosophy of toleration, of sweeping insight into the contradictions of the world. For a fair sample, in translation, of Jean Paul's theory of humor in the *Aesthetics*, see *Theories of Comedy*, ed. Paul Lauter, pp. 314–23. See also W 2:106. Jean Paul considered the subconscious capable of guiding the artist as though by divine wisdom, as well as frightening him. Hazlitt's first lecture is also reprinted in Lauter, pp. 262–94. See Poe on Hazlitt (H 12:226–28) and a reference to Jean Paul (H 11:185–86) that implies familiarity. Selections from Jean Paul were available in numerous anthologies (see Morgan, p. 391), and forty-six items appeared in American periodicals before 1864 (see Pochmann, p. 346). DeQuincey published "Specimens from Flegeljahre" in the *London Magazine* 4 (1821): 606, and "Analects from Richter" and "The Dream of the Universe" in the *London Magazine* 9 (1824): 117, 242. Carlyle included "Schmelzle's Journey" and the "Life of Quintus Fixlein" in *German Romance* (1827), and his essay on Jean Paul in that volume emphasizes his "Humour" with reference to the *Introduction to Aesthetics*; in the essay on Tieck, Carlyle links Jean Paul to the Schlegels, Novalis, and Kant. Carlyle also published a version of his essay on Jean Paul in the *Edinburgh Review*, no. 92 (1827), and in 1830 he published a translation of "Jean Paul Richter's Review of Madame de Stael's 'Allemagne'" in *Fraser's Magazine*, nos. 1 and 4. "The Moon" appeared in Holcraft's *Tales from the German* (London, Edinburgh, Glasgow, 1826), reprinted as *Tales of Humour and Romance* (London, 1829; New York: Francis, 1829). A. Kenney's translated collection of sixty-eight of Jean Paul's prose pieces appeared as *The Death of an Angel, and Other Pieces* (London: Black, 1839). Jean Paul's autobiography, trans. Mrs. Eliza B. Lee, appeared in her *Life of Jean Paul Friedrich Richter* (London: Chapman, 1845), and her translation of *Flegeljahre* appeared as *Walt and Vult; or, the Twins* (New York: Wiley & Putnam, 1846). Miss L. Osgood translated *The Diadem* (Philadelphia: Carey & Hart, 1846).

23. Or as Irving Babbitt in Chapter VII of *Rousseau and Romanticism* (New York, 1955) translates it, "hot baths of sentiment" are followed by "cold douches of irony." Cf. Walzel, *German Romanticism*, pp. 231–32.

24. W 2:102; cf. Muecke, *Compass of Irony* (London: Metheun, 1969), pp. 196–204.
25. Translated by A. R. Thompson in *Dry Mock*, p. 51.
26. Translated by Thompson in *Dry Mock*, pp. 66–67, my italics.
27. See Wimsatt and Brooks, *Literary Criticism*, p. 379.

NOTES TO CHAPTER SEVEN
Romantic Skepticism

1. Edward H. Davidson, *Poe: A Critical Study* (Cambridge, Mass.: Harvard University Press, 1957), pp. 189–94.
2. Notably Davidson, in *Poe: A Critical Study*, Chapters VI, VII, and VIII. Richard Wilbur sees *Eureka* as the key to Poe's work in a seminal essay, "The House of Poe" (The Library of Congress Anniversary Lecture, May 4, 1959), reprinted in *The Recognition of Edgar Allan Poe: Selected Criticism Since 1829*, ed. Eric W. Carlson (Ann Arbor: The University of Michigan Press, 1966), pp. 255–77. *Eureka* and *Arthur Gordon Pym* have received a sudden flood of critical attention recently, as documented subsequently.
3. Killis Campbell in *The Mind of Poe* (1933; reprint ed., New York: Russell & Russell, 1962), p. 163, suggests that Bulwer's "Manuscript Found in a Madhouse" (which appeared in an early edition published in Boston by Phillips, Sampson, and Company) may have suggested the title of "MS. Found in a Bottle." J. S. Wilson in "The Devil Was In It," p. 219, suggests that the tale is told by the Folio Club author Solomon Seadrift and that the literary butt of the satire is Jane Porter's *Narrative of Sir Edward Seaward* (1831). The emphasis on "discovery" and the use of polar openings into the interior of the earth also suggest John Cleves Symmes's *Symzonia: A Voyage of Discovery* (1820) as a satiric butt. Other sources have been suggested, but these are not our concern here. Clark Griffith in "Caves and Cave Dwellers: The Study of a Romantic Image," *Journal of English and Germanic Philology* 62 (1963): 560–63, not only clearly details the change in style from crisp and analytical to cadenced and emotional but also suggests that the discovery is about the self: the narrator discovers that the world can drive one mad and that after death there is only silence. But surely the narrator never discovers anything about himself; he is merely the victim of the tale, of the hoax that perverse fortune (and Poe) plays on him. The theme of ultimate discovery is, however, extended somewhat in "The Pit and the Pendulum" and "A Descent into the Maelström," though each has its ironic reversals. Donald Barlow Stauffer's "The Two Styles of Poe's 'MS. Found in a Bottle,'" *Style* 1 (1967): 107–20, derives from Griffith's article. Randall Helms's "Another Source for Poe's *Arthur*

Gordon Pym," *American Literature* 41 (1970): 572–75, derives from Wilson. See also Claude Richard's speculation on the place of "MS. Found in a Bottle" in the Folio Club sequence, *Poe Newsletter* 2 (1969): 23.

4. The Latin motto to the tale is comic: "My friends said that my troubles would be in some measure relieved if I would visit the tomb of my sweetheart." Hardin Craig suggests that "Berenice" is the story of "ardent imagination in which a logical element is perceived as coming into the control of pure fancy. The hero is a monomaniac conscious of the decay of his reason. The thought takes possession of him that the teeth of Berenice will restore him" (*Edgar Allan Poe: Representative Selections,* ed. Margaret Alterton and Hardin Craig, New York: Hill and Wang, 1962, p. 512); Darrel Abel, "Coleridge's 'Life-in-Death' and Poe's 'Death-in-Life,'" *Notes and Queries* 2 (1955): 218–20, argues unconvincingly for a supernatural interpretation (even while admitting that Berenice may have the cataleptic disorder of Madeline Usher) and tries to expand all apparent psychological devices in Poe into the supernatural—the reverse of the thesis of his seminal article on "Usher."

5. T. O. Mabbott in "The Source of the Title of Poe's 'Morella,'" *Notes and Queries* 172 (1937): 26–27. Walter G. Neale, Jr., in "The Source of Poe's 'Morella,'" *American Literature* 9 (1939): 237–39, points out parallels to Henry Glassford Bell's "The Dead Daughter" in the *Edinburgh Literary Journal* (January 1, 1831). Neale takes "Morella" as a serious tale; but "The Dead Daughter" provides a clear butt for the literary burlesque of the Folio Club. See Killis Campbell, *Mind of Poe,* pp. 14 ff., on Poe's reading of Schelling and Locke; and Palmer C. Holt, "Poe and H. N. Coleridge's *Greek Classical Poets:* 'Pinakidia,' 'Politian, and 'Morella' Sources," *American Literature* 34 (1962): 8–10, for Poe's use of Coleridge on the Platonic Theory of love and unity—which, of course, is inverted in the tale. For an important discussion of Platonic love in Poe, see Richard P. Benton, "Platonic Allegory in Poe's 'Eleonora,'" *Nineteenth Century Fiction* 22 (1967): 293–97.

6. H 16:161. For commentary on "Silence," see J. S. Wilson, "The Devil Was In It," *American Mercury* 24 (1931): 215, and Clark Griffith, "Poe's 'Ligeia' and the English Romantics," *University of Toronto Quarterly* 24 (1954): 14. Other commentary has been essentially repetition of Wilson.

7. The mirror motif in *Pym* also reflects nothing, as discussed later. See Davidson, *Poe: A Critical Study,* pp. 198–201, for an interpretation of "Wilson" as a "Romantic individualist for whom the world is nothing but the externalization of the self: at any instant what the self wills the world must become" until the world and the self annihilates itself—an interesting parallel with the metaphysics of Romantic Irony. Other pertinent discussions of "William Wilson" include two articles by James W. Gargano, "'William Wilson': The Wildest Sublunary Visions," *Wash-*

ington and Jefferson Literary Journal 1 (1967): 9–16, and "Art and Irony in 'William Wilson,'" *Emerson Society Quarterly*, no. 60 Suppl. (1970), pp. 18–22.

8. See Mabbott, *Selected Poetry and Prose of Edgar Allan Poe* (New York: Modern Library, 1951), pp. 419–20. I am indebted to Mr. Athar Murtuza for the observation of the lens motif and the biblical echo. For recent discussion of this tale, see Herbert Rauter, "Edgar Allan Poes *The Man of the Crowd*," in *Amerika: Vision und Wirklichkeit*, ed. Franz H. Link (Frankfurt/Main: Athenäum, 1968), pp. 115–27; and Gisella Vitt-Maucher, "E. T. A. Hoffmans *Ritter Gluck* und E. A. Poes *The Man of the Crowd*: Eine Gegenüberstellung," *German Quarterly* 43 (1970): 35–46.

9. See Margaret J. Yonce, "The Spiritual Descent into the Maelström: A Debt to 'The Rime of the Ancient Mariner,'" *Poe Newsletter* 2 (1969): 26–29.

10. See Clark Griffith, "Caves and Cave Dwellers," pp. 563–64; James Lundquist, "The Moral of Averted Descent: The Failure of Sanity in 'The Pit and the Pendulum,'" *Poe Newsletter* 2 (1969): 25–26; and David H. Hirsch, "The Pit and the Apocalypse," *Sewanee Review* 76 (1968): 632–52.

11. John E. Reilly, "The Lesser Death-Watch and 'The Tell-Tale Heart,'" *American Transcendental Quarterly*, no. 2 (1969), pp. 3–9. Also see James W. Gargano, "The Theme of Time in 'The Tell-Tale Heart,'" *Studies in Short Fiction* 5 (1968): 378–82; E. Arthur Robinson, "Poe's 'The Tell-Tale Heart,'" *Nineteenth Century Fiction* 19 (1965): 369–78.

12. See James W. Gargano, "'The Black Cat': Perverseness Reconsidered," *Texas Studies in Literature and Language* 2 (1960): 172–78.

13. Perversity is not strictly a phrenological term, as some critics assume, but is merely linked with the phrenological category of "combativeness" in "The Imp." Poe specifically says that the phrenologists are limited in their understanding of the human personality. As noted before, Poe is skeptical about the "systems" that psychologists and phrenologists have tried "to dictate" to God the Creator, whom Poe yet seems to hold responsible for man's grotesque condition. The most insightful commentary on this tale yet published is Eugene Kanjo's "'The Imp of the Perverse': Poe's Dark Comedy of Art and Death," *Poe Newsletter* 2 (1969): 41–44.

14. See Barton Levi St. Armand, "Poe's 'Sober Mystification': The Uses of Alchemy in 'The Gold-Bug,'" *Poe Studies* 4 (1971): 1–7. Several other studies of the ratiocinative stories, while excellent, are not pertinent here. I am indebted to Mr. Roger O'Connor for the discovery of several mockingly erroneous details in the story.

15. See Edward H. Davidson, *Poe: A Critical Study*, pp. 156–80, and Patrick F. Quinn, *French Face of Poe* (Carbondale: Southern Illinois University Press, 1949), pp. 169–215 for especially fine discussions of *Pym*;

my own discussion, as will be apparent, relies heavily on theirs, though the perspective is different. *Pym* has received a great deal of critical attention lately. Other relevant, though less pertinent, discussions include: Walter E. Bezanson, "The Troubled Sleep of Arthur Gordon Pym," in *Essays in Literary History Presented to J. Milton French*, ed. Rudolf Kirk and C. F. Main (New Brunswick, N.J.: Rutgers University Press, 1960), pp. 149–75; L. Moffitt Cecil, "The Two Narratives of Arthur Gordon Pym," *Texas Studies in Literature and Language* 5 (1963): 232–41; Pascal Covici, Jr., "Toward a Reading of Poe's *Narrative of A. Gordon Pym*," *Mississippi Quarterly* 21 (1968): 111–18; Leslie Fiedler, *Love and Death in the American Novel*, rev. ed. (New York: Stein and Day, 1966), pp. 392–400; Evelyn J. Hinz, " 'Tekeli-li': The Narrative of Arthur Gordon Pym as Satire," *Genre* 3 (1970): 379–97; Sidney Kaplan, Introduction to *The Narrative of Arthur Gordon Pym* (New York: Hill and Wang, 1960), pp. vii–xxv; Richard A. Levine, "The Downward Journey of Purgation: Notes on an Imagistic Leitmotif in *The Narrative of Arthur Gordon Pym*," *Poe Newsletter* 2 (1969): 29–31; Joseph J. Moldenhauer, "Imagination and Perversity in *The Narrative of Arthur Gordon Pym*," *Texas Studies in Literature and Language* 13 (1971): 267–80; Sidney P. Moss, *Arthur Gordon Pym or the Fallacy of Thematic Interpretation*," *University Review* 33 (1967): 299–306; Charles O'Donnell, "From Earth to Ether: Poe's Flight into Space," *PMLA* 77 (1962): 85–91; Joel Porte, "The Ultimate Romance," in *The Romance in America* (Middleton, Conn: Wesleyan University Press, 1969), pp. 84–94; Jean Ricardou, "Le Caractère singulier de cette eau," *Critique* 243 and 244 (1967): 718–33; Joseph V. Ridgely, "The Continuing Puzzle of *Arthur Gordon Pym*: Some Notes and Queries," *Poe Newsletter* 3 (1970): 5–6; Joseph V. Ridgely and Iola S. Haverstick, "Chartless Voyage: The Many Narratives of Arthur Gordon Pym," *Texas Studies in Literature and Language* 7 (1966): 63–80; John H. Stroupe, "Poe's Imaginary Voyage: Pym as Hero," *Studies in Short Fiction* 4 (1967): 315–21.

16. Pym is from Edgarton (H 3:5), a real place, it may be noted.

17. See Patrick F. Quinn, "*Arthur Gordon Pym*: 'A Journey to the End of the Page'?" *Poe Newsletter* 1 (1968): 13–14.

18. Cf. Fiedler, *Love and Death in the American Novel*, pp. 399–400.

19. See Joseph J. Moldenhauer, "Murder as a Fine Art: Basic Connections between Poe's Aesthetics, Psychology, and Moral Vision," *PMLA* 83 (1968): 284–97. Craig anthologizes "Monos and Una" as "philosophy" and juxtaposes it with *Eureka* in *Representative Selections*, pp. 427ff.

20. See H 6:295. "Mellonta Tauta" until recently had never been thoroughly explicated either in terms of specific satiric thrusts or large outline, though Burton R. Pollin has now identified several satiric targets in his "Politics and History in Poe's 'Mellonta Tauta': Two Allusions Explained," *Studies in Short Fiction* 8 (1971): 627–31. I am indebted to Mrs. Roberta Sharp for the suggestion that the balloon is a minia-

ture image of the cosmos, and that its collapse is a comic variation on the collapse of the universe in *Eureka*, from which work the tale's dissertation on logic and the degradation of society is directly derived.

21. See Richard Wilbur's Introduction to the Laurel Poetry Series *Poe* (New York: Dell, 1959), pp. 11–13, and "The House of Poe," reprinted in *The Recognition of Edgar Allan Poe*, pp. 255–77.

22. Moldenhauer, "Murder as a Fine Art," p. 296*n*.

23. Like *Pym*, *Eureka* has received much attention lately. Most relevant here are Patrick F. Quinn's "Poe's *Eureka* and Emerson's *Nature*," *Emerson Society Quarterly*, no. 31 (1963), pp. 4–7; and Harriet R. Holman's "Hog, Bacon, Ram, and Other 'Savans' in *Eureka*: Notes Toward Decoding Poe's Encyclopedic Satire," *Poe Newsletter* 2 (1969): 49–55.

24. Davidson, *Poe: A Critical Study*, pp. 222–53; Eliot, "From Poe to Valéry," in *To Criticize the Critic* (New York: Harcourt Brace, 1965), pp. 27–42.

25. In this connection, see Robert Martin Adams, *NIL: Episodes in the Literary Conquest of Void During the Nineteenth Century* (New York: Oxford University Press, 1966), pp. 41–50.

26. Robert Mallet, ed., *André Gide—Paul Valéry: Correspondence 1890–1942*, (Paris: Gallimard, 1955).

27. Eliot, "From Poe to Valéry," pp. 35, 40–41. Morse Peckham's formulation of the concept of "Negative Romanticism" also describes Poe's stance. The Negative Romantic is caught between two value-systems (the static eighteenth-century mechanistic universe and the dynamic nineteenth-century organic universe), no longer content with the old nor quite able to accept fully the new orientation. See Part I, "Theory," Chapters 1–4, of Peckham's *The Triumph of Romanticism: Collected Essays* (Columbia: University of South Carolina Press, 1970), pp. 3–83; and also Peckham's *Beyond the Tragic Vision: The Quest for Identity in the Nineteenth Century* (New York: George Braziller, 1962), passim.

Index

Addison, Joseph, 70

Alazon, 11. *See also* Eiron, eironeia

Alchemy. *See* "The Gold-Bug"

Alciphron (verse tale by Thomas Moore): Poe on, 11

Allan, John, 5, 52

Allen, Ethan: *Reason the Only Oracle of Man,* 56; "treasonable" correspondence, 220–21 n34

Animal magnetism. *See* Mesmerism

Antinous, 127, 129

Apollo Belvedere, 127

Arabesque: geometrical design in Kant, 24, 123; "Arabic" style of Gothic architecture, 69–70, 73, 80–81, 114, 122; as a deceptive and confusing pattern, 69–70, 102–3, 105–6, 131, 132, 134; complex interior design, 121, 123–25, 130; related to exterior and landscape design, 131, 229 n11; style sanctioned by the Koran, 227 n2

—as a "madman's rhapsody," 103; as the influence of setting on an overwrought mind, 120, 130–34 passim; as writhing light geometrically patterned, 121, 124–25, 129, 130, 134; as delirious dream-visions, 121–22, 130–31, 134

—as irony of narrative design, 13, 68, 105–6, 108–9, 137; associated with Quixotic tradition, 27, 108–9, 209–10 n10; related to the grotesque, 105–6, 109, 114–15; related to Romantic Irony, 108–9, 212 n18; associated with the burlesque, 137

—critical and historical studies, 223 n5, 227–28 n2. *See also* Cervantes; Gothic; Grotesque; Irony; Poe

Ariosto, Ludovico, 37, 108, 113

Aristotle: *Nicomachean Ethics,* 11

Arnim, Achim von, 161

"Assignation, The" ("The Visionary"): discussed, 126–30; Benton on, 127–28; grotesque and arabesque decor in, 128–30; criticism on, 229 n11; mentioned, 6, 40, 42, 104, 124, 168

Bacon, Francis, 83, 84

Banter: and verisimilitude, 77, 158, 160

"Bargain Lost, The." *See* "Bon-Bon"

Barrett, Elizabeth. *See* Browning

Baudelaire, Charles, 4

Bell, Henry Glassford: "The Dead Daughter" as a source of "Morella," 236 n5

Berkeley, George, 68, 70

Berni, Francesco, 108, 113

"Berenice": *Southern Literary Messenger* on the "German horror" in, 19; Poe on the "ludicrous heightened into the grotesque" in, 43; discussed, 168; criticism on, 236 n4; mentioned, 6, 42, 66

Black, John: translator of A. W. Schlegel's *Lectures on Dramatic Art and Literature,* 30

"Black Cat, The": discussed, 172; criticism on, 237 n12; mentioned, 13

"Bon-Bon" ("The Bargain Lost"): discussed, 47; mentioned, 6, 40, 44, 54, 217 n13, 220 n31

Bosch, Hieronymous, 107

Brentano, Clemans: *Godwi* indirectly alluded to, 12; mentioned, 161

Brown, Charles Brockden: *Wieland,* 76, 103; *Edgar Huntly,* 103, 151–52, 232 n11; mentioned, 75, 148

Browning, Elizabeth Barrett, 34

TEXT DESIGNED

BY IRVING PERKINS

JACKET DESIGNED BY KAREN FOGET

MANUFACTURED BY IMPRESSIONS, INC., MADISON, WISCONSIN

TEXT LINES ARE SET IN CALEDONIA, DISPLAY LINES IN CENTURY NOVA AND CRAW MODERN

Library of Congress Cataloging in Publication Data
Thompson, G   R   1937–
Poe's fiction, romantic irony in the Gothic tales.
1. Poe, Edgar Allan, 1809–1849.   I. Title.
PS2638.T5   813'.3   72–7996
ISBN 0–299–06380–1